THE UNNAMING OF ALIASS

Before you start to read this book, take this moment to think about making a donation to punctum books, an independent non-profit press

@ https://punctumbooks.com/support

If you're reading the e-book, you can click on the image below to go directly to our donations site. Any amount, no matter the size, is appreciated and will help us to keep our ship of fools afloat. Contributions from dedicated readers will also help us to keep our commons open and to cultivate new work that can't find a welcoming port elsewhere. Our adventure is not possible without your support.

Vive la Open Access.

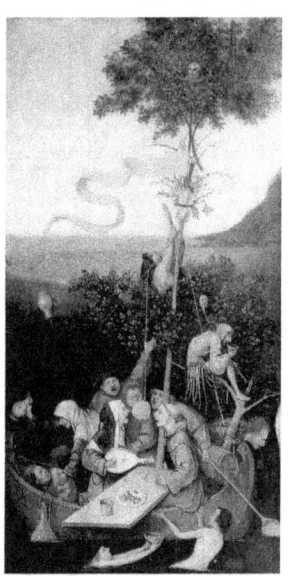

Fig. 1. Hieronymus Bosch, *Ship of Fools* (1490–1500)

Parts of chapter 6 were previously published in "If Not for Her Spots: On the Arts of Un/naming a New Ass Breed," *Humanimalia* 10, no. 1 (Spring 2019). Parts of chapter 3 appear in "The Unnaming of 'Aliass'," *Performance Research* 22, no. 6 (December 2017). Earlier versions of chapter 8 were published as a chapbook, *R.A.W. Assmilk Soap: (Parapoetics for a Posthuman Barnyard)*, in the LABAE Parapoetics Series (Berlin: Broken Dimanche Press, 2016), and earlier as "R.A.W. Assmilk Soap," in *The Multispecies Salon*, ed. Eben Kirksey (Durham: Duke University Press, 2014), 64–86. Some of the material in chapter 1 was revised from "'What You Gonna do About Yer Ass?': Or, an Answer to Sun Ra via Journeys of Incarnated Poetics and Interdisciplinary Art Practice," in *Collision: Interarts Practice and Research*, eds. David Ceccetto, Nancy Cuthbert, Julie Lassonde, and Dylan Robinson (London: Cambridge Scholars Press, 2009), 149–61. Excerpts also appear in "Gut Sounds Lullaby: Listening with Karen Barad," *Antennae* 32 (Winter 2014).

First published in 2020 by 3Ecologies Books/Immediations, an imprint of punctum books.
https://punctumbooks.com

ISBN-13: 978-1-953035-12-7 (print)
ISBN-13: 978-1-953035-13-4 (ePDF)

DOI: 10.21983/P3.0299.1.00

LCCN: 2020945733
Library of Congress Cataloging Data is available from the Library of Congress

Book design: Vincent W.J. van Gerven Oei
Cover photograph: The shadow of a lovely spotted she-ass, yet to be unnamed, in Whites Creek, Tennessee in April 2002. Photograph by the artist.

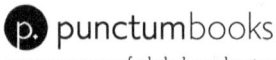

punctumbooks

spontaneous acts of scholarly combustion

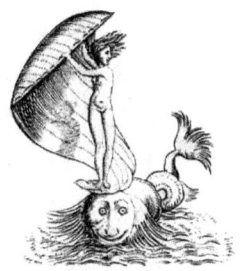

HIC SVNT MONSTRA

Karin Bolender

The

Unnaming

of

Aliass

Contents

~×~×~×~

~×~×~×~

PART II: ART OF A SULL

Preamble &
Assnowledgments

Despite thousands of hours spent huddled over its contents, gnawing on roots and bones, I am still not sure this ought to be a book – at least not in the guise of a monograph with a lone author's name on it. At the same time, this seems like a good spot to recognize the particular ways that this project has been a reckoning with the limits, possibilities, and troubling assumptions of the Book from the get-go. Nothing is resolved here; in an effort to honor the involvements of all those whose tales one cannot possibly claim to tell, this volume puts the prickly question of whether or not it ought to be a book at the core of its proceedings.

Over the course of a long-ass journey across the US South in 2002 – born as it was of a book-that-wasn't – the idea has stuck in my mind that my companion Aliass carried a few special books in the black synthetic saddlebag, along with our pink plastic sunblock and bug spray, notebooks and water-bottles and crumbled rice cakes. One book, I am pretty certain, was my tattered copy of *Watt*. I also recall, from the Wilderness Trail campsite the night before, reading William James at the graffiti-laden picnic table... but no, I don't think that was one on the road with us that day. Anyway I don't remember, and no catalog exists of that little lost library. So, despite a certain hunger to archive, this lacuna leads me to wonder: is it not for the best that I have forgotten, since the premise of that original journey was that the exclusively human linguistic apparatus of a book – whether as fat papery codex or pulsing digital record of syntactical thought – could not contain, and might indeed compromise, the seamy flux of living tales that comprise our passages in timeplaces?

Well, yes. This was a premise of sorts, a paradoxical passion that originally drove me and Aliass to hoof it all those back-road miles that summer long ago. And the desire to buck the assumptions of the Book, to resist exclusive rights to human authorship, remains at the heart of our dusty barnyard becomings to this day. One could certainly make a case that Aliass has unfairly borne the burden of a voluminous mass of human expressions, desires, fears, hopes, and longings for a long time. So while I admit to certain poetic and narrative urges to commit fuzzy memories to prose – to somehow cling with words to, say, the bygone billowing curtains of fireflies that lit our path in a darkening Tennessee forest, or full-blown moonlight sifting through barn slats, or the bite of fat wild blackberries on our tongues – one thing I have always known for sure is that this project must resist the reflective lure of encompassing memoir, in which the ass herself is but a foil, antagonist, or comely sidekick. What unfolds going forward must be otherwise, must do otherwise.

One other thing I can say for certain is that Aliass and I never would have made it one blasted mile without the assistance and encouragement of swarms of friendly strangers, strangely wonderful friends, and myriad mysterious others encountered in the places we have passed through, all of whom nourished and sheltered us in different ways. Many generous and brilliant humans have woven their creative wisdoms, wit, friendship, and support through this project over many years: Adam Brinton, Christine Cearnal, Jack Christian, Rennie Elliot, Adam Lore, Kelly Marksbury, Jacob Mitas, Melanie Moser, George Murer, Alex Ney, Beth Sale, Emily Stone, Julie Stein, Christine Toth, and many other friends, students, and fellow wanderers of varying species we met along the way. I owe deep thanks for care and support to Alice Beretta DVM, Maria Cortes, Amy Krohn, Philomath Montessori School, Marie Skersick, Richard and Pam Skersick, and the Smiths. Sebastian Black, Jessica Bozek, Shane Carpenter, Layne Garrett, Kate Herron, Susanna Hill, Richard Lucyshyn, Douglas Smith, and Eli Queen shared their reflective lenses, improvisational brilliance, and illuminating poetic visions.

In certain spectral ways, the dream of Aliass-to-come was born in the barn on Maple Hill Farm, where the Mutt of Gold and I were lucky enough to live next door to the lofty studio where our dear friend Alice Provensen created wonderful picture books about the farm's inhabitants and beloved ghosts. Later on down the road, we were welcomed into other special barns, guest rooms, basements, backyards, and pastures by old friends and new: Vanessa Batts, Maria McFadden Beek, Don Eulert, Becky and Judy Gale Roberts, Amos and Coulter Fussell Harvey, Karen Hawthorne, Kevin Hayes, Kristina Holm, Laura Rittall, Oak Ridge Riding Club, Ketch Secor, Charlie Strothers, Jeanne Thompson, Libby Tucker, and many others who offered gifts of gnarly crabapples, dusty memories, and shady places to graze or lay down in the leaf litter along the way. And to all the nameless others and friendly roadside grasses in places we passed through, regards and gratitudes: in places known (more or less) as Abbeville, Badlands, Betty Davis Grocery, Bluebird Road, Boyd Tavern, Carnesville, Cedars of Lebanon, Clinton Hollow, Como, Damascus, Fincastle, Mosset, Naked Creek, Nameless, Noon, One Mile Lane, Orland, Paradise, Paris (Tennessee), Perigord Noir, Pleasant Valley, Philomath, Roanoke and Rowan Oak, the bygone Tallahatchie Bridge (and what's below), Whites Creek, Wilderness Trail, Valley of Dooms, Weyers Cave, Les Eyzies... and so many overflowings between and beyond.

I cannot possibly say what all we owe to Mariann Black, who not only brought me and Aliass together and outfitted us radically for the road but who also saved our ass more times than anyone could know. Also in unforgettable ways, Tom Bolender was there for me and Aliass at the ragged end of the trail. Down the road in Roanoke, Cheryl Haas welcomed us into the long-eared camaraderie of her rambunctious herd and cared for me and Aliass and Pass in many ways. On what has to be the most beautiful farm in the galaxy, Fred Taylor offered us boundless friendship, radical mechanical genius, and a wondrous place to come to ground.

The shaping of a slow-ass poetic implosion into an enduring art-research practice over almost two decades owes massive gratitude and reverence to my exquisite mentors Laiwan, Ruth Wallen, Ju-Pong Lin, and Goddard College's singular MFA–Interdisciplinary Arts program. Lately the Rural Alchemy Workshop has been richly augmented by fertile, dirty glimmerings and earthly wisdoms of Annie Sprinkle and Beth Stephens, Laboratory for Aesthetics and Ecology, Kultivator, and dance for plants. Pamela Albanese has been a steadfast friend and inspiration since we were seven on Green End Avenue. L-Haw (Lydia Peelle) has lit spiraling and deliciously thistly paths since (Mule) Day One, and on and on they g((o)).

Wrangling our R.A.W. ass storying experiments into rippling realms of multispecies studies and art-research in surprising ways, Eben Kirksey has been an enthusiastic champion of this work for a decade. Engagement with vital creative-critical research nodes owes much to the support of Environmental Humanities at UNSW in Sydney. I am especially grateful for the inspiring guidance of Thom van Dooren and Stephen Muecke. For infusions of hot feminist compost, I bow to Astrida Neimanis, Jennifer Mae Hamilton, and Lindsey Kelly. Insights came from early readers Jay Babcock, Jennifer Blair, Mark Bilbrey, Nathaniel Brodie, Emily Crawford, Nancy Cuthbert, Richard Dillard, Jeff Fearnside, Julia Johnson, Inman Majors, and Bonnie Roop Bowles. More recently the project was gifted reassurance and brilliant provocations from Ida Bencke, Sophie Chao, Felicity Fenton, Kristin Guest, Tessa Laird, Stephanie LeMenager, Natalie Loveless, and Laura McLauchlan. Out of the blue, Erin Manning, Brian Massumi, and the global 3Ecologies posse entertained a rather odd not-book proposal and embraced its ass-backwards ways. It is an utter thrill to be associated with their radiant immediations, and another gift to be part of the radical generosity of punctum books, piloted by the miraculous Vincent W.J. van Gerven Oei and Eileen A. Fradenburg Joy.

The most onerous burdens of this project have been borne by those I hold dearest, especially the unnamed one(s). Whatever is good here is dedicated to them. For the gifts of implosive words and sustaining barnyard kinships and care, my mother Christie Bolender has my muddiest, hoofworn gratitude and love. Here I stand in grateful awe of the generosity and brilliance of my partners in rural alchemy: Sean Hart, who builds, hangs true and holds open the most beautiful barn doors and postlibraries I could ever imagine, and Rolly Kestrel, who listens and cares deeply for the wild secret tales of you-no-hoos and m<other tongues to come.

Invitation to an Unnaming
(or, Untold Stories from the Road to Nameless)

Nameless, Tennessee is a small unincorporated patchwork of farmlands and home plots that sits atop a Cumberland hill, east of Nashville, west of Knoxville, and not far from a manmade lake called Cordell Hull, managed by the US Army Corps of Engineers. Nameless is barely a dot on the map – grid coordinates G12 in the *Tennessee Gazetteer,* to be exact. On that day we passed through it in the summer of 2002, Nameless came across as a fairly ordinary Middle Tennessee settlement, typical of the rural, early twenty-first-century US mid-South: a rolling landscape of mostly single-family homes with shades drawn against the heat of day, mostly on paved driveways and an acre or two of mown lawn, and spaced amid crop fields, thickets of prickers and creeper vines, and patches of hardwood forest. A rural American palimpsest much like any other, perhaps, stitched together by shady backroads that turned from asphalt to gravel and back again, flickering with shadows of global petrochemical and other extractive industries and a vague postindustrial malaise.

Ordinary though it may have seemed, I must say this about Nameless, Tennessee: that day in late June 2002 –

spent meandering slowly along shady hills and rolling byways of Jackson County amid constant birdsong, leafy brilliance, lawnmower hums, far-off thunder rumbles, and the occasional bray of an unseen mule – was one of the most extraordinary outings I've ever experienced. What made this particular passage through Nameless so special that bright-dark summer day was not just the pro-vocative allure of the town's unlikely name, nor the frag-ile beauties of its glistening understories, thick as they were with ghostly histories and lively unreckoned mesh-es. Rather, the most extraordinary thing about Nameless, Tennessee on that particular day was this: I found my-self passing through it with a certain wise, luminous, and quietly otherworldly American Spotted Ass.

Who shall remain unnamed.

"Aliass" is a handle by which I have come to know (in some ways), love (a lot), and honor (I hope) the embod-ied mortal beasthood of a certain wondrous companion, member of the species *Equus asinus* and also (significant-ly) a registered American Spotted Ass. This lovely inscru-table beast, whom I was lucky enough to find in Tennes-see, helped carry a ridiculous burden of human longings and quandaries into a maze of hot, harrowing miles over a seven-week walking journey across the American South in that summer of 2002 – beginning in Mississippi, weav-ing through Tennessee, ending in Virginia – all the while bearing her own untold burdens and histories. And so she has been carrying various specialized and mostly less onerous loads ever since, with hardly ever a wrinkled nos tril of complaint. And nary a stumble, even in the most uncertain of territories.

In a certain sense, the special she-ass of whom I speak is the unwitting hero of the story at hand. More than that, "Aliass" also stands for something harder to grasp than the body of a lovely little ass: familiar forms of pro-tagonist, setting, and even common narrative tropes turn inside-out inside this "name-that-ain't," making room for unwritten tales and lacunae that abound within shapes and shadows of the myriad lives that interweave in any environment. Over almost two decades now, Aliass and a herd of long-eared associates have been hearty companions within an ongoing, slow and steady negotiation with slippery names, shifting ways of (un)knowing and composing, and ontological grasping-at-straws, all grounded in the daily demands of good ass husbandry in rural US barnyards and roadsides.

As it happens, it was a specific twenty-first-century human morass of conflicted impulses, longings, and shames that drove me and Aliass out on the road that summer of 2002, across three Southern states and beyond. Most of all, though, what drove me (and so her, too) was a ferocious desire to compose truer-to-life and more inclusive stories. We are never really alone in our life stories, after all. Centuries of Western tales spotlight (certain) human enterprises and leave everybody else outside, yet animate worlds are always meshes of thinking, feeling, perceiving, and responding lives that connect and communicate across tissues, membranes, and senses of all kinds. While *Homo sapiens* may be uniquely adapted to the arts of storytelling (such as we recognize them), attentions to wildly diverse lives find significant sequences of events playing out across cells, neural pathways, and porous bodies of many different kinds – from cooperative strivings of bacteria, mycelia, and roots within forest understories to dolphins who make visual puns, rats who laugh, and foxes who mourn and bury their dead. The field of cognitive ethology explores arrays of behaviors that Western thought has long guarded as Exclusively Human, from altruism to self-awareness in species as diverse as primates and mollusks. Crows, sheep, and wasps recognize and remember faces (of their own species and others); elephants express rumblesome joys and suffer PTSD; octopuses plan for the future; even the nematode *C. elegans* has neurochemical states akin to emotions in other species. Plants communicate in mind-blowing ways with allies and predators, cooperate with microbial communities, listen and respond to who is chewing on them, and remember and adapt routes of growth to accommodate others.[1]

As new insights about others' lives emerge through scientific and cultural shifts of awareness, we begin to understand how ecologies we inhabit, and the companions we live among and care for, already and always have their own stories – however ignored or denied. In light of all this liveliness, how can we crack open anthropocentric modes of naming and storytelling so that all kinds of bodies might inscribe ongoing life stories, in their own specific ways and idioms, into the mapping of timeplaces?[2]

1   On the human predilection for storytelling and its underlying evolutionary meshes, see Brian Boyd, *On the Origin of Stories: Evolution, Cognition, and Fiction* (Cambridge: Harvard University Press, 2009), 42–79; on advances in cognitive ethology, see Frans de Waal, *Are We Smart Enough to Know How Smart Animals Are?* (New York: W.W. Norton and Co., 2016); on moody worms, see Scott W. Emmons, "The Mood of a Worm," *Science* 338, no. 6106 (2012): 475; on the complexity of plants' social lives, see Matthew Hall, *Plants as Persons* (New York: SUNY Press, 2011) and Meeri Kim, "Can Plants Hear? In a Study, Vibrations Prompt Some to Boost Their Defenses," *Washington Post*, July 6, 2014, https://www.washingtonpost.com/national/health-science/can-plants-hear-study-finds-that-vibrations-prompt-some-to-boost-their-defenses/2014/07/06/8b2455ca-02e8-11e4-8fd0-3a663dfa68ac_story.html.

2   As Deborah Bird Rose and Libby Robin assert: "We would compound the Cartesian epistemological error if we were to ignore (or forget) that the world already has its own stories. Scientists approach this issue through theories of communication, proposing, for example, that all living things (cells, plants, bladderworts, etc.) are expressive communicators [...]. In the social sciences and humanities we are challenged to foster an expressivity that is suited to the connectivities we are exploring and communicating, and that is both vigorous and rigorous." Deborah Bird Rose and Libby Robin, "Ecological Humanities in Action: An Invitation," *Australian Humanities Review* 31–32 (2004). See also Eben Kirksey and Stefan Helmreich, "The Emergence of Multispecies Ethnography," *Cultural Anthropology* 25, no. 4 (2010): 545–76 and Maria Puig de la Bellacasa, *Matters*

In a paroxysmal mission to make room for new kinds of stories, then, the first journey with Aliass departed with a flourish from traditional, humanly exclusive modes of word-bound narrative: literally, swerving off from a little literary pilgrimage to Rowan Oak, the country estate of late modernist Southern author William Faulkner, in Oxford, Mississippi. We set out on this quest as a pair of embodied beasts – one wracked with ethical and poetic conflicts and questions, and the other bound to bear the burdens of them – into these uniquely storied realms of Faulkner's fictional Yoknapawtapha County and beyond, with the intent of immersing into otherwise place-bound stories. Departing quite literally from sidetracked dreams of authoring an epic (anti)hero's journey novel, that original trek with Aliass from Mississippi to Virginia in 2002 sought instead to honor tales of untold others, composed with countless millions of other inscrutable lives and erased histories in all the places we passed through. The first long-ass journey sought to gesture toward fullblown embodied-biological-ecological storyings that a lone mind (of any kind) could never author alone but always participates in, in both known and unknown ways.

This particular quest for untold stories (or the more precise, if bulkier "storyings with untold others") has guided my own specific "assthetic" aims and art practices for nearly two decades. Meanwhile, untold stories composed with Aliass wrangle with authority that is shot through with conflicted desires from the get-go: whatever I might say of the restless dreams and anxious hankerings that motivated that initial excursion for me, the intentions, desires, and feelings endured by my sweet ass companion through those days of harrowing hot highway miles and sweltering gas-station parking lots are another story – and never mine alone to tell. In bottomless grati-

of Care: Speculative Ethics in More Than Human Worlds (Minneapolis: University of Minnesota Press, 2017).

tude and humility, I can say one thing for sure about our adventures together, from that first revelatory and onerous trek across the mid-South to the different dwellings and kinships we've inhabited together ever since: The fact that this wise and dainty, white-lashed and graceful long-eared equine is the one I ended up with for the long haul, rather than some ornerier ass antagonist, must be the boon of a lifetime. If she was not who she is, we would have died in a Mississippi ditch. By some lucky stars, she is who she is, and we are still alive.

All this and much more brought me and Aliass to find ourselves wandering the shady hills and hollows of Nameless, Tennessee that day in June 2002 – in many ways a crazy-ass dream come true. We set out early that day from our campsite by the lake at the Wilderness Trail horse camp. Fresh in the early-morning coolness and encouraged by faint and far-off rumbles of thunder, we departed from an empty Baptist church parking lot in Liberty and slowly ascended a long, steep, gravelly hill. We paused often on the ascent, to bask in a passing cloudburst, scrawl notes, remove an eager tick questing for a warm crevice, or to grab a mouthful of roadside grasses. After some time, we arrived, slightly wet, at the crest of that big hill, just as the little storm passed and the sun broke over the land. The tobacco was glistening in the furrowed fields, and the blackberries were fat on the vines. All of Nameless glowed and twinkled in post-thunderstorm light. After clipping along for another half mile or so, we came upon a friendly white-haired lady in her yard, tending to flowerbeds full of towering cosmos and tiger-lilies and other bright blooms. She invited us to stay for lunch and rest a while in the shade of her carport. She offered Aliass an apple and a drink of water and me a sandwich and some sweet tea. When I asked how Nameless got its name, she drew a blank, and then said it must have been that none of its founders could come up with a better one.

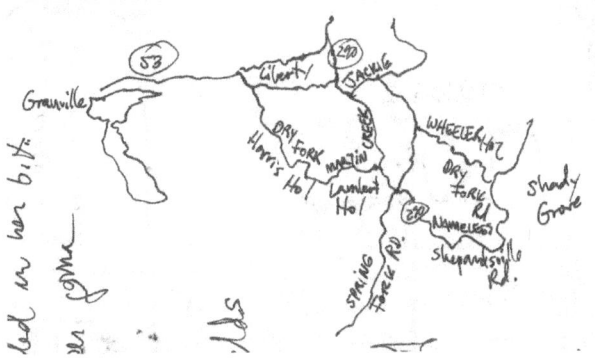

Fig. 1. Sketched map of roads around Nameless, Tennessee, copied from a gazetteer as a pocket-guide for navigating a loop with Aliass one midsummer day in 2002. Courtesy of the artist.

I admit to passing through Nameless that day with no small measure of poetic reverie, and even homage to beloved fictions. (I wore a t-shirt that said "Molloy" in homemade yellow iron-on bubble letters). And in a way, this entire project bears the burden of an assbackwards desire to dwell inside one haunting and bitingly paradisiacal line from Beckett's inimitable novel: "Yes even then, when all was fading, there could be no things but nameless things, no names but thingless names."[3] If only in a dreamy way – dreaming of a quiet escape, that is, from the serrated blades of names and classifications that unjustly cut and cleave bodies (via Karen Barad, "onto-epistemologically") from each other and from the ecological meshes that sustain earthly lives – we nonetheless plodded on with the full expectation of surveying an average, if pleasantly pastoral, twenty-first-century rural us Southern settlement, with its driveways full of shiny suvs, trash-strewn creek-beds with rusty runoff pipes dripping suspicious chemicals, and festoons of synthetic yard decor from Walmart. And we did find all this. But we

3   Samuel Beckett, *Molloy* (1955; rpt. New York: Grove Press, 1991), 31.

also encountered other things, less easily traced or identifiable.[4]

Yes even here, in places exhaustively roaded and signposted and mapped and mined by bottomless colonial rapacities, haunted by historical erasures and trashed by global economies, the experience of passing through living places in the bright penumbra of Aliass's special company has the capacity to dissolve static certainties of maps and names, to open flow-ways for new kinds of attentions and attunements. In Aliass's presence, it becomes possible to notice anew how every place we pass through is comprised of shifting, vibrantly mysterious life-ways – always more than the sum of geographic, material, even perceivable parts and energies. Passing through Nameless, Tennessee in the company of an unnamed she-ass, a person might quietly dwell for a time in the implications and possibilities of Gregory Bateson's assertion in *Mind and Nature: A Necessary Unity*: "The map is not the territory, and the name is not the thing named."[5]

I might go so far as to say that this special mode of dissolution we tasted along the road to Nameless that day was the hoped-for aim of that entire long-ass adventure in 2002, and so too all its ongoing hope-ridden barnyard habitations. So let us embark, then, from this auspicious point of departure, on an ongoing quest to

4 Karen Barad, *Meeting the Universe Halfway* (Durham: Duke University Press, 2007), 185.
5 As Bateson explains: "This principle, made famous by Alfred Korzybski [...] reminds us in a general way that when we think of coconuts or pigs, there are no coconuts or pigs in the brain. Korzybski's statement asserts that in all thought or perception or communication about perception, there is a transformation, a coding, between the report and the thing reported, the *Ding an sich*. Above all, the relation between the report and that mysterious thing reported tends to have the nature of a *classification*, an assignment of the thing to a class. Naming is always classifying, and mapping is essentially the same thing as naming." Gregory Bateson, *Mind and Nature: A Necessary Unity* (Cresskill: Hampton Press, 2002), 27.

make new spaces for more radically inclusive modes of storying. Even untold stories have to begin somewhere. In the fertile cracks where words and maps and bodies-in-places implode, slowly but surely, in full-blown, never-to-be-told adventures, we proceed in the company of a certain inscrutable and humbly beautiful spotted beast of burden, respectfully (un)known as Aliass.

"Ass"

Paradoxically, perhaps, this adventure into seamy territories between words and bodies-in-places was initially enabled by the discovery of one small but powerful three-letter word, and a dirty one, no less: the word was "ass." In creative practice, certain loaded words or images sometimes ignite, like fireworks or dynamite, to blow open unforeseen openings across some previously intractable impasse. Artists have no choice but to trust such implosive obsessions; potent metaphors can sometimes be our only means of getting through. Unlikely figures can lead the way into territories that might otherwise spook the rational mind. Sometimes such passions even offer illuminated paths, like lights that shine along the smoky aisle of an airplane cabin, shining forth to carry cracked hopes through the cold black winds of terrible times.

This is how it was on that wondrous, fateful day I discovered my true ass – the American Spotted Ass, that is. True to the twenty-first-century, I first encountered this enchanting and transformative figure in cyberspace, on the website of the American Council of Spotted Asses (http://www.spottedass.com). At first I thought it might have been a joke. This preposterous website asserted that people all around the US, and especially Texas and the West Coast, were breeding donkeys for what is called "color" in the parlance of equine enthusiasts: that is, a genetic inheritance of multicolored haircoat, also known as "pinto," "piebald," "Paint" or, in this case, "Spotted."

Though I could not have said why at the time, the notion of breeding and thus classifying piebald donkeys struck me at the gut level as ridiculous, possibly even sinister. In the very same breath, I was instantly enflamed with a full-blown passion for a newfangled breed called the American Spotted Ass.

In later years, I would come to unpack certain racist colonial histories inscribed in this genetic coding for equine coat color. Once anathema in the early-twentieth-century US among colonial horse people – loosely due to associations with "half-breed" Indian ponies or gypsy steeds in Europe – the same pinto/paint/spotted coloring on horses began to get appropriated in the later twentieth century as a popular (if ambiguous and shifting) symbol of American patriotism. Though these cultural nodes are scattered and diffuse, the shift of spotted equine hides from a stain of "bad breeding" to hot commodity hit me gut-wise, and sparked both intuitive discomfort and an implosive frisson of radical possibility. Years later, I would come to explore and play with these shifts and their implications more deeply. At first blush, though, the call of this chimeric Spotted Ass figure was primarily visceral. I sensed worlds unfolding in the flickering promise of this humble and unassuming donkey breed, splatted with spots and saddled with a dubious name.[6] Worlds where a person might find detours around cer-

---

6   Presumably the founding and naming of a breed is a fairly high-stakes endeavor that one should always take seriously. Harriet Ritvo's *Platypus and the Mermaid* describes what was at stake in the classification and naming of a breeder's product in the English eighteenth and nineteenth centuries – how early breeders of domestic livestock competed with multiple claims to scientific authority, whether in burgeoning species classifications or dubbing their own variations on them. The stakes are high indeed; naming a breed is an act of reification, after all, making certain biological traits into a unique exchange of words and flesh. Harriet Ritvo, *The Platypus and the Mermaid, and Other Figments of the Classifying Imagination* (Boston: Harvard University Press, 1997), 75.

tain colonial Western traps and myths, and even find new paths (however slow and assbackwards) into tangles of language and bodies, names and unnamables, and barbed quandaries of gender and species enmeshed in questionable ethics of companion animal and livestock breeding.[7]

Another aspect of the implosive power of "ass" was the fact that it was the one so-called dirty word my mother discouraged me from uttering as a child. She claimed it was "unladylike" and even "crass." This is one of very few linguistic prohibitions that came down from a mother who had her own mouth washed out with soap as a teenager for telling her little brother to "shut up." Raising her own daughter, she frowned on "fuck" and "shit," yes, but for some reason "ass" was the only bad word that she forbade, and in fact I refrained from using it into adolescence and onward.[8] And yet... within the stirring

7 Drawing me into feminist science studies viscerally through the lure of warmly beloved (in this case, canine) bodies, Donna Haraway's *Companion Species Manifesto* opened my critical awareness to deeper histories, responsibilities, and challenges inherent in the privileges of breeding domestic species to suit cultural and personal tastes, along with the mind-bending ethical issues that arise with cloning and other technoscientific adventures. Donna J. Haraway, *The Companion Species Manifesto: Dog, People, and Significant Otherness* (Chicago: Prickly Paradigm Press, 2003).

8 So the word "ass" was loaded with baggage of class and gender from the get-go. Meanwhile, this might be a good opening for a psychoanalytic theorist to probe my tale to explore why I still, to this day, shy away from using the word "ass" in reference to the human body. No doubt this hesitation lies at the root of some deep shit in my own mother tongue, beckoning deeper exploration. I am grateful for the vital and liberatory wisdom in lively ass spaces reclaimed and explored by Maggie Nelson in *The Argonauts* (Minneapolis: Gray Wolf Press, 2015), 84–85; and by Julietta Singh throughout her work, and especially in a scene of poignant mother/daughter ass-wisdom becomings in *No Archive Will Restore You* (Earth: punctum books, 2018), 103. But my own passion in this realm roots less in the precisely anatomical, and more in the promiscuously grammatical and mysteriously metonymic openings of this dirty three-letter word and its special beyond-human possibilities.

possibilities of "ass" as transformed by the multifarious modifiers of "American" and "Spotted" – here representing a relatively rare, humble, and spectacular breed of domestic beast of burden – this dirty word's forbidden nature bloomed with lovely ambiguities and radical possibilities. Even better, it flipped inside-out with the slip-'n-slide felicity of the double-meaning pun, which by nature undermines the hold of any human tongue on bodies and things it is supposed to grasp. I believe "ass" is the only so-called "dirty" word in the American vernacular that also appears in Holy Scripture.[9]

"Ass" was just what I needed to implode certain impasses in the mother tongue, to blast through the seams between words and animate worlds that pester every aspiring poet, artist, or philosopher. As the taproot of an idiom, "ass" became something like a skeleton key.[10] Mixed with these extraordinary and complex modifiers, "American" and "Spotted," "ass" became over time a secret and blassphemous password, unlocking gate after gate into labyrinthine depths of psycholinguistic imagination and material incarnation. In other words, I had no better option than to seize upon this kaleidoscopic portal that was the American Spotted Ass, with all the forces of longing for misplaced family of mammals and lost sites of barnyard belonging.

9   That is to say, the Old Testament of the Christian Bible, a text that suffuses and shapes the social and political landscapes of the Southern "Bible Belt" states Aliass and I passed through in 2002 and beyond, as a sociocultural force that is arguably as much if not more powerful than the local/global industries and infrastructures.

10 In *Cosmopolitics I*, contemporary philosopher of science Isabelle Stengers presents what she calls "a question of creating words that are meaningful only when they bring about their own reinvention, words whose greatest ambitions would be to become elements of histories that, without them, might have been slightly different." Isabelle Stengers, *Cosmopolitics I* (Minneapolis: University of Minnesota Press, 2010), 13.

On the Road with an American Spotted Ass

This implosive affair with the American Spotted Ass, as such, kicked off a cascade of events and implications that eventually led me and Aliass to find ourselves zigzagging our ways across three Southern states, from Mississippi to Virginia, in the summer of 2002. Haunted as I was by the seeming impasse between human naming and other embodied ways of knowing and becoming, I delighted in the sweet-ass pun because it figured the vast gulf between knowing the name of a species and knowing lives of any kind more deeply. It opened a kind of vital crack in certain assumptions about human language and the authority of the "classifying imagination." And it was from that wondrous crack of "ass" that possibilities for new modes of storying – toward new ways of making worlds with untold others – emerged.[11] In the years that followed, those seven intense weeks Aliass and I spent navigating asphalt and concrete infrastructures, (cosmo)political crevasses and crossings, and tracing otherwordly paths (through slatted barn-darks, colonial pastures, and seedy parking lot carnivals) gave way to decades of making homes in different places, with the aid of specific artistic, poetic, and critical practices. In every opening, I have sought ways to slip through divisive, barbed-wire assumptions laced through languages and the names, hierarchies, and dominant narratives we pass through and pass on.[12]

11 In *Thinking Animals*, Kari Weil sidles gracefully from Claude Lévi-Strauss's well-known statement that "animals are good to think with" to her own book's "premise that it is good to 'unthink' animals and so to rethink our conclusions about who we are, who they are, and how we are all entwined." Kari Weil, *Thinking Animals: Why Animal Studies Now?* (New York: Columbia University Press, 2012), xvii. In this regard, the linguistic crack of "ass" invited a space in which to dissolve and "unthink" particular acts and implications of classifications like "animal" and "ass," as appended to laconic equine friends.

12 This project as a whole makes the claim that un/naming a she-ass companion is an act of resistance and even hopeful remediation, in

At the beginning of the first long-ass journey, I still operated under the guise of "author." Secretly, though, I was already determined that our time on the road itself comprised the stories that mattered – not whatever words or sentences or scenes might be wrung from it in the long run. Over those weeks of traveling with Aliass, I became more and more assured that the truest, most beautiful book I could imagine must be a collective enterprise, indeterminately writ (if writ at all), with the full participation of the she-ass in question and every other trace of lives and becomings we passed through. The unnamed ass must be co-author, in her own inscrutable way, as much as I was in mine, along with all those bright little cedarlings and stray dogs and red-eyed cicadas and parking lots brimming with brightly clad Baptists on Wednesday evenings, and all the muds and lichens and roadside creeper vines, turtles and thunderclouds, blowsy thistles, and even that old yellow goat who watched idly from her rope on the tiny porch of an aquamarine, single wide trailer home, while a ferocious pack of Pomeranians yapped from inside a chain-link pen as Aliass and I wandered past on Bluebird Road one Tennessee evening.... The author of such a journey, any journey for that matter, could never be one human alone. A journey, as such, is always co-composed, however inscrutably, with teeming meshes of lives: every undulating knot of ways, affects,

---

light of the false ways that names tend to cleave bodies and ecologies. But Mel Chen writes in *Animacies* that naming practices are always fraught with matterings of all kinds and beyond control, however we pitch them, whether as affectionate nicknames or racial slurs (or sometimes hybrid combinations). Chen reminds us that names are unavoidable as "cognitive processes of mundane object-rendering as a result of everyday cognizing and discourse. [...] Yet it is important to recognize that linguistic objectification is framed by historical, national, and social configurations of power, and is not always able to be recuperated into realms of pleasure." Mel Chen, *Animacies: Biopolitics, Racial Mattering, and Queer Affect* (Durham: Duke University Press, 2012), 49.

and "becomings-with" that ravels visibly and invisibly in all those places in time.[13]

Both inside and beyond that original journey, though, I struggled to negotiate between sweet-ass dissolutions borne in timeplaces and the seemingly opposing task of sitting down at the keyboard to conscript shared experiences into text, given only limited perspective and vocabulary to draw from. What I really wanted most was to find ways to let wordless interweavings of bodies-in-timeplaces tell their own stories. Co-authored a million times over, and all somehow respectfully (un)told.

Assmilk

Although her condition was not apparent that day we met in the dusty gloom of a Maury County cowshed, Aliass was nearly seven months in foal. Fetal asses gestate for twelve months, often to the day, so at this stage we had a good five months of journeying before we'd need to find a safe place to settle down and raise a little ass family. (Only later, after Passenger was born on September 17, 2002, did I calculate that she must have been conceived around the week of September 11, 2001.) Over the many miles of that first harrowing trek from Mississippi to Virginia – as I walked behind Aliass day after day on

13   The kinds of companion-species "becomings-with" elaborated in the works of Vinciane Despret and Donna Haraway, and in affect theory – particularly by Brian Massumi at the intersection of literary/aesthetic and animal studies, and Kathleen Stewart and others in ficto-critical fashion – are key touchstones for the process of un/telling slippery-ass stories. See Vinciane Despret, *What Would Animals Say If We Asked the Right Questions?* (Minneapolis: University of Minnesota Press, 2016); Donna Haraway, *When Species Meet* (Minneapolis: University of Minnesota Press, 2008); Brian Massumi, "Becoming-Animal in the Literary Field," in *Animals, Animality, and Literature,* eds. Bruce Boehrer, Molly Hand, and Brian Massumi (Cambridge: Cambridge University Press, 2018), 265–83; and Kathleen Stewart, *Ordinary Affects* (Durham: Duke University Press, 2007).

city streets and rural backroads, and as we slept nights in random churchyards and patches of woods – a biological fact I absorbed years before in an equine-husbandry class kept coming back to me: a pregnant mammal should never leave her local environment just before giving birth, because her thick first milk, known as *colostrum*, contains antibodies to the specific pathogens where she has been gestating. By extension, then, all milk is enmeshed with places, made of everything the mammalian mother body eats, drinks, and breathes as she feeds the growing fetus and eventually the newborn.

All across the ferociously hot, haunted, weedy, and bastard-beautiful South that summer, Aliass's gut and blood and mammaries brewed antibodies to hidden, harmful elements in the places we passed through. Aliass was percolating a super-charged fetal-ass healing brew! This colostrum she made held residual traces of all the places we traveled through, as we waded through roadside weeds and trash and broken glass, glysophate hazes and thistle-grown hayfields, lonesome crossroads and abandoned train-tracks, and the harrowed traces of bygone mules and ghosts and other invisible residues of the American South. Aliass's body made this special milk night and day, in the paralyzing heat and in the shade, and from every blade of roadside grass, handful of blackberries, and drink of water from a trickling creek or cracked-edge pond along the way, from the ditch where she sipped as the red sun went down on the Peace Park in Oak Ridge, Tennessee – the formerly secret city where they refined uranium for the atom bombs that destroyed Hiroshima and Nagasaki – to the melting Creamsicles we shared with local kids who followed us for blocks along the blazing, broken sidewalks of Nashville housing projects. So Aliass's milk-to-be held traces of borrowed pastures and border-crossings, wakeful nights in strangers' woods, and infinite encounters with countless other beings, both familiar and unseen – held it all like memory is supposed to.

Meanwhile, milks of all earthly mammals these days hold unseen elements that are not so wholesome or hopeful. From flame-retardant fabrics to phthalates to carcinogenic and endocrine-disrupting PCBs and neurotoxins we collect from drinking water and conventional wheat, mammalian bodies accumulate byproducts of industrial processes and chemical pollutions through air, soil, water, and food. Processes of biomagnification, by which toxic chemicals in the environment become concentrated in mammary glands, make that first vital nourishment of newborns into a poisonous cocktail laced with toxic chemicals. As Mirium Simun writes in her recipe for "Human Cheese": "The list of chemical toxins found in human milk reads something like an acronym alphabet – it includes CDDS, CDFS, DDT, NPS, OWCS, PCBS, and PBDE, as well as dibenzofurans, Triclosan, heavy metals, and bromine-based flame retardants."[14] And yet somehow – from Rachel Carson's 1960s revelations about the effects of DDT on wildlife to unrelenting discoveries of human runoffs harming marine life, birds, amphibians, and countless other lives – news of biological porosity continues to shock us. Maybe because the same false distinctions that allow humans to imagine our bodies as singularly impervious to environmental pollutions persist in other ways, in mother tongues where names and classifications supposedly hold humans separate from surrounding webs of

---

14 Mirum Simun, "Human Cheese," in *The Multispecies Salon* (Durham: Duke University Press, 2014), 137. On biomagnification in breastmilk, also see Eva Simms, "Eating One's Mother," *Environmental Ethics* 31 (2009): 263–77 and Winona LaDuke, "Akwesasne: Mohawk Mother's Milk and PCBs," in *Sing, Whisper, Shout, Pray! Feminist Visions for a Just World*, eds. M. Jacqui Alexander, Lisa Albrecht, Sharon Day, and Mab Segrest (Fort Bragg: Edgework, 2003), 159–71.

life.[15] At the same time, milk also holds traces of unspoken intimacies and nourishing exchanges we gather on our journeys through times and places. From this thick mix of pollutions and possibilities comes the tainted hope that milk of compromised earthly bodies might still hold unique powers to heal and protect, and perhaps (in the tricky logic of the *pharmakon*) these powers might even be warily amplified by contaminations.[16]

In the late summer of 2002, after seven weeks on the road from Mississippi, Aliass and I settled on a magnificent hundred-acre farm near the small hilltop town of Fincastle in the Appalachian foothills of southwest Virginia. Beyond the slatted walls and lofty, owl-habited beams of the rambling barn, a stunning landscape of wooded ridges, vast pastures, and secret pawpaw groves spread out in splendorous wild mystery along a rolling mountain creek. Here we dug in and waited, as Aliass grew rounder and wider into the coming autumn. Passenger was born at long last in mid-September. After riding along *in utero* the whole way, the newborn spotted she-ass stood wobbly to suckle on that rich colostrum, which

15 Manmade toxins move through biologies of all kinds, affirming in fearsome ways that bodies are less impervious to environments than we like to suppose. While not an antidote, exactly, Stacey Alaimo elaborates on the generative rethinking of this ill-conceived separation through the "material turn in feminist theory," whereby scholars theoretically extend "the paradigms of poststructuralism, postmodernism, and cultural studies in ways that can more productively account for the agency, 'thought,' and dynamics of bodies and natures." Stacey Alaimo, "Trans-Corporeal Feminisms and the Ethical Space of Nature," in *Material Feminisms*, eds. Stacey Alaimo and Susan Hekman (Bloomington: Indiana University Press, 2008), 242.

16 As Brian Massumi notes, we might be alert to a troublesome, "dominant self-defining" characteristic embedded in the notion of the *pharmakon*, wherein humans tend to pitch ourselves as the only antidote to our own earthly poisonings: "What gives pause is that this maintains unchanged the human sense of its own nature, and its position at the apex of the pyramid of nature in the wider sense." Massumi, "Becoming-Animal in the Literary Field," 265.

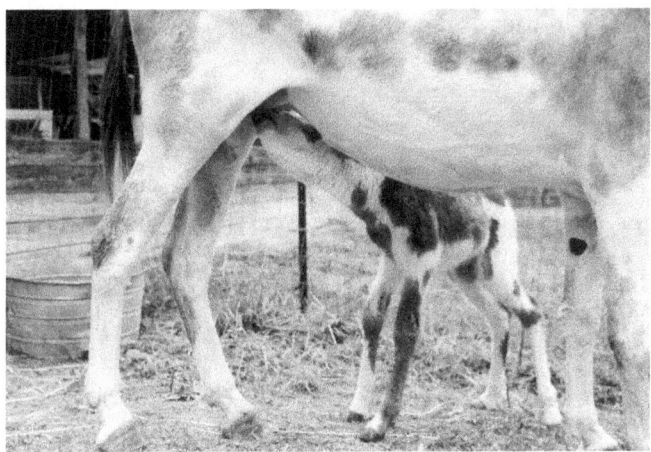

Fig. 2. Aliass nurses newborn Passenger in Fincastle, September 2002.
Photograph by the artist.

held traces of our whole long-ass journey, along with sustenance from the sweetly fleeting peace-of-ass we found,
tucked in those old hills in its aftermath. Passenger grew
up her bones and thick fur and gut on the microbial, nu-
tritional, and other elements of Aliass's milk. Meanwhile,
from its pasture grasses and woods and local hayfields,
Fincastle nourished all of us in sublime material and affective ways. But as the years passed, and our adventures
on the road began to fade, the notion of Aliass's milk
holding unnamable immunological essences and epige-
netic residues of places we had passed through became
more and more potent in my imaginings.

We all live in landscapes and languages that hold –
and mostly hide – traces of lost kinships and human and
ecological atrocities. I pondered this often through that
summer of wandering the South with Aliass. I liked to
imagine that somehow the elements of weeds she ate
along that byway in Tennessee that parallels the Trail of
Tears, or her sips from the murky Tallahatchie waters silt-
ed with traces of racial violence in Mississippi, could be

transformed as they passed through her muzzle tongue, stomach, blood, and glands, to become something more wholesome: foremost, of course, as the colostrum that would nourish Passenger, but also a metaphorical substance. So Aliass's milk became a figural container for all the unique encounters and onerous hopes and longings we each carried all that distance, from Oxford, Mississippi to Nameless, Tennessee to Fincastle, Virginia and beyond. Assmilk came to hold the untellable stories, and all the experiences and becomings a person could never find words for.

On the Road Again...

Ways of being on the road are ways of being in worlds. Living stories unroll with their own momentum and casts of untold millions. After the first journey with Aliass, I could not get past the sense that representing our shared experiences by traditional narrative tropes seemed both ethically inadequate and woefully narrow. Because time lived on steamy summer roadsides in meshes of mammalian senses and plants and microbes and weathering waters is not linear. It is looping, recursive, slow, and repetitive – not a human hero's journey but "something more warped and glancing," as poet Fanny Howe describes a state of bewildered, wide-open wandering.[17] At the same time, most of the Western monomyths and tropes I grew up with – especially those that erase violent colonial tracks and bear hidden assumptions of teleological Human Progress – trample efforts to attend to delicate and fleeting configurations.[18] The bulldozing forces of heroic Human Progress too often blunt our ability to notice and respond

---

17 Fanny Howe, "Bewilderment, or, Incarnation and the Author," *Raddle Moon* 18, no. 2 (2002): 13.
18 Robert Jewett and J.S. Lawrence, *The American Monomyth*, 2nd edn. (Lanham: University Press of America, 1988).

within what Thom van Dooren and Deborah Bird Rose call "entangled storyings."[19]

How we make stories within living places matters, because as Thom van Dooren describes, "the stories we live by" shape worlds, as "they 'rearticulate' us as beings at stake in one another's lives in various ways."[20] Yet the dominion of Eurocentric human exceptionalism most often excludes other species' ways of knowing and narrating, thereby vanquishing prospects for more inclusive worldings in the stories we make and pass on. On the road with Aliass, I wanted to inhabit and frame such entangled storyings, to invite all kinds of meaning-making bodies, forms, and substances into the journey's unfolding – or at least to gesture to various shaping contributions and experiences of all kinds of bodies and affects. Being a human hitched irrevocably to language, though, I continued to be moved by a desire to let nameless interweavings of bodies in time somehow *be the text*. I found that even in the aftermath of that first journey with Aliass, this desire remained stuck in a double bind, a kind of poetic no-man's land: with no choice, it seemed, but to suck it up and claim the sacred burden of human authorship, or... what?

To this day, this "what" remains an open question at the heart of a slow, site-specific, interdisciplinary ass

19 As Van Dooren and Rose write, "[P]laces are co-constituted in processes of overlapping and entangled 'storying' in which different participants may have very different ideas about where we have come from and where we are going." Thom van Dooren and Deborah Bird Rose, "Storied-Places in a Multispecies City," *Humanimalia* 3, no. 2 (2012): 3.

20 Following philosophers Val Plumwood and Vinciane Despret, Thom van Dooren goes on to say in *Flightways* that, "The affective separation of human exceptionalism holds the more-than-human world at arm's length: human exceptionalism plays a central role in the active process of our learning not to be affected by nonhuman others." Thom van Dooren, *Flightways: Life and Loss at the Edge of Extinction* (New York: Columbia University Press, 2014), 150–51.

art practice. And so with bottomless apologies to the donkeys in question, I have to report that our forays on Southern US roadways did not end with arrival in the pastoral peace-of-ass of those exquisitely beautiful, mountain-ringed pastures of Fincastle, Virginia. In the summer of 2004, a team of asses (Aliass and a big-boned ringer named Brawnson) hauled a strange and peculiarly American vehicle known as the Dead-Car Wagon on a slow crossing. (Passenger, who was still too young to pull, tagged alongside.) Departing from the gates of a rural Virginia NASCAR speedway, the Dead-Car Wagon rolled south, over the state line, to end its travels in an abandoned church parking lot in Eden, North Carolina.

The Dead-Car Wagon's material body was resurrected from the stripped-down carcass of a rusty orange 1980 Ford Pinto, pulled by the ass team and driven by two human drivers with questionable aspirations to move poetic imagination off the page and out into the world in new ways. The Dead-Car Wagon was incarnated in collaboration with poet Jack Christian, whose ideas, words, and labors shaped the Wagon's form and fate. It was physically powered by the brave team of Aliass and Brawnson, after it found its ever-precarious form with the help of badass visionary engineer Fred Taylor and local angel-of-asses Cheryl Haas. This Wagon, as such, was an ironically post-Fordist vehicular articulation, heaving with specific burdens of troubled (agri)cultural and industrial histories and cultural appropriations and other cargo, powered by the reluctant labors of sensitive bodies who were harnessed to its fearsome and unwieldy bulk. For three beastly hot days, the Dead-Car crossing performed a creaky meditation on American senses of place and passage, in light of car-culture infrastructures and suburban sprawl, Manifest Destiny and colonial ravages. The Dead-Car Wagon nodded in passing to hordes and herds of rural ghosts along the way, in the kinds of wayside exchanges that become impossible when landscapes and all their

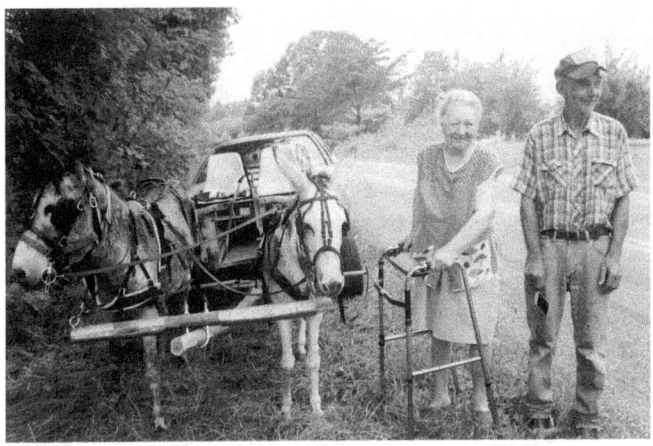

Fig. 3. Brawnson and Aliass take a rest from pulling the Dead-Car Wagon in the blazing heat, stopping across the road from the home of Bertha "Granny" Lankford and her son David Harris in Ridgeway, Virginia. Photograph by Jack Christian.

slower, photosynthetic and plasmodial lifeways – never mind the more or less familiar mammalian ones – are nothing but terminal blurs in windshield glass.

As an in-car-nation of poetic imagination, fretful environmental aspirations, and a surprising (and slightly ominous) material articulation, the Dead-Car Wagon opened spaces for unpredictable conversations with/in places it passed through. Almost every human inhabitant of that haggard rural stretch of Henry County backroads had a sparked memory to share, from Kodachrome-tinted recollections of their own ill-fated Ford Pintos to Granny Lankford's recollections of riding bareback on her daddy's mule to local country dances. One may speculate on other affective connections, but a certain assurance came with the sense that the dead-car crossing resonated in local environs in ways a written text on a page could never do, especially in a region where most (human and otherwise) do not read poetry as a pastime. One afternoon as the Wagon creaked past a row of dilapidated, abandoned-looking mobile homes on a rural Virginia backroad, an old woman came out of her trailer holding a quivering Chihuahua to her chest. As the Wagon rolled past, she pointed at the strange equipage and talked softly to the little dog. Her words, audible only to the Chihuahua, were part of the weaves of unwritten tales and possible poems that the Dead-Car Wagon rolled out to compose-with-others, from its origins in a strange vehicular vision to its final sad abandonment under a weepy black walnut tree, in a lot beside a doomed home-appliance store in postindustrial Eden.

All of the projects performed in the (un)name of Aliass navigate a push-and-pull between traditional expressive forms for creative imagination and a drive to honor and explore nameless ways of knowing and becoming. The Dead-Car crossing, in particular, began to articulate certain implosive "assthetic" impulses of the first long-ass journey in relation to historical and contemporary performance-art forms, theories, and practices – specifically durational, site-specific, and ecological performance. Through years of living with Aliass, what began as a stubborn refusal to claim sole authorship of shared stories became an apprenticeship in what I have come to call "the art of a sull." The sull takes its name – and so too its assbackwards method of resistance – from the old-fashioned term for a specific mode of refusal-to-move practiced by long-eared equines in the face of un-welcome coercion. The sull is, in fact, what gives asses their worldwide infamy as paragons of stubbornness. In the sull, every atom of an ass's (or half-ass's) embodied life is fully dedicated to the act of not-moving in a given direction, which of course is most often the direction some willful human wants that ass to move. We will take up the unique dynamics and wisdoms of the sull in more depth later on, but suffice to say its spirit of resistance infiltrates the shape and methodology of this text through and through. As incorporated in the arts of un-naming Aliass, the sull becomes a distinct *Equus asinus*-affected performative mode of refusing certain colonial human(ist) assumptions of linear progress and narrative, toward the aims of framing multispecies tales we invari-ably make together. Different forays with Aliass over the years have all hoped to open vital cracks in anthropocen-tric modes of storytelling, seeking ways to more deeply attend to different whos and whats and hows of places we pass through.

In this sense, our journeys-as-performance follow paths explored by some contemporary artists, curators, and critics who aim to make space for perspectives and experiences often excluded from art institutions: The art of the sull stands for a different breed of art practice, as a kind of rural-roadside and barnyard-bound "relational assthetics." Yet in their nomadic wakes, projects like the Dead-Car Crossing and subsequent forays left frayed questions of who and what actually benefits from these seemingly well-intentioned excursions. As art critics He-lena Reckitt and Miwon Kwon illustrate in their respec-tive critiques of relational and site-specific art practices, many contemporary socially engaged projects erase vital histories, labors, and experiences both within and be-yond art institutions, even as they open new spaces for others.[21]

21 Nicholas Bourriaud articulated theories of relational aesthetics that have been taken up by many contemporary artists and curators. In an important essay called "Forgotten Relations," Reckitt draws at-tention to the ways that Bourriaud's deployment of relational aes-thetics fails to acknowledge the political and artistic groundwork laid by feminist artists like Mierle Laderman Ukeles and others in the late twentieth century, while she also describes curatorial tactics that combat this erasure. Meanwhile, Miwon Kwon offers a critique of relational art practices that intervene "site-specifically" but re-main heedless of deeper ways in which every place has its own com-plicated, mostly unknown histories, partial connections, and im-plosive energies. See Nicholas Bourriaud, "Relational Aesthetics," in

Fraught questions of inclusion and exclusion become even more complex when the others-in-question are not humans. In places where interconnected lives of all kinds are threatened by toxic chemical and cultural legacies and uncertain climate futures, all relations (assthetic or otherwise) are haunted by questions of belonging and responsibility that lace through soils and waterways, roots and tissues and mother tongues. Beyond dominant artistic forms, systems, and institutions, how can we practice modes of storying so inclusive that they might hold spaces for unknown (even unimaginable) biographical agents, from asses to grasses to microscopic bacillus?

R.A.W. Assmilk Soap

In the spring of 2005, I received a surprise gift from my friend Chris, who had just returned from a trip to France. There she had happened upon the phenomenon of *savon au lait d'ânesse,* or "assmilk soap." Aliass was no longer making milk for Passenger by this time, but even so, when I first held in my hand that paper-wrapped, ylang-ylang-scented French ass soap, all the metaphorical possibilities of assmilk that I had pondered back on the road with Aliass took a sudden and surprising physical form. It felt like somebody had just given me a formula for a foamy Philosopher's Stone, or the blueprint for a *Magnum Opass.* Here suddenly was a material form in which to hold the wordless bodies' storying, inscrutable tales traced in substances made of time and places and suspended, present but untold, in a solid inscrutable bar of Assmilk Soap.

Participation, edited by Claire Bishop (London: Whitechapel, 2006), 160–71; Helena Reckitt, "Forgotten Relations: Feminist Artists and Relational Aesthetics," in *Politics in a Glass: Case Feminism, Exhibition Cultures and Curatorial Transgressions,* eds. Angela Dimitrakaki and Lara Perry (Liverpool: Liverpool University Press, 2013); and Miwon Kwon, *One Place after Another: Site-Specific Art and Locational Identity* (Cambridge: MIT Press, 2004).

This synthesized material object offered a way to hold and solidify assmilk, a substance by nature perishable and elusive, and to transform its immunoglobulins and phospholipids into a cool magical little stone, with properties of both cleansing and healing.[22] With its double-barreled (material and metaphorical) cleansing powers – combining the immunobiology of milk and the unique chemistry of an artisanal cleansing product – Assmilk Soap became an even thicker figural substance for holding untold stories. Here was a form that could hold both the material–biological and parapoetic elements of assmilk and perhaps nourish hopeful, imaginative action. Assmilk Soap presented a foamy, rarefied solvent for polluted environments, languages, and psyches.[23]

As an artistic project, Assmilk Soap aspires to the modes of contemporary ecological artworks that involve both material and metaphorical acts of biological remediation, where artists frame systemic processes to address particular environmental woes. For instance, Jackie Brookner's 1996 installation, *Prima Lingua* (First Language/First Tongue), demonstrates a cycle whereby the biochemical filtering processes of mosses, plants, and volcanic rocks cleanse water polluted by agricultural runoff. As the dirty water runs over the rock – shaped pro-

22 Here with "magic stone" I echo the French poet Francis Ponge, who wrote an entire treatise (simply titled *Soap*) on the nature of a slippery proposition that poetic figurations could cleanse languages of their latent stains. Francis Ponge, *Soap*, trans. Lane Dunlop (Stanford: Stanford University Press, 1998), 19.

23 I am grateful to Ida Bencke and Dea Antonsen of the Laboratory for Aesthetics and Ecology, who have sewn R.A.W. Assmilk Soap into their vital curatorial platform through the lens of parapoetics. The Parapoetics Series, edited by Bencke and featuring innovative works by poets Amanda Ackerman, a. rawlings, and others, pitches parapoetics as "investigation into the array of possibilities and problems for a transspecies semiotics in various aesthetic modulations. Parapoetics exorcises the all-too-human quest for monopoly over voice, inscription, worlding..." http://www.labae.org/past#/para-poetics/.

vocatively like an extended human tongue – the plants
and minerals absorb pollutants, over time cleansing the
water and also the surrounding air. Drawing on its own
sources of pollution and possible remediative actions,
Assmilk Soap seeks to dissolve residues of sticky exceptionalism that separate "human" and "animal" – distinctions that tend to justify the ways many human systems
exploit and desecrate earthly others and exclude embodied wisdoms.[24]

It took another few years to assemble the material
means to actually manufacture Assmilk Soap. In 2008, I
made a first experimental batch under the auspices of a
long-term barnyard-based performance called the Rural
Alchemy Workshop (R.A.W.). The R.A.W. was founded in
Carnesville, Georgia, where for several years our familial
herd lived in a long-neglected, hardscrabble homestead
on a ten-acre plot of forested hills full of majestic oaks
and poplars, gnarly old fruit and nut trees, and piney
paddocks of patchy grass and mud. To make the place
habitable, Sean and I spent the first sweltering summer
in Carnesville building fences, clearing invasive privet,
poison ivy, and plastic trash from the paddocks, and en-
gaging in a surreal and SF-esque battle with the ferocious
reign of fire ants (which, by the way, they almost won).
We labored to make an amenable home within the farm's

24 R.A.W. Assmilk Soap is informed and inspired by ecological artists
like Brookner, Ruth Wallen, Deanna Pindell, Helen and Newton Har-
rison, Mierle Ukeles, and Suzanne Lacy, along with contemporary
indigenous artists like Anne Riley and Cease Wyss who practice
forms of decolonial remediation of bodies, languages, and places.
A now-classic example, Mel Chin's *Revival Field* (1990–ongoing) uses
several different plant species called hyperaccumulators to draw
up toxins from poisoned soil in the Pig's Eye Landfill in Minnesota; Chin draws poetic resonance from cycles of plant growth and
harvest as they cleanse the soil over time. See Linda Weintraub, *To
Life! Eco Art for a Sustainable Planet* (Berkeley: University of California
Press, 2012); and Eben Kirksey, ed., *The Multispecies Salon* (Durham:
Duke University Press, 2014).

old weathered wood and cinderblock structures, and so too within the dominant political, municipal, and neo-liberal asphalt-and-phthalate Dollar-Store and interstate truck-stop infrastructures of rural northeast Georgia. Though ultimately doomed, this enterprise changed all of our lives. For all its compromised beauties, the Carnesville farm offered a shady place on a forested dirt road in which to ground radical forms of husbandry. And it was here that a secret ass dairy operation came to produce R.A.W. Assmilk Soap, on a very small scale, in a landscape that goes a long way toward demonstrating how "the Dirty South" got its name.

Every time it rained on our little ass farm, shards of broken glass and shattered mirrors, scraps of burnt plastic, and bent tangles of rusty metal surfaced from the paddock dirt. This trash was left behind by the farm's previous inhabitants, buried in the heart of the barnyard where the herd lived on bare hooves. In a pile in the feed room, I collected artifacts that surfaced from the mud, until it got too overwhelming. Trashy treasures included old cassette tapes and pink plastic mud-filled My Little Pony™ change purses, jagged metal lightbulb ends, whole antique medicine bottles, and ancient rusty pull-tab beer cans. But mostly the collection was just sharp and dangerous shards of old burnt and broken things. These dangers in the Carnesville barnyard haunted me with a deeper need to know: How deep down does the pollution go? What about the other side of the hill, where the municipal/global powers-that-be bulldozed the hardwood forest and left an apocalyptic mess of ruts and slash for the buzzards to patrol in advance of the coming industrial park? If I dug down deep enough, could I ever find earth that's fertile, dark, and clean?

The proposed cleansing powers of R.A.W. Assmilk Soap are not just about apprehending visible scars of industrial wastelands, but more so attending to hidden pollutions – poisons born of exploited bodies, lands, minerals, and other earthly systems – and the ways these toxic residues linger in tissues, thoughts, and utterances. So the inner realm is where Assmilk Soap really finds its potency, calling upon imagination to bring buried stains to the surface, at least to attend (if not to assuage) them. But what kinds of stains are we talking about here? What kinds of shames and fears? And how can I claim R.A.W. Assmilk Soap works to cleanse them, or even acts as a conduit for hopeful gestures in specific landscapes blasted by past horrors and present complex global economic and biopolitical forces?

These are questions of home, belonging, and home-making in cosmopolitical American ass barnyards: Who all lives here? How can we make any place safe and clean for the bodies we care for, while at the same time recognizing that every caring gesture toward loved ones is also often a killing blow to others? As we grasp the many different ways that lives matter in places, we become responsible even to "unloved others" whose fates are entwined with those we knowingly care for.[25] Can we find ways to move beyond the paralyses of fear and shame, knowing our global systems flood some places more than others with invisible toxins, poisoning soil and watersheds and entangled livelihoods that depend on them? How can we reckon with all that is being lost at our hands?

For all its claims to attend to various contaminations, R.A.W. Assmilk Soap is by no means itself clean or free of stains – not by any stretch of the imagination. It is a product of its time and place, which is to say, its manufacture is tied up (often blindly) with global petrochemi-

---

25 Deborah Bird Rose and Thom van Dooren explore the concept of "unloved others" in the context of extinction studies; in an issue of the *Australian Humanities Review,* they gather multispecies scholars to ask: "what hope could there possibly be for the other creatures who are less visible, less beautiful, less a part of our cultural lives?" Rose and van Dooren, "Guest Editors' Introduction," *Australian Humanities Review* 50 (2011): 1.

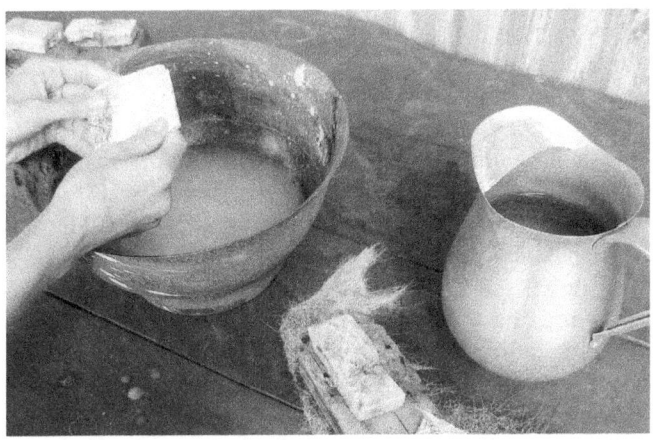

Fig. 4. R.A.W. Assmilk Soap installation at the Multispecies Salon Ironworks exhibition in New Orleans, Louisiana in 2010. Photograph by Sean Hart.

cal and agribusiness industries, and its material form is suspended in tense, quivering webs of domestic exploits that connect even the most intimate ass dairy to industrial feedlots, far-flung research labs, and slick-floored slaughterhouses. Every gnarly soap bar is a composite of myriad lives and labors, mostly unrecognized and asymmetrically rewarded. I may seek to justify the questionable ethical knots of everyday barnyard exchanges with my beloved asses by caring for their well-being in both practical and artistic ways. But what can I say to the naked plantations of Indonesian oil palm trees, whose plundered fruity seeds make up the bulk of this soap, at the expense of so many untold others?[26] What can a limited parapoetic gesture like this offer in the way of antidote to, say, billions of invertebrates ushered to extinction by chemical manufacturers like those who produce the so-

26 Sophie Chao, "In the Shadow of the Palm: Dispersed Ontologies among Marind, West Papua," *Cultural Anthropology* 33, no. 4 (November 2018): 621–49.

dium hydroxide (lye) I use to invest Assmilk Soap with the bite of its supposed cleansing powers?

As an artifact of an art practice that hopes to honor earthly wisdoms and recollect that our embodied lives are always composed with innumerable others, Assmilk Soap must also reckon with its own inherent stains. From reliance on chemical-industrial systems to its requisition of others' bodies to feed a distinctly human hunger for meaning, Assmilk Soap is sullied with murky accumulations and omissions. Yet it remains the most potent "material-semiotic" form I've found in which to hold space for messy, ineffable stories, composed through knotted generations, at multiple scales of loving and living with one unnamed ass and a herd of significant familial others.[27] As we grasp that all bodies-in-places have their own stories – most of which human perception may not even fathom – how can we learn to participate with humility and careful respect in the present lives and possible futures of others, rather than always asserting the dubious authority of names, maps, and capitalist ventures that too often erase or bulldoze worlds of living tales and territories?

Untold Stories from the Road to Nameless (and then some...)

As Vinciane Despret writes in *What Would Animals Say if We Asked the Right Questions?*: "To create stories, to make history, is to reconstruct, to fabulate, in a way that opens other possibilities for the past in the present and in the future."[28] Let's imagine the same could be true of creating untold stories, too. Such stories are "un-told" in more

---

27 On "material-semiotic" as a framework for recognizing significant, signifying others, see Haraway, *When Species Meet*, 26.

28 Vinciane Despret, *What Would Animals Say if We Asked the Right Questions?*, 178.

ways than one. First, perhaps, through unraveling certain worn-out, violently exclusive Western colonial narrative forms that assume only (certain) human protagonists are capable of making and inhabiting meaningful (auto)biographies. Still other stories are untold because they cannot be grasped, as such – at least not by narrators who lack means to transcribe or even recognize them.

All of this musing brings us back (if assbackwards) to the quietly fabulous day Aliass and I spent wandering through Nameless, Tennessee in the middle of our journey in 2002 – and more so to the ways any given timeplace is full of stories no one authoring body can tell or know. For all the thinking and writing, scheming and dreaming one human author might do, the true ass story remains beyond the grasp of even the most dexterous tongue. Cracking open the ancient human hero's journey to diverse and ineffable becomings is a task that matters urgently, if we hope to make truer stories in the places we pass through.

What follows aims to be as true as possible to meshes of storying woven by and through myriad protagonists with whom we cross paths on the road to Nameless and beyond. All kinds of earthly storytellers (never only human) recognize each other in creative ways and go on composing novel assemblages, even while struggling with rising tides of extinction, changing climates, and toxic burdens. In honor of diverse forms of storying both in and beyond any known library or database, let us explore what life stories can do when their supposed boundaries imaginatively crack open to the multitudes who are always co-composing hybrid bodies, secret maps, and inscrutable autobiographies.[29] In this quest, we plot

29 From (para)poetic forays that billow and press against the limits of human language, to artistic collaborations that hold new spaces for commingled agencies, contemporary artists are expanding wild possibilities for multispecies thinking, acting, and storying. Despite certain impasses between traditional humanist tales and respect

a course by what Donna Haraway describes as a "very interesting definition of truth, one rooted in material-semiotic dancing, in which everybody has face but no one relies on names."[30] And so, in the dusty penumbra of the Name-that-Ain't, in the glow of an otherworldly, laconic, and beautiful white-lashed beast of burden – and most of all in honor of what we might cultivate in the fertile spaces-between assumed names and unnamed meshes of lives in timeplaces – let the untellings begin.

for worldly complexity, Brian Massumi describes instances of literary writing that sustain generative relational modes of becoming, wherein "[a]ffective distance, the asymmetry of otherness, the unease of difference [are] honored." Massumi, "Becoming-Animal in the Literary Field," 279. For more on hybrid creative practices that cultivate relational ecologies, see Erin Manning and Brian Massumi, *Thought in the Act: Passages in the Ecology of Experience* (Minneapolis: University of Minnesota Press, 2014).

30 As Haraway goes on, "I like to think that this is one treasure for Derrida's hunt 'to think the absence of the name as something other than privation." Haraway, *When Species Meet*, 26.

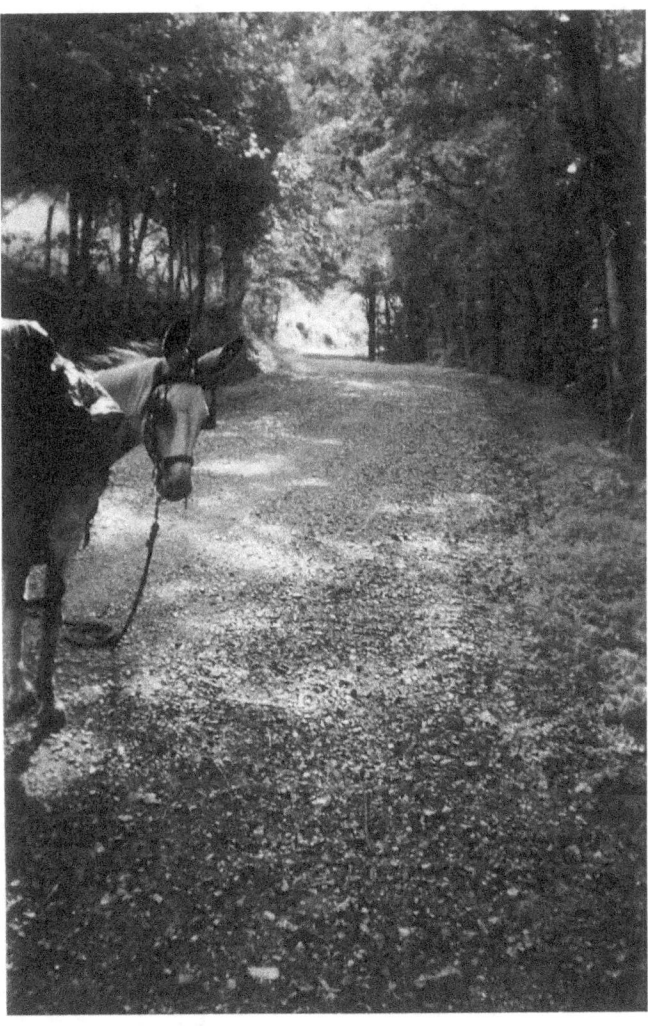

Fig. 5. Aliass on the road to Nameless, Tennessee, June 2002. Photograph by the artist.

PART I

"WHAT YOU GONNA DO ABOUT YER ASS?"

1

EXIT MUSIC
(for a Road Trip)

"What you gonna do about yer ass?"
– Sun Ra, "Nuclear War"[1]

Yes, even untold stories must begin somewhere. So let us set off from a crossroads where a certain cocked-and-loaded question, posed by Sun Ra in a song, collides with the velocity of a big black American luxury sedan, a gas-guzzling Chevy Caprice Classic speeding down the length of Mississippi on Interstate 55 on New Year's Day, 2001. This is a firsthand report, as I was the driver of the Black Caprice in question, intent on gleaning inspiration from passing landscapes beyond the glass and prone to scrawling cryptic postcards on the steering wheel while

1   The motto of this chapter reflects the pervasive influence of Sun Ra and especially the song titled "Nuclear War" in which this provocative query is found. There isn't enough time or space to encompass the full scope of entwined musical, visual, poetic, and performance legacies that Sun Ra gifted to earthlings before he left the planet in 1993. But I wish to pay homage to Sun Ra's resounding influence as a provocateur of "space" and "race" in US cultural discourse. For more, see John F. Szwed's biography, *Space Is the Place: The Lives and Times of Sun Ra* (New York: Da Capo Press, 1998). More importantly, you gotta listen to the music, especially: Sun Ra and His Outer Space Arkestra, "Nuclear War," *Nuclear War* (Atavistic, 2009).

speeding down the interstate. Still in the early days of a weeklong cross-country road trip, the Mutt of Gold and I had rolled out of upstate New York a few days earlier with the aim of witnessing a breadth of American places as we headed for winter refuge with friends in the mossy milds of the Pacific Northwest. The trusty Mutt was in her spot in the backseat. Riding shotgun were a copy of the *Collected Poems of Wallace Stevens* and a slew of mix-tapes that my buddy Adam Lore had sent along as soundtracks to the rolling transcontinental quest.[2] I thrust the first of these into the Caprice's cassette player as we headed south from the smokestacks and pyramids of Memphis, Tennessee and rolled on down into the piney unfoldings of North Mississippi hill country.

I had not planned to take the Mississippi way, but Mississippi happens to be a place with a certain special gravity that can pull a gas-guzzling nomad in, again and again – just as it did this day. After a steamy neon New Year's Eve in Nashville saloons the night before, I lit out with the Mutt of Gold early that morning, heading west. I had hoped to take Interstate 40 all the way to Oklahoma before dropping down into Texas, but the empty highway was laced with the remains of a terrific ice-storm that had paralyzed the Mid-South and shut down all of Arkansas. Hell-bent on making the Texas border by nightfall, but with Interstate 40 closed west of the Mississippi River, my only possible route was to cut south at Memphis and roll down the length of Mississippi on I-55 through that clear, cold, icy New Year's Day 2001.

So it happened that we were in North Mississippi, just approaching the exit for Senatobia/Como, when I first heard "Nuclear War" by Sun Ra and his Intergalac-

---

2   Adam Lore is always eager to share his passion for rare, radical, and wildly transformative social music, and he spreads his gospel of musical intoxication through his Brooklyn-based imprint, *Fifty Miles of Elbow Room*, https://www.50milesofelbowroom.com/.

tic Arkestra. From the first strange thrums of bass and synthesizer hums that came through the Caprice's speakers, I felt the song throb deep inside my skin and bones. As the song murmured on through those miles of rolling hill country, past frozen swamps, furrowed fields, and scraggly stands of pine, a welter of uneasy feelings began to stir beneath the blur of passing landscapes. I rode on with my heavy foot on the gas pedal of the Black Caprice, deeper into the roiling Mississippi hills, listening to the lyrical refrains and strange intonations of "Nuclear War": "Nuclear war, yeeeaaahhhhhh, nuclear war, yeeaahhh.... It's a motherfucker, don't you know? When they push that button, your ass got to go. What you gonna do about yer ass?"[3] I listened to the song over and over, utterly mesmerized. With every mile certain tensions of those times, not to mention other dim pasts and futures, trembled deep below. By the time I reached the Louisiana border in the late afternoon, forbidding revelations rumbled under the surface of that romantic American road trip like a rickety Gulf oil rig about to blow.

Looking back now on that wayward trip – and really that entire fraught millennial time – I might hazard a guess as to what came to pass on that headlong westward drive. The more miles I drove, the more I realized that I experienced nothing of the places I passed through and left behind nothing but toxic fumes. The sense of American places I was supposedly gathering on this trip was more like a subtraction. I only smelled or felt the native air when I stopped for gas somewhere, wherever. From my plush seat in the Caprice, the country was all the same big truck-stop parking lot. I hardly ever met a soul of any species in those towns I blew through. It didn't have to be this way, but I was caught up in compulsive, need-for-speed highway adventure mythos that ultimately cost much more than the price of gasoline. I was on the verge

3   Sun Ra and His Outer Space Arkestra, "Nuclear War."

of grasping that my great cross-country drive was less an exploration than a compulsion, shaped by specific histories of industrial and capitalist exploits, a symptom of a manifest reaping of false freedoms that wring rapacious loss of places and unknown ways of being.

I was at a truck-stop in Tallulah, Louisiana late that afternoon when the full force of Sun Ra's question hit me. In a burst of frustration born of friction between myths of American "freedom" and all the knowns and unknowns that their consequences obscure and harm, I scrawled a desperate message on a scrap of old '80s rainbow-unicorn stationary and mailed it back home to my future self. The missive said only this: "What you gonna do about yer ass?"

*   *   *

Now I need to pause from the driving tale to ruminate more fully on the word "ass." What is one's ass, in this context of ethical action (i.e., what to *do* about it)? And where is it located? There's the ancient beast of burden, and there's the lower human body part, but neither of these denotations encompasses the ass-entire that Sun Ra's Intergalactic Arkestra invokes as they chant: "Gonna blast you so high in the sky, you can kiss yer ass goodbye."

The *Oxford English Dictionary* grants "ass" the status of what they call a postpositive intensive, which means one can append it to any descriptive term to intensify the meaning: i.e., "badass," "crazy-ass," and "sorry-ass," to name a few. My personal favorite example of this construction is uttered by the long-lost mother in a gut-wrenching scene from the 2012 film, *Beasts of the Southern Wild,* when she tells her estranged six-year-old daughter, Hushpuppy, "Nobody likes a pity-party-havin'-ass woman."[4] Clearly, "ass" is one little word that gives a good bang for your buck in the American vernacular. As I have said before, I was forbidden as a girl to say this word, which my mother claimed was not "ladylike." But as I listened over and over again to the Arkestra's melancholy chant that day, I got a sense that this "ass" they sing of embodies much more than one little word can contain, because enmeshed within the question of what to do about "yer ass" is a challenge to every one of us as a special agent and earthbound beastly becomer, an old and deep question of action, belief, and desire that reaches beyond bounded bodies in timeplaces, far-outward into the meshes of worlding paths and the varying speeds we travel them, and even into a kind of swarming void where knowing and the edges of specific beings dissolve.

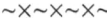

So back to the cross-country road-trip, then, where as a bewildered American interstate motorist and aspiring poet-artist, I heard the sly resonance of the song's call but had no clue how to respond. So I just kept driving west. At that stage, I was dimly beginning to gather the implications of the "ass" as put forth in "Nuclear War" – that we all have one, that is, and that it might not be just another static possession or asset but rather something we *do*, something we are *responsible to*, that is, the ass as an instrument of ethical, aesthetic, even ontological action that embodies what we desire, honor, and hope to see thrive within the worlds we care for. Meanwhile, I was dimly coming to understand the ways that most of the special privileges and freedoms I took for granted often compromise bodies, ecologies, and tangled ways of life in earthly places. And yet, in the course of this westward

4 Behn Zeitlin, dir., *Beasts of the Southern Wild,* screenplay by Lucy Alibar (Fox Searchlight, 2012).

drive, I wantonly indulged in the same destructive, slippery global resource-extractionist forces that my ass, in this sense, was supposed to stand against.

The days of that doom-ridden road trip wore on, mile after mile. I just kept driving west and flipping the "Nuclear War" cassette. Every time the song came around again, the Arkestra's chant that pulses through it seemed more strange and urgent: "Nuclear war, yeeeaaaaahhh, nuclear war, yeeeaaahhh... it's a motherfucker, don't you know, when they push that button, yer ass got to go. *What you gonna do about yer ass?*"

The pressing urgency of this question brings us (perhaps inevitably) to the crash in the desert. Two days after Tallulah, dazed by miles and the lull of spectacular desert landscapes rolling past in the window panes, the Mutt and I were coming down into Arizona, out of the Apache National Forest where I had strayed from the interstate for a night to stay with acquaintances in a prefab model home in the middle of an arid llama pasture in New Mexico. It was late morning. I raced through the dazzling desert light toward the I-10 in hopes of making it to California by sundown, with a long way still to go. Winding down the two-lane highway among striated pink cliffs and stands of gnarly pine, I was in too much of a hurry to do more than gawk at the rock monoliths and swathes of dry cactus landscape, and then in turn at the makeshift desert homesteads of plywood and hand-painted signs that lined the roadsides through the outskirts and town of Safford, Arizona.

I was listening to "Nuclear War" again as I came around a curve and saw the two-lane county route stretch out long and straight ahead of us toward the interstate. After so many days on the road, highway speed gets to be a habit. I let my foot go heavy on the pedal as I zoned into the hypnotic flow of the song and shot west toward California, watching the pale unfamiliar colors of the desert unfurl in the windshield. Right about then I passed a scratched-dirt lot full of fighting cocks, each chained by a leg to a tiny triangular hut. In my hermetic, maroon-upholstered capsule of the Caprice, I was teasing out some vague notion about suppressed violence, speed, and the compression of mortal time – as witnessed in the shimmer of sunlight sliding along the iridescent rainbow blade of one rooster's tail-feather as it lifted lightly in the wind, reminding me of a Wallace Stevens line I could not quite bring to mind... when I crashed into an orange pickup truck and skidded into the broken glass and weeds at the edge of the highway.

Here in this split second of the crash, I crossed over from easy, unhindered speed into an abrupt caesura. I sat frozen and watched a silver hubcap go rolling off into the ditch in slow motion. After a long, shaky moment, I got out of the driver's seat and stood on the roadside, knowing with all the certainty of mangled metal and oily rising smoke that it was time to take responsibility, in more ways than one, for the destructive forces, assumptions, and half-baked beliefs that manifested in my lone westward drive. As I stood there beside the mangled right fender of the Caprice, "Nuclear War" blaring out of the car speakers, eerily. The Mutt of Gold was panting like a locomotive in the backseat, and I swear on my future American ass that a sourceless ash was falling like light snow or fallout from the cloudless desert sky.[5]

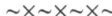

---

5   Astrid Schrader investigates residues of past nuclear disasters like the Chernobyl meltdown alongside questions of how to cultivate broader ecological awareness and care in light of ongoing and forthcoming catastrophes. Astrid Schrader, "Abyssal Intimacies and Temporalities of Care: How (Not) to Care about Deformed Leaf Bugs in the Aftermath of Chernobyl," *Social Studies of Science* 45, no. 5 (2015): 665–90.

The collision in the Arizona desert was a shock to the system, and it gave me new ears for the ever-more haunting ethical and aesthetic admonitions borne in Sun Ra's pressing-ass question. For one thing, the faded but ever-present threat of nuclear holocaust. US Cold War kids grew up in a late century where images of mushroom clouds seemed as iconic to desert landscapes as the saguaro cactus, not to mention the globally significant reverberations of the Chernobyl meltdown and the psychic residues of a widely watched 1983 Hollywood television miniseries called *The Day After*. Even as specific Cold War-era memories fade and rise, the specter of annihilation and swelling waves of extinction becomes ever more real, complicated, and immediate in a fearsome era of ecological woe and grief, where countless species and places are caught up in skeins of melting ecosystems and rapacious capital extractive schemes. How much more fraught do questions of "what to do about our asses?' become as we witness slow devastations of earthly ecosystems already well underway and realize the inextricable ways we are all implicated in their decline?

If this all sounds like vague doom-saying, so it is and was – vaguely understood and articulated, that is. But Doom was what I knew best, growing up – apocalyptic extremes to which thinking defaults when it lacks critical tools to parse complicated environmental conundrums. This sense of doom remains a dominant mode within environmental politics, where, as Susan Harding points out, discourse often crystallizes around preacher's son Al Gore's powerful cooptation of the Christian "jeremiad," as deployed in the documentary *An Inconvenient Truth* to motivate a sense of guilt and urgent need for redemptive action in regard to global climate change. In other words, we are all born sinners in global industrial technoculture: *How we gonna get clean?*[6]

The crash in the Arizona desert was a kind of wake-up call to unreckoned complexities and unimagined possibilities of material realities I was failing to attend to, especially the energy systems, infrastructures, and assumptions of seemingly inescapable oil-driven lifeways that are "shot through with largely unexamined cultural values, with ethical and ecological consequences," as Stephanie LeMenager demonstrates in *Living Oil.*[7] Oozing and lurking at the periphery of awareness, ethical provocations and hidden energies trembled through "what you gonna do about yer ass?" How might a person learn to live in the frictional complexities of neoliberal petro-global capitalist times, within exhausted tropes, impossible desires, and irresolvable conflicts? Swinging between easy extremes, with pastoral bliss on the one side and mostly invisible multispecies holocaust on the other, the challenge lies in finding immediate, inventive, DIY (or better yet, DIT or Do-It-Together) ways to imagine worldly becomings that match the complexities at hand.[8] Over

6 Susan Harding, "Get Religion," in *The Insecure American: How We Got Here and What We Should Do About It,* eds. Hugh Gusterson and Catherine Besteman (Berkeley: University of California Press, 2009), 376. Indeed, this dynamic laces through all kinds of environmental discourses and ecological art practices.

7 Stephanie LeMenager, *Living Oil: Petroleum Culture in the American Century* (Oxford: Oxford University Press, 2014), 2. My nomadic road-trip wanderings in this era of the Black Caprice were laden with literary tropes of (US American) freedom and self-discovery that obscured the fossil-fueled material realities of these drives.

8 Questioning the assumptions of individualism that often characterize Do-It-Yourself (DIY) and some hacker cultures, ecofeminist collectives in Australia have proposed alternative models of Do-It-Together (DIT). Hosted in Melbourne in 2019 by the Ecofeminist Fridays research collective, the 4th Hacking the Anthropocene Symposium proposed a DIT theme in order to explore: "What does it mean to strive for collective action when queer, Indigenous, anticolonial and posthumanist artists, scholars, and activists have so deeply prob-

time, the embarrassment and shame that steamed up through the cracks of that crash carried a nascent sense of newfound responsibilities to complex hidden systems and the "shadow places" that make pretty windshield vistas and pastoral idylls possible, as Val Plumwood asserts – crazy webs from which a person could no longer withdraw in quaint dreams of innocent communion with tadpoles and wild grasses.[9]

The slow and radical cultural shift to ecological awareness over the last decades of the twentieth century took hold slowly in the cockpit of the Black Caprice, within a growing astonishment that these vital others I was just discovering had been right here all along – the low-growing plants and trees, all the hot- and cold-blooded and carapaced bodies, alive and aware, present and mattering – along with the ever-growing grief born of the ways industrial cultures have and continue to compromise all of them (and some much more than others). I should say that it was not for lack of spending time outdoors as a kid that I was so ignorant of ecologies. Like many subur-

---

lematized the anthropocentrism underpinning taken-for-granted colonial understandings of both collectives and agency?" https://hackingtheanthropoceneiv.wordpress.com/.

9 Val Plumwood describes the dangers of "dematerialization" and blindness to global inequities and interconnection that certain types of "place-based" ecological thinking unwittingly encourage. See Val Plumwood, "Shadow Places and the Politics of Dwelling," *Australian Humanities Review* 44 (2008). Meanwhile, tropes of hermitic withdrawal into semi-wild or rural solitude are often linked with traditions of Nature Writing and its sister environmentalisms in the US and abroad. Such ideas persist, despite warnings from contemporary critics who call out the dangers of allowing romantic nostalgia for wild Nature to obscure complex histories and global connections, perpetuating dualisms that hold humans as separate from the so-called Natural World (i.e., all other-than-human life). See William Cronon, "The Trouble with Wilderness: or Getting Back to the Wrong Nature," in *Uncommon Ground: Rethinking the Human Place in Nature,* ed. William Cronon (New York: W.W. Norton & Co., 1995), 69–90.

ban kids, I grew up in the view that the beyond-human world was a mere backdrop – an undifferentiated and fairly static mass called "Nature," which was more or less an empty stage set in which human actors and our charismatic familiars in the spotlight were the only significant players. So much of what we learned in those days worked to reinforce the separation of the Human subject from the muddy mass of raw and ruder forms of being. At the same time, lived experience, body memory, and gut instincts – visceral, bone-deep ways of worlding amidst others' ways of knowing and becoming – told a different and deeply conflicting (if for the most part untold) story.

"Longing for Old Virginia"

So the road trip rolls on. We made it to the West Coast, the Black Caprice banged up and mangled on the passenger side fender but otherwise more or less intact. After eight weeks of couch-surfing between Portland, Oregon and Olympia, Washington that winter of 2001, the Mutt and I returned home to Maple Hill Farm (aka the Hollow) in early March. The Hollow was a farm where we had been holed up for several years, as tenants in a beautiful, bare-beamed converted barn apartment on an old Hudson Valley estate that was fifty-some acres of rolling, stone-walled pastures bordered by stately maples, special oaks, and deep hardwood forests where the tang of leaf litter changed rapturously with the seasons. In the Hollow we had brought in the new millennium (the Y2K hullabaloo) in true Luddite style, with an antique pinball machine and a handmade old-time mountain banjo.[10] And there in

10 It may be worth mentioning that I was one of many in a cohort of mostly white, middle-class, liberal-arts-inclined young folks who became fascinated in a deep way with what Greil Marcus called "the old, weird America" in his liner notes to Harry Smith's *Anthology of American Folk Music*. This bizarre collection was reissued in 1997 and

the pastoral Hudson Valley, I was enmeshed in the writing of a slowly unfolding fictional narrative, a novel-in-
the-making that tracked the adventures of a raw-boned
renegade wrangler and barn-burner named Juniper Ales,
who was in the midst of a secret southward journey on a
stolen, blue-eyed pinto horse named Totem.[11]

From the Adirondack foothills to the darkly folded
Appalachians of Virginia, Juniper and Totem plodded
south in search of redemption and resolution of unnamable losses. Scene by scene they slowly made their ways
toward a final reckoning with troubled pasts and uncertain futures. They waded at dusk and dawn along backroads, through withering chicory and Queen Anne's lace
chest-high to the horse, and they clip-clopped mile after
mile under swooping wires and weird buzzings of blasted power-lines terrain. They took shelter in abandoned
barns, roadside rest-area picnic shelters, and thin patches
of woods that skirted the edges of interstates, driveways,
and endless mown lawns.

This tale was driven, as fiction often is, by a feverish
desire for something lost or scattered or hoped-for and

precipitated a groundswell of passionate exploration of antiquated American musical traditions – if not always into the depths
of seamy histories in which they are situated. Greil Marcus, "The
Old, Weird America," liner notes in *Anthology of American Folk Music*
(Smithsonian Folkways, 1997).

11 Hidden histories were embedded, if obscured, in the fictive figure of
Totem, who was inspired by a real pinto horse I met while working
one summer as a wrangler at a dude ranch in upstate New York. This
ranch boasted "the only cattle drive east of the Mississippi" and a familiar cowboys-and-Indians Western theme. Kin to appropriations
of native names for American car models in the 1970s and beyond,
most of the trail horses working at the ranch had names that appropriated and flattened histories of colonial conquest and native
genocides. Folks ambled the woodsy trails aboard Cherokee, Apache,
Cochise, Navaho, and so on. Scores of native critics have called such
appropriations into question over recent decades. For an analysis of
the broader phenomenon, see Philip Deloria, *Playing Indian* (New
Haven: Yale University Press, 1999).

hidden. Meanwhile, certain well-worn tropes undergird the quasi-Western narrative drive of any renegade rider in search of redemption. What exactly did the lone pale rider on a blue-eyed paint horse hope to redeem or rediscover in her desperate ride toward a lost Virginia home? In the figure of the iconic horseback hero trespassing through forbidding postindustrial landscapes, the narrative carried persistent American/Western legacies, even as the wasted places along a specific US Appalachian north–south axis – trash-strewn highway-sides, seamy rural cinderblock roadhouses, and convenience-store parking lots where bad things happen – replaced the spectacular backdrops of striated Western basin-and-range canyons and horizons.[12]

Not surprisingly, the adventures and reckonings of this fictive (anti-)heroine Juniper Ales drew on a raw adolescent biography riddled with festering buckshot memories of lost, cedar-blown hills and sweaty, adolescent days full of pounding hoofbeats and red dust. "Longing for Old Virginia" (as the old Carter Family song goes), I holed up in the upstate Hollow for years, hoping to tap-tap-tap

---

12 Late-twentieth-century Westerns in film and literature – from Clint Eastwood's *Outlaw Josey Wales* and Jim Jarmusch's *Dead Man* to the devastations of McCarthy's *Blood Meridian* and Border Trilogy – complicate the genre of the Hollywood Western and dash old-time expectations of happy endings. Juniper and Totem would never see a happy end, either. But even as it navigated postmodern simulacra and traversed the ruins of postindustrial landscapes, The Ride's teleology still clung to charred remnants of what Joseph Campbell famously identified as "the Hero's Journey," along with what cultural theorists Jewett and Lawrence call "the Western monomyth": a narrative structure wherein the stability of an Edenic white settler home/family is threatened by some dark force of evil or chaos, and the hero rides in to redeem or restore it – or if all else fails, to paint the town red and burn it to the ground, as in Eastwood's *High Plains Drifter*. Meanwhile, in real places, the mythos of the lost "homeland" to which the hero returns often rests on erased histories of indigenous genocide, slave labor, and essentialist white settler claims to tenuous belonging and Manifest Destiny.

(on an antique typewriter, of course) into the lofty realms of high-blown lyrical Southern fictive prose like William Faulkner's monumental modernist tomes and Cormac McCarthy's opaque Southern Gothic Tennessee novels, believing (after memorizing Faulkner's 1950 Nobel-Prize acceptance speech) that both personal redemption of past losses and the supreme task of artistic imagination lay in the (modernist) effort to "create out of the materials of the human spirit something which did not exist before."[13] I dreamed of authoring as heir to that grand, thunderous legacy of hyper-lyrical Southern fiction – never mind the inimitable Western – and I devoted myself to hammering out a novel that bore south a wayward tale, wherein a renegade wrangler on a stolen pinto plodded inimitably toward fiery reckoning with a lost Appalachian home.

Still, beneath all the old on-the-road tropes and formal contrivances, the fictive Ride I sought to write strained to reckon with the crumbling of older figurations and possibilities of emergent becomings. Even the ancient horse-and-rider copula, silhouetted against an empty landscape, was no longer as clean-lined as it once seemed.[14] This relation, like all the others, was troubled by new fric-

---

13 William Faulkner, "Nobel Prize Acceptance Speech," *Southern Cultures* 12, no. 1 (2006): 71. Faulkner's speech is also available in full on the Nobel Prize website, in both textual and audio form: https://www.nobelprize.org/nobel_prizes/literature/laureates/1949/faulkner-speech.html/.

14 In *Coming Home to the Pleistocene*, Paul Shepard makes this assertion: "The long shadow thrown over the earth's ecology is that of a man on a horse, the domestic animal which, more than any other consolidated central power, energized the world-wide debacle of the skinning of the earth, the creation of modern war, and the ideological dissociation from the earthbound realm." Paul Shepard, *Coming Home to the Pleistocene* (Washington, DC: Island Press, 1998), 109. These are strong words, and they leave aside many of the brighter aspects of human-equine coevolution; but inevitably the shadow-plays of horseback power and domination are part of the figure in question, from ancient wars to modern-day rodeos.

tions, old longings, and barbed conflicts that to this day rub certain tender, fleshy spots raw.

Palomino of the Past

James Clifford warns that "[q]uestionable acts of puri-fication are involved in any attainment of a promised land, return to 'original sources,' or gathering up of a true tradition."[15] Taking this admonition seriously, I ought to steer clear of casting nostalgic glances toward my earliest years in Vacaville, that northern California "Cowtown" now idealized as a far-off, hazy land of childhood inno-cence (despite the fact that I came bawling into the world on a US military base in Fairfield). But I just can't resist the hazy scene, where in a patina of pale dust and wonder a primal horse rises up on the Western horizon, a palo-mino named Eggshell that my mother used to take me to visit on the edge of town. This glowing Palomino of the Past appears across the field, camouflaged against the pale parched hills of Solano County, as we stand in the roadside dust and offer withered apple slices across the barbed wire. (Eggshell merges with my mother's reminis-cence of her own childhood love for cowboy movie star Roy Rogers's gilded stallion Trigger, whose tail hairs she treasured as a girl.) Golden hills rise and roll in the haze of that old Vacaville where I was born, which of course no longer and maybe never did exist, where I hearken back to the childhood wonder of billowing self-in-others, blurry becomings amidst trees and snakes and mimosa blossoms and the slippery tadpoles of Alamo Creek.

Vacaville was where I first felt the electric thrill of touching whiskery-velvet muzzles at the rundown lo-cal stable known as RancHotel. And naturally Vacaville was where I began to grasp a mother tongue: beginning

15 James Clifford, *Predicament of Culture* (Cambridge: Harvard Univer-sity Press, 1988), 11.

with domestic animal sounds, the "moo" and "meow" and "hee-haw," followed inevitably by names and nouns. Eventually grammars took hold and enfolded a budding humanity in all the old Western hierarchies, classification systems, and dualisms that seek to separate it from the flowing wholeness of that old wild world. Like so many of us, I suspect I grew up seeking redemption of this original mythic breach – a sense of separation that began way back in Vacaville (that hazy and fluid timespace of early childhood) with the linguistic and ontological cleaving of "Human being" from other "animals."

Later in life I learned and even reveled in deeper nuances of naming practices, such as the distinctions between nicknames and proper names, or between pet names and taxonomic classifications. In worlds of domestic-species breeding and showing, for instance, horses, dogs, donkeys, and others often have two names: registered names, which range from succinct or poetic (American Pharaoh, Secretariat, Cloud Computing, Dare Me, Junior Pro, Perfection, and so on) to spews of nouns and adjectives seemingly strung together at random, which often include some form of the name or branding of the enterprise that bred them. Take, for instance, a champion Guernsey Bull from Missouri in the early twentieth century, who was dubbed "Dolly Dimple's May King of Langwater."[16] Hard to imagine farmhands addressing or even speaking about the heifers and bulls and rams and sows they cared for by proper names like these, however much affection they might feel for them. Show horses have their "stable names" – that is, what their friends call them – and these can be affectionate, silly, or at the very least expedient: Buddy, Bob, Blue, or Boo-Boo. And then there are the other names, the ones beyond words, which we either never know or, if we heed trainer–philosopher Vicki Hearne, we

16 *The Book of Live Stock Champions 1912* (St. Louis: Hale Publishing, 1912), 191.

may with respect and careful attention earn the right to grasp – if only in our limited human ways.[17]

However dominant practices might assert distinct separations of species based on names and categories – most especially "human" and animal" – experiences of entangled lives assert otherwise. In spite of flesh-tearing barbed-wire fences and other material and linguistic barriers set up between species, we come to be and recognize ourselves and others through processes of fluid *intra-action*, a concept described by scholar Karen Barad to expand the more limiting "interaction."[18] Barad's insights, from within a radical practice of feminist particle physics, hold that bodily boundaries do not break along material differences so much as they are imagined, constructed, and maintained by human habits. Rather than the discrete division of kinds of bodies – male/female, animal/human, and so on – Barad offers the simple (yet radical in terms of Western philosophical and religious traditions) assertion that human bodies are not distinct from other biologies, even as we proceed with ordering worlds through "onto-epistemological cuts."[19] In other

17 Vicki Hearne, *Adam's Task: Calling Animals by Name* (New York: Harper Perennial, 1989), 166–71.
18 Barad coined the term "intra-action," which critiques the more limiting sense by which "interaction" implies entities are essentially discrete material bodies. The concept of "intra-action" dissolves "relata" – things and bodies – into webs of relations where everything is in a constant material process of becoming with everything else. Karen Barad, *Meeting the Universe Halfway* (Durham: Duke University Press, 2007), 139.
19 The posthumanist relational ontology that Barad calls agential realism "refuses the representationalist fixation on 'words' and 'things' and the problematic of their relationality, advocating instead *a causal relationship between specific exclusionary practices embodied as specific material configurations of the world* (i.e., discursive practices/ (con) figurations rather than 'words') and specific material phenomena (i.e., relations rather than 'things')." Karen Barad, "Posthumanist Performativity: Toward an Understanding of How Matter Comes to Matter," *Signs* 28, no. 3 (2003): 814.

words, what we know and believe about the world, and the ways we make and unmake each other within it, are not so much determined by transcendent material truths as by the ways we learn to cut and cleave bodies by various means. More often than not, for humans, these cuts are done by acts of naming and hierarchical storying.

In spite of efforts to classify and sort animals, insects, plants, and microbes in clean-lined categories of static being, muddy, messy snarls of bodies-in-places reign. They shake off tight-laced names and grammars that hope to contain them, as surely and exuberantly as a dog shakes off a waterlogged coat and splatters everything in her midst. This vibrant mess was the truth of my growing-up and remains the substrate of a way of life, but not because my mother raised me up on animal alphabets and endless stories of great dogs and horses. Rather, it was the immersion in fur and flesh, a life enmeshed in mud and sweat, manure and dust and sweet-smelling roughage. Because when my mother fell in love and married for the second time, it was not a man she fell for but a tangled knot of dog–man–horse. For better or worse, richer or poorer, this family knot of different bodies we became remains to this day a swirling centripetal force that pulls all matters of care, desire, and responsibility into its multispecies field of gravity.

Man–Dog–Horse

So many gut feelings flit through childhood viscera – those sick little rushes and flutterings that come, whether as premonitions or fleet recognitions of some irreconcilable shift, dim knowledge of a border being crossed that can't ever be crossed back. I had feelings like this every time we watched Johnny get up into his saddle to ride Aquarius.

It always began like the genteel first step of an old country dance. The man in his boots and cowboy hat stepped up to the withers of the quivering roan mare, and she in turn would raise her blazed head high, nostrils flared and eyes white and wild. They would stand frozen like this for a moment, like a monument, suspended with every tissue tensed. And then they'd begin to furiously spin. Sparks would fly as the mare pivoted and stamped her shod hooves on the gravel or asphalt. The man, stepping nimbly at her shoulder, angled for a chance to grab the saddle horn and slip the toe of his boot like a bolt of lightning into the flapping stirrup at her side. Meanwhile his golden dog, Scrapper, would bound around the pair in tight circles, a blur that orbited the spinning man and mare, weaving amidst the tangle of boots and hooves and letting out an occasional excited yelp. It was like this every time Johnny got on Aquarius to lead us out for a ride. Sometimes it was over fast; other times it took twenty minutes or more. Once, only once that I witnessed, the mare reared and lost her footing in slippery grass at the edge of a reservoir and fell over backwards, pinning Johnny to the ground for a long moment, where he lay still and ghostly pale beneath her weight with a strange expression on his face before she rolled sideways and leapt to her feet. Still holding the reins, Johnny rose slowly and went back to her side, where she stood a little dazed, spraddle-legged and blowing. He moved his fist that held the reins toward her withers and the saddlehorn, and the crazy spinning began all over again.

In spite of the chaos, Johnny never failed to make his quick-draw move. And he never missed his aim, that lightning leap of his left boot into the flapping stirrup always hit just right in mid-air as he vaulted over her back, where he'd settle into his saddle like he was easing into an armchair. The golden dog would dart forward and back again, round and round the whirling pair, as once in the saddle Johnny gathered up the reins, adjusted his seat slightly, and just barely touched the mare's flank with his boot-heel. At this, all three (man and dog and mare) would spring forward as one in a graceful flow of motion. Aquarius would raise her silver-tufted tail and off they would sail, sucking the rest of us into their wake. If Johnny happened to have lost his cowboy hat, which was often the case, he'd double back and swoop down and grab it off the ground, leaning down nimbly and barely coming out of the saddle. And so we'd be off on our way, out on the roadsides to ride through the days.

A horse of her own is a privilege so many postdomestic girls dream of. So it was a dream-come-true for me at age seven, and a coming-true of my mother's dream, too, made possible in the flesh when Johnny came spinning into our lives with his half-wild, red-roan mare and halo of a golden dog.[20] From the first encounter one April afternoon at the ramshackle riding stable operated by Johnny's older brother, Bobby, this wild whorl of boots and paws, hooves and dirt and braided reins became a familial way of life. Who could blame a young single mother for falling in love and getting roped into the mythic, centripetal force of this? After all, she had moved us all that way to the old colonial shores of Rhode Island in search of a certain grit and salt-of-the-earthiness she felt suburban California lacked; if nothing else, she wanted a place where she could have a backyard pony for her kid. And lo and behold, there at the rundown riding stable, she found a seam of true grit and golden fur that ran straight down into a deep, dark motherlode.

---

20 In *Hunters, Herders and Hamburgers,* historian Richard Bulliet presents his concept of the "postdomestic" as a recent phase of human–animal relations where humans in the developed world, no longer integrated in the practical lives, deaths, and sex of other animals, tend to accord them higher social status. In broad strokes, Bulliet cites the widespread keeping of pets, animal rights, and "elective vegetarianism" in the West (mainly the UK, US, and Australia) as evidence of postdomestic trends. Richard Bulliet, *Hunters, Herders and Hamburgers* (New York: Columbia University Press, 2007).

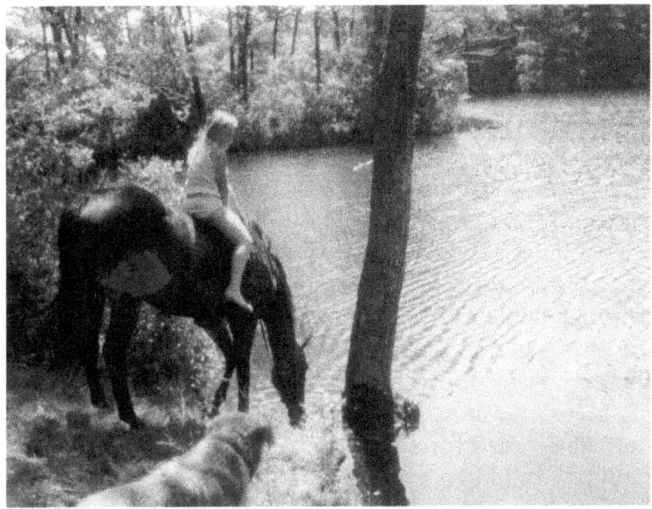

Fig. 1. A family of mammals on a camping trip come upon a lake in the woods, somewhere in the wilds of Massachusetts, sometime in the 1980s. Photograph courtesy of Christie Bolender.

For years, our weekend family pastime was to saddle up the horses in the backyard and ride out around the suburban neighborhoods where we lived, cutting through brambly primrose thickets behind strip malls and housing developments and paying surprise visits on horseback to Johnny's extended family and friends all over the island. We would clop up and stand in their driveways to "shoot the shit," as if it was the 1890s instead of 1986. The horses would sidle and chomp their bits; they sometimes got to graze on clipped lawns or rip silky corn off the thick wall of whispering stalks as we rode along raspy edges of cornfields in late summer. We paraded around the settlements of the colonial island as if paved sidewalks were old cattle trails, as if the gas-station parking lots – where we'd hold the restless horses while Johnny ran in for a pack of smokes and another six-pack for the saddlebag – were weathered Western trading posts rather than the outposts of global corporations. On the soil of old Rhode Island, where the only visible traces of pre-colonial cultures were the Native place-names that rolled off our tongues as if we owned them, we rode tall in our saddles along the roadsides, iconic shorelines, and secret muddy paths through estuaries and shadowy patches of old hardwood forests.

What matters of this past to present-ass unfoldings is that certain ways of worlding and belonging took shape through domestic knots of humans, dogs, and horses, immersed together as we all were in specific trees, grasses, rocks, waters, and infinite nameless other lives tangled in places we inhabited and explored. This world was forged as much through daily routines of care for shared hungers and hygiene as it was lit by the special wonders of exploring unknown forests, fields, littoral wetlands, and beaches inside an array of overlapping mammalian senses. Places, as such, were made of distinct odors and visual recognitions of bark, leaves, mosses, soils, rocks, and seaweeds that my human sensory organs could make out; but environments were also woven through with acquired sensitivities to flickering shadows or suspicious sounds that equines care about, and to the meshes of hot invisibilities that excite dogs, who invite us into their newsflashes with such exuberant generosity.

But then here is the rub again: elaborate knots of species never reveal all their twists and turns at once. Often we attend to bright bulges of outer surfaces and forget about darker twists hidden within. Twining bright and sinister threads through histories of biocultural gives-and-takes, domestic knots of *Canus familiarus–Homo sapiens–Equus caballus* and others bind us in ethical quandaries and responsibilities that come with loving other social mammals in societies where they are both "flexible persons" and disposable commodities.[21]

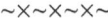

I was an idealistic teenager in 1989, newly attuned to animal rights and environmental discourses (if not a critical politics of the full and foul scope of global industrial capitalism), when our family moved to the rolling colonial farmscapes of central Virginia with the dream of developing a horse business. The farm we found was a neglected landscape of rough magic and exquisite beauty: sixty acres of secret lives lived in cedar-shot cattle pastures, wooded hills, winding creeks, a massive old oak-beamed barn, and a deep mysterious lake at the heart of it all. On this plot of land, we grounded a horse boarding stable and training enterprise. It was a manifest family dream. For years we moved day-in and day-out through slatted barn light and dewy pastures and swinging gates, as the farm's daily workings honed specific skills and habitual ways of caring and belonging with other bright-eyed, sensitive mammals – each of whom we loved, admired, and also enslaved to specific economies and customs that decided the lives of (mostly Thoroughbred) equines in that American place and time.[22] The business struggled,

---

21 Studying "animal children" in human households, Eben Kirksey builds on Israeli scholar Dafna Shir-Vertesh's concept of "flexible persons," describing how she "coined this term to understand how animals are shuttled among moral spheres where they enjoy different rights and privileges. Pets are often loved, incorporated into human families, but they can be demoted at any moment, moved outside the home and family, as household income or personal circumstances shift." Eben Kirksey, *Emergent Ecologies* (Durham: Duke University Press, 2015), 106.

22 The thoroughbred racing industry is one major contributor to both the longstanding public passion for horse heroes and the darker side of myths and markets that revolve around them. Thousands of long-legged equine athletes who fail to become Seabiscuit or Smarty

as they tend to do, barely if ever breaking even. The family foundered, as they do, too. Eventually the farm was lost, through a series of baroque financial and legal unravelings that hardly matter anymore.

What does matter still, in the haunted barn light of present-ass questions, is the sense of estrangement from that specific place – an "ecology of care," in artist-researcher Natalie Loveless's words – and so the kinships and belongings grounded in it.[23] Exile from "homelands" real or imagined breeds bewildering experiences that often lead humans to nomadic and nostalgic turns of mind and politics, even as contemporary awareness of diasporas, mass extinctions, and genocides through the ages herald the dangers of rooting any essential sense of belonging in bounded plots of land or ways of life within them, as Emily O'Gorman writes.[24] In some cases, estrangement from places of belonging lends itself to artistic attempts to conjure lost communions through the traces that remain of bodies in places: memories, im-

Jones end up trundling off to the Glue Factory in the long run. See Rebecca Cassidy, *The Sport of Kings: Kinship, Class and Thoroughbred Breeding in Newmarket* (London: Cambridge University Press, 2002); and Richard Nash, "'Honest English Breed': The Thoroughbred as Cultural Metaphor," in *The Culture of the Horse*, eds. Karen Raber and Treva J. Tucker (New York: Palgrave MacMillan, 2005), 245–72.

23 Natalie Loveless, "Maternal Ecologies: A Story in Three Parts," in *Performing Motherhood: Artistic, Activist, and Everyday Enactments*, eds. Amber E. Kinser, Terri Hawkes, and Kryn Freehling-Burton (Bradford: Demeter Press, 2014), 149.

24 Environmental historian Emily O'Gorman offers both powerful critique and hopeful proposal for "belonging" in her entry on the word for the *Living Lexicon for Environmental Humanities*: "While belonging has been taken up in ways that promote essentialist categories of inclusion and exclusion, and that disguise specific relationships, the promise of this concept is that its emphasis on fit might be usefully reimagined to provide insight into contested spaces of biocultural relationships, how they are created and contested and with what consequences for whom? Both critique and relationality can help us open new possibilities for belonging." Emily O'Gorman, "Belonging," *Environmental Humanities* 5, no. 1 (2014): 286.

ages, names, and familiar and shadowy figures. This urge, I suspect, is what brings this story crashing back to the Hollow, where holed up with the faithful golden Mutt, I furiously tracked the ill-fated quest of an imaginary protagonist on horseback, a ragged wrangler heroine hell-bent on riding south to reckon with a lost home, buried in a Virginia-bound way of life sunk in mortal time.

Exit Music ("Adapt or Die")

Even in the pastoral peace of the Hollow, specific emergencies of the age wailed like tsunami sirens. While ecological concerns and postcolonial critiques eroded any essential sense of a safe, stable, and innocent homeland in which to dwell, the vast implications of genomics, cloning, and other technoscientific wonders worked from the inside-out to loosen epistemological holds on "natural" biological bodies as stable entities. Back at the writing desk, I tried hard to hold tight to the reins of a renegade wrangler's fate and ignore all this twenty-first-century biopolitical hocus-pocus.[25]

Each morning, I sought to pick up where I'd left off with the tale, a heap of scattered scenes through which Juniper and Totem clopped on through thick roadside weeds, cracked leather and asphalt, sweat-caked fur and barn-beam ashes. But then each day, after a light lunch, I would settle back down at the very same laptop and make the rent by copyediting articles for BioMedNet's late webzine, The *HMS Beagle* – the tag line of which happened to be "Adapt or Die." I checked links to databases and web-

25 Science-studies scholar Joseph Dumit points at that, whether or not we are aware of it, we live in the "Biological Century": "There is quite simply no space outside the laboratory, no space that isn't kin to a lab, and no part of the lab that isn't a site of social, political, and artistic regulation and invention." Joseph Dumit, "Foreword: Biological Feedback," in *Tactical Biopolitics*, eds. Beatriz da Costa and Kavita Philip (Boston: MIT Press, 2010), xiv.

sites of burgeoning biotech firms, and I added basic HTML code while listening to Radiohead's OK Computer over and over and over again. After the fall of dark, it was back to the past-present where Juniper and her spotted companion plodded on in a sort of rebellious anachronism, as doomed in her era as Billy the Kid had been in his own, immersed in the groundswell of changing landscapes, economies, and obscured realities both geographical and psychic.

Season after season we went on living like this in the lovely, rough-beamed barn apartment in the pastoral Hollow, roughly a hundred miles north of New York City, liking to imagine this mode of dwelling as an aesthetic withdrawal from unsavory economic and global/local political pressures.[26] During the day, I engaged (if reluctantly and from afar) with the demands of the market for freelance copyeditors in the New York publishing industry. But amid the lofty whitewashed beams of my quiet dwelling with the Mutt in the renovated barn, I fed and sheltered a solitary beast of poetic imagination as if it was a secret unicorn or rare wild orchid – fragile and flighty and liable to be destroyed (or at least soiled and disenfranchised) by "the Real World."

All this brings us back to the crash in the desert, where with this mess of tanglesome tensions as a backdrop, Sun Ra's "what you gonna do about yer ass?" koan demanded new reckonings with energies known and unknown, in places full of others, and in time became a catalyst for action. In his own sly idiom, Sun Ra partook of an ancient cross-cultural hope that human acts of imaginative ex-

---

26 The barn I speak of happens to be both real and imaginary, having sheltered generations of inhabitants of Maple Hill Farm. This storied barn appears in a number of beloved, frank, and funny children's books by Alice and Martin Provensen; see especially Alice and Martin Provensen, *The Year at Maple Hill Farm* (London: Jonathan Cape, 1978) and *Our Animal Friends at Maple Hill Farm* (New York: Random House, 1974).

pression have a certain power to transform the material world.[27] Rooted in a far-seeing cosmic crossroads of the far and near, the "out there" and right here – where Ancient Egypt intertwines mythopoetically with the rings of Saturn – Sun Ra's Astro Black Mythology invests in the capacity of creative acts to shape the material world, with special love for the transformative possibilities of words turned inside-out.

I had sensed the pulse of all this volatile possibility throbbing through the fateful Sun Ra song that New Year's Day, as we sped obliviously southward through the rolling Mississippi pine forests and fields: What you gonna do about yer ass? But I had yet to fully grasp the catalytic charge hidden in words turned inside-out and the slippery possibilities of the pun to blast us (back) down into dirty, fleshly, root-bound earthly assemblages. Soon enough, an unexpected figure would reveal itself. And so I would come to discover the explosive, secret powers of a chimeric (if humble) beast of burden, who was hidden in the loaded ass question all along.

---

27 Sun Ra proposed that music and lyric can move us in more than just metaphorical ways. In the opening sequence of the film *Space Is the Place*, Ra declares that the Arkestra will play a song that, by means of a process he calls "transmolecularization," will literally transport its audience away from this planet, where his people have suffered too much, to a distant and better galaxy where all beings can be whole and free. Sun Ra's Astro Black Mythology calls for a greater consciousness of the ways that lyric acts, music, and all forms of performance blur boundaries between static categories; from his insistence that his music could "transmolecularize" listeners from one place to another to his deep plays on the double meanings of words like "race" and "space," all of Sun Ra's colorful talk about the Space Age was arguably a sly call for all listeners to be present and work for a more harmonious place where we are, as much a matter of the transformation of the Here as transportation to Elsewhere. John Coney, dir., *Space Is the Place* (North American Star System, 1974). See also Szwed, *Space Is the Place*, 51–109.

2

On Puns, Passwords,
and American Spotted Asses

At first the whole "ass" thing was more or less a joke, a glib and ironic play on a hinged word that swings both ways, with only vaguest intimations of explosive blasphemies packed into it. But the joke was, after all, a little bomb waiting to go off, if in exquisitely slow-motion. And as the slow-ass joke blew open in the midst of word-bound, material bodies, it opened new spaces in static habits of thought and naming, through which new idiomatic "as-sthetic" enterprises could flow. And so we set off to trace asphalt cracks and weedier paths, toward a newfangled American ass dream.

Like flowering weeds growing up through broken con-crete on abandoned military bases, a kind of idiom took root within an unexpected opening in a seemingly im-pervious manmade surface. The surface, in this case, is the ironfisted claim of words on the things and bodies they are supposed to name. And the crack, of course, is the darkly luminous and fertile space between, where "ass" blossoms and blooms, that is, the wondrous double-some pun. Here the "ass" in question grows forth in all its troublesome glory, as by nature any pun destabilizes the assumed grip of names on mysterious, inscrutable, "involutionary" bodily matters.[1] Where the doubled-up word becomes a gap that fails to encompass its supposed subject, I first caught a solid whiff of alternate ways to think and act with bodies inside/outside language, with all due respect for the meshes of fur and flesh and leaves and seeds that make life worth living (not to mention possible).

Here is how it came to pass. Spring came with dizzying profusion to the Hollow in upstate New York that year, with the deep moans of bullfrogs from the ponds in the woods and pasture, wildflowers (with names like hop-clover and butter-'n-eggs) popping up all over the place, and the big maples budding out with slower oaks in their wake. Like many other blooming things, the radical figure in question blossomed with sudden force in this tremblesome greening. One shiny May morning, I was sidetracked from some unfolding fictive scene of Juniper and Totem's wayward renegade ride (i.e., the novel-that-never-was), when all of a sudden I couldn't stop thinking about mules.

1   I am promiscuously mixing metaphors of bomb blasts and floral forms and energies here, but mixing metaphors in this case may be a strategy akin to what Carla Hustak and Natasha Myers call "involutionary momentum," which turns from the hard distinctions of individual organisms in evolutionary competition toward a way of becoming that "involves" diversely interwoven "affective ecologies" of many kinds of bodies – specifically, in this case, the interlaced bodily becomings of certain orchids, insects, and human scientists. Carla Hustak and Natasha Myers, "Involutionary Momentum: Affective Ecologies and the Sciences of Plant/Insect Encounters," *differences* 23, no. 3 (2012): 74–118. Also vaguely present in this floral mix are images of young protesters holding up flowers in the face of soldiers in iconic photographs of 20th-century anti-war and civil rights uprisings, Paris and Prague to name two. This is just one little spot in which to assert the subtle influence of the ongoing US Culture Wars, as they press at the edges and/or implode within this particular American Spotted Ass(backwards) love story. See Susan Harding, *The Book of Jerry Falwell: Fundamentalist Language and Politics* (Princeton: Princeton University Press, 2001).

Mules? This was an unexpected intrusion; I had never met a mule in the flesh or paid much attention to these hybrid beasts, who were alien hybrid outsiders to the colonial, "pureblooded"-Thoroughbred New England horse worlds I grew up in. More than just weird strangers in that world, mules were charged figures as hybrid, "half-breed," and queerish, long-eared outsiders (the Ziggy Stardusts of equines, perhaps), but I had known them only as objects of derision when they happened to appear in the stone-walled landscapes of (casually racist and homophobic) late-twentieth-century Northeastern equestrian cultures. The night before, though, I happened to have been reading *Mule Trader*, William Ferris's colorful ethnography of a Mississippi-based horse trader named Ray Lum, who travelled around the Southern US in the early and mid twentieth century peddling equine livestock. That next morning, the phrase "spotted mule" kept sneaking into my thoughts like a ceaseless, creaky carousel music coming from some indeterminable location. So I did what anybody would do, seated at a laptop screen in the cybernetic rosy-fingered dawn of 2001. I clicked on Internet Explorer, waited through the old dial-up static pop and buzz, and entered the search phrase "spotted mule" at the blinking cursor.

The next click was as fateful as they come. I found myself at spottedass.com.

What appeared on the laptop screen was a confabulated beast, an uncanny hybrid mix of familiar and strange in a pixel-borne form I could barely conceive. It was love at first sight, mixed with horror and disgust, this first vertiginous encounter with the chimeric beast of burden known as the American Spotted Ass. The blast of intuitive recognition when I saw the variegated equine shapes shining and pulsing on the screen was dizzying and gut-deep. This first visual encounter with the figure of the

American Spotted Ass was like coming upon a carnival, or perhaps an old casino, in a supposed wilderness.[2]

Foremost was the equine beast itself, this so-called "ass," otherwise known as a donkey – an odd, vaguely abject cousin of the inimitable Horse that reigned over my sense of beauty and desire and the fortunes of my family as far back as I can remember.[3] "Donkey" (*Equus asinus*) is among the many familiar domestic species I and my peers learned to recognize and name as a child, one of many naturalized inhabitants of Old Macdonald's Farm; but beyond appearances in children's books, I more or less dismissed donkeys, as their rarely seen, humble beast-of-burden status is eclipsed by the showy, elegant magnificence of their equine cousins, *Equus caballus*. Part of the buzz of this first encounter was in the fact that, in spite of being one of the most anciently domestic beasts, donkeys get little respect. And yet, this newfangled "ass" I saw blazing out from the laptop screen was another story altogether, a distorted version of a familiar figure, as in a funhouse mirror. The spectacular alterations to an otherwise unassuming barnyard beast caught my attention like a backhand slap – the kind a child might get for uttering a dirty word, but given back.

2   Wallace Stevens writes in "Academic Discourse at Havana": "Life is an old casino in a wood." Wallace Stevens, *The Collected Poems* (New York: Vintage Books, 1990), 142.

3   Horses maintain a distinct place of honor in the American imaginary – whether or not this translates to actual care for the real lives of individual equines. Asses, on the other hand, do not enjoy the same honors in the broader American culture, with the exceptions of certain circles that laud illustrious mammoth jacks used to sire mules and the ever-growing and much adored population of pet miniature donkeys. Both mammoth donkeys (over 54 inches tall) and miniatures (under 36 inches) are hot rural commodities, rarely selling for under $500, whereas I have seen ads on Craigslist offering to throw in an average-sized standard donkey jack (36"–54") for free if you bought the seller's chicken coop for sixty bucks. In the world of American asses, size definitely matters. Indeed, it can be a matter of life and death.

In light of all the years I've since devoted to playing back this slow-motion explosion, I can safely say the most significant aspect of this seminal encounter was the opening I glimpsed in the chosen branding of this confabulated breed. The choice of "ass" by the wily founders of the American Council of Spotted Asses (ACOSA) – instead of, say, the perfectly respectable "donkey" or even "burro" – was so blatant in its word-ness, and with that little kick of unseemliness to boot. Given my personal linguistic history with the word "ass," it hit me obliquely in just such a way, hinting at slippage of boundaries that logos takes for granted – between bodies and the names by which we aim to contain and render them to our purposes. Classifications tend to stand as the bedrock of Western, language-bound species exceptionalism. On these foundations we prop up the complex of assumptions whereby "human" stands apart from "animal." In that regard, to disrupt our sense of things being just what we call them, whether in the wake of Adam or Linnaeus, is a disturbance that cuts to the quick of epistemological stability. So the word "ass" presented a promising rupture, an intuitive breach of otherwise unassailable boundaries.[4]

On Puns (and Other Wordly Associations)

I found sudden, unforeseen power in the doubled-up meanings of "ass," but it is important to note that puns are dismissed as mere idiocy by some. What is it about puns, these slips between stable meanings, that so unsettle some listeners while delighting others? Even at their cleverest, listeners often receive puns as "low" and

4 I was primed for this embrace of word-as-object by a raw, unschooled passion for *écriture féminine*, in particular the work of Hélène Cixous, along with a certain postmodernly ironic and deconstructive atmosphere. But these were not the deepest forces at work, as I would eventually discover.

"cheap" jokes, as likely to provoke groans as a good guf-
faw. Literary scholar Jonathan Culler suggests that puns
draw ire because they upset the satisfying grasp of names
on material things. They undermine the authority of logos and make our most sensible pronouncements precarious.[5] On a different note, pun enthusiast Walter Redfern
has it that, "The associative mind clearly revels in simi-
larities, recurrences, echoes, reminders, assonances, and
rhymes."[6] Oh those associative assonances! More subversive, perhaps, is the call of their raw animal music, where
puns expose almighty language's roots in toothy, lispy,
guttural grunts and warbles, that crowning glory that it
is supposed to hold humans above all other species – the
Word, that is – becomes just so much idiotic scatting,
where meaning and authority give way to mere sounds
and music.

Drawing on the laconic protagonist of Melville's *Bar-
tleby the Scrivener*, philosopher Isabelle Stengers proposes that the mumblings of an idiot (whether in slippery
doubled meanings or incomprehensible speaking-in-

5 Jonathan Culler, "The Call of the Phoneme: Introduction," in *On Puns:
   The Foundation of Letters*, ed. Jonathan Culler (Oxford: Basil Blackwell,
   1988), 1–16. Lucky for me, my most intimate human associates tend
   to appreciate both puns and their underlying ontological mood. Old
   friends and I recall together some of our best wordplays, such as
   when Alex Ney and I were in the midst of a Sam Peckinpah Western
   film fest and one of us suggested we "Peckin-pause" the movie for a
   popcorn break. And then there was the unforgettable moment in a
   basement bar called The White Rabbit in Portland, when Alex, Jacob
   "Pastor My-Ass" Mitas, and I were talking about a foiled terrorist
   plot in the news, where a guy was caught with a bomb hidden in
   the rear wheel well of his car. And it burst from me like an episode
   of speaking-in-tongues: "Well, the bomb wasn't wheel-well hidden,
   was it?" In the spirit of great punster-provocateurs like Sun Ra and
   Samuel Beckett, we reminisce about old puns like over-the-hill radi-
   cals remembering a good protest prank. That is to say, groan if you
   must, but puns matter – not least in the ways they subtly unite and
   affirm kindred ontologies and politics.
6 Walter Redfern, *Puns* (London: Basil Blackwell, 1984), 11.

tongues) undermine the kinds of certainty we ascribe to linguistic articulation: "We know, knowledge there is, but the idiot demands that we slow down, that we don't consider ourselves authorized to believe we possess the meaning of what we know."[7] Indeed, to embrace the "low" pun is to harness the power of its precarity and radical possibilities for rethinking the hold of language on material, epistemological, and political matters. Perhaps this is why Chinese authorities tried to publicly ban puns in 2015.[8] Just how dangerous could puns possibly be, that they would provoke ire in social situations and even compel prohibition by massive global powers?

As it happens, puns also hold great and powerful allure for philosopher Jacques Derrida. The "possibility of puns" sits at the very heart of Derrida's philosophy of deconstruction, the massively influential mode of postmodern thought wherein language becomes a playful surface, cut loose of its bedrock grounding in transcendent human logos. Derrida says, "If I had a single definition of deconstruction, one as brief, elliptical, and economical as a password, I would say simply and without overstatement: *plus d'une langue* – both more than a language and no more of a language."[9]

Jonathan Culler takes the power of the pun even further in "The Call of the Phoneme," to assert that, "Puns present us with a model of language as phonemes or letters combining in various ways to evoke prior meaning

7   Isabelle Stengers deploys the idiot toward this end: "The idea is precisely to slow down the construction of the common world, to create a space for hesitation regarding what it means to say 'good.'" Isabelle Stengers, "A Cosmopolitical Proposal," in *Making Things Public*, eds. Bruno Latour and Peter Weibel (Boston: MIT Press, 2005), 995.

8   Tania Branigan, "China Bans Wordplay in an Effort to Control Puns," *The Guardian*, November 28, 2014. https://www.theguardian.com/world/2014/nov/28/china-media-watchdog-bans-wordplay-puns/.

9   Jacques Derrida, *Memoires: For Paul de Man*, trans. Trans. Cecile Lindsay, Jonathan Culler, and Eduardo Cadava (New York: Columbia University Press, 1986), 15.

and to produce effects of meaning – with a looseness, unpredictability, excessiveness, shall we say, that cannot but disrupt the model of language as nomenclature."[10] Derrida scholar Gregory Ulmer develops this instrumentation into a form he calls the "puncept," or "the relationship between the pun and concept formation or the order of knowledge."[11] Indeed, I found that when it comes to the special power of hinged, double-meaning words to open hidden histories and alternate ways of knowing untold others in full-blown places, puns give us the possibility of other stories altogether. As Culler asserts, "Puns can inspire momentous action, as well as narrative. They may also be an instrument of knowledge."[12]

Beckett said it best (as with so many things): "In the beginning was the pun."[13] And so it was: Like dynamite in the darkest mines, the slip-knotty nature of one specific beastly-burdensome pun came to guide a brand new quest, to blast new paths into a seeming impasse between named human enterprises and nameless intra-mammalian silences. "Ass" was and is precisely this kind of "*pass*word" – an abracadabra magic spell that promises to open lively possibilities of lives-lived between more-than-language and language-no-more.

Spotty Histories

While this readymade detourn of "ass" was the first glimpse into the volatile payloads with which this lowly beast of burden is loaded, it was the addition and admixture of "American" and "Spotted" that really set fire to the fuse.[14] Despite genes for spotted coats cropping up

10 Culler, "The Call of the Phoneme," 14.
11 Ibid., 14–15.
12 Ibid., 15.
13 Samuel Beckett, *Murphy* (New York: Grove Press, 1955), 65.
14 "Readymade" is a term borrowed from Marcel Duchamp's radical move to shift the boundaries of art by framing and making mean-

in donkeys all over the world, ACOSA, founded in 1969, is the first organization to maintain a breed registry for this trait in donkeys, and as a result, to stake a certain national claim on asses's spots as "American." Hidden layers of American cultural history and Western mythos were splattered across those little long-eared equine bodies in the spectacle of "spots" – a genetic inheritance of splotch-patterned coat color that in horses is called "paint" or "pinto" or even Appaloosa, depending on the colors and pattern involved and their specific biocultural histories. Meanwhile, the sense of play and seeming irreverence in the naming of this new ass breed is complicated by a statement from John Conter, who co-founded the ACOSA and dubbed its primary product as such: "Now, we could call them 'pinto donkeys,' you understand that, but there's no romance in 'pinto donkeys.' Whereas when you say 'spotted asses,' well then, that means something."[15]

As another human whose lifelong passion was catalyzed by this breed and its surprising choice of name, I can attest that "Spotted Asses" is indeed packed with meaning – as laden with it, in fact, as the little burros who have carried human burdens worldwide for millennia. Recognition of these loaded aspects of the ass's spots was intuitive in that first encounter, but I have since come to explore some of the ciphers at play in that swirling massquerade of species and national/cultural identities, where these newfangled spotted hides conjured (and simultaneously made a joke of) latent and watered-down

ing with objects that artists did not physically make, most famously a signed urinal in 1917's *Fountain*. "Detourn" here is a verb form of "detournment," which is a form of radical aesthetic interventions proposed and practiced by Guy Debord's Situationist International movement in the late twentieth century. Guy Debord, "Towards a Situationist International," in *Participation*, ed. Claire Bishop (London: Whitechapel, 2006), 96–101.

15 Ruth Kalenian, "The American Council of Spotted Asses and John Conter," personal website no longer extant.

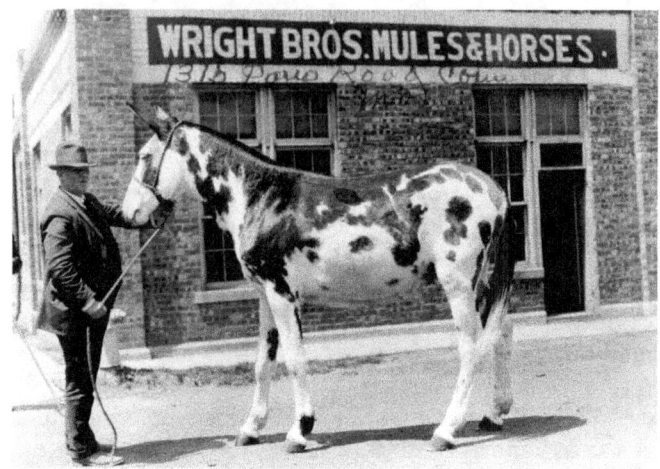

Fig. 1. A rather spectacularly "loud" spotted mule, shown off by dealer B.C. Wright of Columbia, Tennessee and sold to a St. Louis mule trader as the hot commodity they were in the early twentieth-century USA. Photograph courtesy of the State Historical Society of Missouri Digital Collections, Missouri Equine and Equestrian Collection of Photographs, P0993-021051.

Wild-West, cowboys-and-Indians associations, which in turn hold violent erasures of specific histories of Westward colonial expansion and genocide in co-opted traces of Native American names and cultural patterns.[16]

16 The founding of the American Council of Spotted Asses in 1969 parallels the shift in popularity of pinto horses, from early rejection in certain circles of settler-colonist American horse culture due to associations with half-breed Indian ponies to its current status as the virtual American flag of horse-coat colors, as witnessed in the phenomenal and ever-growing worldwide popularity of the American Paint Horse. The American Paint Horse Association was founded in 1962 by Rebecca Tyler Lockhart, in support of her beloved paint-horse underdogs and with a significant fight at the time against racist and misogynistic forces in her native Oklahoma. Penny Owen, "A Colorful Life, She's Riding Ol' Paint to Fame: Ryan Woman to Join Cowgirl Hall of Fame," *Daily Oklahoman*, October 29, 2000.

Meanwhile, in this swirl of images and hidden associations, the spectacle was working its magic on me. As
the "American" and "Spotted" shot through these humble domestic equine bodies evoked the burn-and-twitch
of a commodity fetish, a certain horror rose up along
with the haunting desires sparked by this alter-equine
form. This desire, even as it rooted in longings for absent
friends and places in the past, nonetheless implicated me
in dominant biocultural regimes of livestock breeding for
consumer markets, among other human habits that reduce living bodies and deeper wisdoms they contain to
surfaces, pixels, and dollar values.

Yet this is precisely where – in a carnivalesque atmosphere of fant*ass*tic possibility that turned everything
inside-out and upside-down – the crack opened a breach
between the word "ass" and the familiar/unfamiliar beast
it was supposed to name, and that crack gave forth a faint
glimmer of possibility for creative interventions. The
moment was a vital pause at the edge of what Michael
Taussig describes as "the exchange-value arc of the market circuit, where the general equivalence rules the roost,
where all particularity and sensuosity is meat-grindered
into abstract identity and the homogenous substance of
quantifiable money-value."[17] Of course, commodification
of bodies – "meat-grindered" as Taussig writes in an apt

17 Michael Taussig writes: "We need to note that as the commodity
    passes through and is held by the exchange-value arc of the mar-
    ket circuit, where the general equivalence rules the roost, where
    all particularity and sensuosity is meat-grindered into abstract identity
    and the homogenous substance of quantifiable money-value, the
    commodity yet conceals in its innermost being not only the myster-
    ies of the socially constructed nature of value and price, but also all
    its particulate sensuosity – and this subtle interaction of sensous
    perceptibility and imperceptibility accounts for the fetish quality,
    the animism and spiritual glow of commodities, so adroitly chan-
    neled by advertising (not to mention the avant-garde) since the late
    nineteenth century." Michael Taussig, *Mimesis and Alterity: A Particu-
    lar History of the Senses* (New York: Routledge, 1993), 23.

metaphor for what happens to many equines, cattle, and even cast-off dogs and cats in hungry regimes of global capitalism – compromises not only long-eared beasts of burden but all of our mortal bodies and embodied biographies. In the loaded figure of the American Spotted Ass, animated by lively ghosts, I glimpsed what Taussig calls the "phantasmogorical potential" of Walter Benjamin's take on the commodity fetish, that is, "the surreal and revolutionary possibilities provided by the culture of capitalism for its own undoing, its own transcendence"[18] The asses staring out at me from the screen seemed to be asking: How much more vital can this inversion of a commodity become when the object looks back as a full-blown subject, a blinking and breathing body that bucks representation with her own untold biography, fears and desires, cares and hungers?

As I clicked in breathless wonder through image after image on the Gallery pages of spottedass.com, the patterns laced across spotted donkey hides hinted at futures full of mixed promise and possibility, and also danger and doom. In other words, I was falling in love. Like Alice's long, colorful fall down the rabbit-hole, this head-over-heels (or "ass-over-teakettle," as my friend Chris would say) tumble bumped and twisted down through an underground labyrinth of images and phonemes, colors and shadows, beloved bodies and mixed-family phylogenies, as if descending deeply earthward toward the common linguistic root of "spectacle," "seeing," and "species" somewhere at the core. Indeed, this spiraling journey is one that anthropologist Paige West traces in hopes that we could eventually arrive at some new place, where human ways of worlding through visual re/cognition and naming-calling – so grievously exploited in our age by

18 Ibid., 29.

humanist hierarchies and capitalist schemes – might instead offer fertile grounds for multispecies futures.[19]

For my part, the feeling of falling head over heels for this spectacular ass breed has never yet hit any kind of bottom. I suspect this dream hath no bottom, as a matter of fact.[20] From the first encounter onward, the unassuming donkey "enterprised-up" in a coat of many colors became an inexorable calling.[21] And if we should need further testament to the power of images (whether for good or evil, haw) in human experience, it is worth noting that all this passion came to pass through the mysterious workings of a slow-loading, haphazard gallery of low-resolution JPEGs, long before I ever met a Spotted Ass in the flesh. Indeed, this clash with the hybrid, Western-

19 In her entry for "Spectacular" on the *ABCs of Multispecies Studies* website, West writes: "If we returned to the Latin origins of the Old French word *spectacle* (the word from which the Middle English term arose in the 14th century) we get *Spectacle* from the Latin *spectacu-lum*, which means 'a show' or 'a place from which shows are seen' and *spectaculum* is from the older *spectare*, which means 'to see' or 'to behold.' In Latin *speciō* also means 'see' and gave rise to the Latin word species which meant 'the appearance of a thing' or 'its outline or shape' and which gave us the Modern English word species. So, at its roots, deep in the history of utterances, *spectacle* connects to *species*. What if we started to reclaim the idea of *The Spectacular* from corporations and marketers and big conservation? What if we went back to the beginning of its linguistic roots and decided to see every species intersection as spectacular; something extraordinary to behold? That is part, in my sense, of the multispecies project. To revive the wonder in and of our world through understanding the processes – political, social, historical – that worked to convince us that 'nature' was somehow distinct from 'culture'........... utterly SPECTACULAR." Paige West, "Spectacular," *ABCs of Multispecies Studies*, http://www.multispecies-salon.org/spectacular/.
20 But of course: "Man is but an ass if he go about to expound this dream. [...] The eye of man hath not heard, the ear of man hath not seen, man's hand is not able to taste, his tongue to conceive, nor his heart to report what my dream was." William Shakespeare, *A Midsummer Night's Dream* (New York: Penguin, 1967), IV.1–2, 200–210.
21 Donna Haraway, *When Species Meet* (Minneapolis: University of Minnesota Press, 2008), 46–67.

historied beast of burden in question was no less than an explosive bray-to-becoming, so thick with transformative possibilities that it may yet take the rest of my mortal days to grasp it. Lo, I stand in wonder here and now, that after all these years of living with Aliass and our rough-furred herd of rowdy kin, I have yet to get to the bottom of that shimmering pool of vague hopes, bright curiosities, and promising inside-outings that rose up in that first laptop glimpse of the so-called American Spotted Ass.

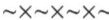

While this call-to-becoming of the American Spotted Ass was loud and clear at the time, the source of its issuance was harder to ascertain. "Ass" was a password, no doubt. It glowed like a hot golden key into landscapes of passtoral promise, even as these places glimmered invitingly on the other side of an opaque, impassable present. Thanks to Lewis Carroll (who, like Coyote, Cixous, Duchamp, Frederick Douglass, Sun Ra, and other tricksters, knows that logic is seldom the surest road to a destination whence imaginative vision beckons us), I surmised that merely having a key in hand is no guarantee of easy passage.[22] There I sat at the laptop day after day, not knowing what to do about my strange newfangled Ass or how to find the places it may haunt. The promise of the Spotted Ass hung in a wondrous space opened by a hinged and double-edged name, but the fervent hopes and desires attached to this odd equine welled up from within a material body whose ways of knowing and inhabiting places have always been pulled and pushed, shaped and affected

---

22 Lewis Hyde's *Trickster Makes This World* elaborates the trickster's role and how these particular tricksters powerfully enacted it in their specific cultural situations. Lewis Hyde, *Trickster Makes This World: Mischief, Myth, and Art* (New York: Farrar, Straus, and Giroux, 2010).

by the presences of domestic equines, canines, and many others. What I sought in the crack of "ass," then, could only be found amidst tangles of real, hot, furry hides, shining eyes, hay and grasses, and odd, long-eared sensitive bodies, and in the mysterious, material mesh of shared experiences in unknown woods and fields and weedy roadsides.

Alas, there in the new-millennial spring of 2001, the American Spotted Ass beckoned from somewhere ambiguously "out there," beyond the peaceful rolling pastures and wooded, stone-walled horizons of old pastoral upstate New York. Here the ecstasy of the American Spotted Ass grew as spring turned to a deep, dark summer, with a growing sense that this urgent calling was also a calling-out that would demand massive transformation. Like Alice peering through a keyhole into a strange landscape into which she watches the White Rabbit beckoningly vanish, I saw limned in the shape of the Spotted Ass a world I had to find my way into somehow. The mottled hides of these mimsy beasts seemed like a shimmering penumbra of a distant magical place, a land of wondersome, inside-out adventures, where one might even stumble into a forest, field, or barnyard where things have no names, and names no things.[23] Needless to say, I became a

23 Incidentally but not insignificantly, I once numinously fell into a site like this myself for a hot minute, after an intoxicating series of solo rollercoaster loops on the Tennessee Tornado at Dollywood in Pigeon Forge, Tennessee. Come to think of it, that revelatory evening at Dolly Parton's homegrown Smoky Mountain theme park had proffered such profound and surprising revelations and unravelings – mind-bending fluidities of genders and geologies, seamy-sweet-insectoid dissolutions of species and kingdoms – that I might have guessed it from the get-go. This briary path onto which I stumbled in search of my American Spotted Ass must lead (back) to Tennessee in the long run, and go deep and deeper into its most clandestine, sequined wildernesses. Yes, in the fantastic (if slow and assbackwards) lines of flight and fancy that would eventually lead to meeting Aliass in the dim, loamy light of that Maury County pole-barn on Monsanto Road, I would need to find and follow all kinds of buck-

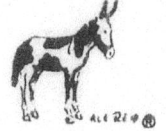

American Council of Spotted Asses, Inc.

MEMBERSHIP CARD
Year 2001
Jan. 1 - Dec. 31
To Promote & Preserve the American
Spotted Ass & Half-Ass
Miniature, Standard, Mammoth

KARIN BOLENDER

Is A Member In Good Standing Of This Association

Fig. 2. ACOSA membership card from that fateful ass year, 2001. Courtesy of the artist.

passionate card-carrying, t-shirt-wearing member of the American Council of Spotted Asses, with a sense of irony that hid deeper desires, lacks, and longings that were embedded in this figure like barbed-wire swallowed in the flesh of a tree.

While somewhat geographically isolated in this regard, I was not alone in falling hard for the romantic allure of American Spotted Asses. On a homegrown website made in the early 1990s by a former Arabian horse-breeder-*cum*-Spotted-Ass aficionado named Ruth Kalenian, I fell into a swirl of images, personal anecdotes/travelogues, and gems of information detailing what happens when a person's dreams are suddenly and unexpectedly hijacked by colorful asses.[24] One particular photograph on this web-

some, elusive, and fluid figures – friends and foes, too, who would pop up along the way to guide and perplex the quest through barbed and strange and dangerous territories. See Karin Bolender, "Silly Beasts in Sacred Places," *Arthur Magazine* 8 (January 2004): 24–34.

24 More than decade later, when researching events around my discovery of spotted asses, I happened again upon Ruth Kalenian's website, which to my astonishment still floated in cyberspace like a relic of

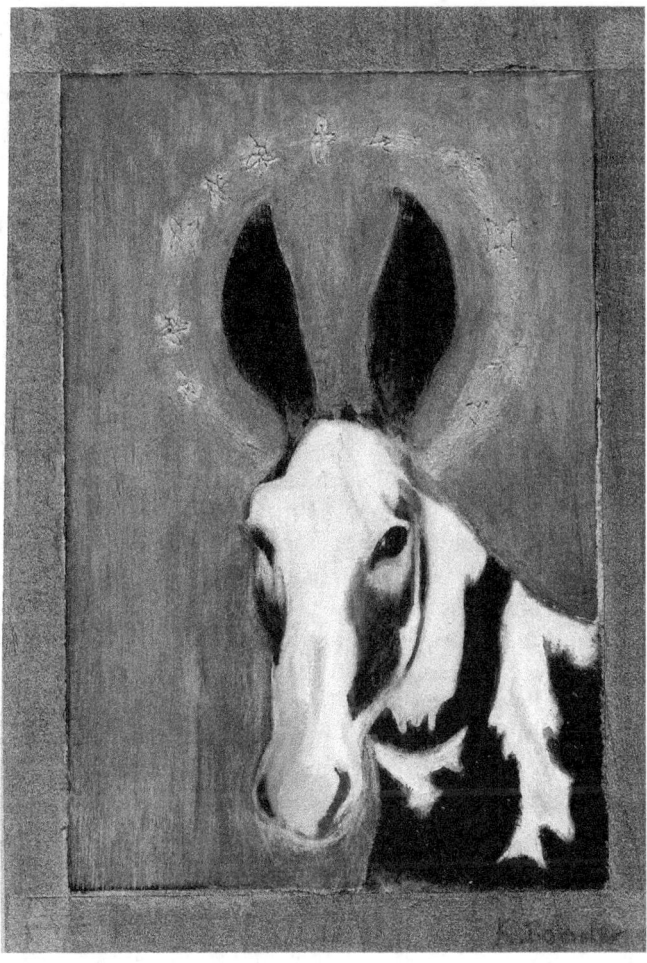

Fig. 3. Heart B Mister. Oil on wood. 2001. Courtesy of the artist.

site captured me so fiercely that I can still recall the trem-blesome, quicksandy sensations I felt when I would gaze at it in those early times. It was almost like a promise of pastoral paradise (almost pornographic in the intensity of sensations it stirred). The image revealed an endless spotted-ass pasture somewhere in the wild western Mon-tana territory, so glowingly full of lively promise that I felt it could not possibly be a real place. But what if it was out there somewhere, this magical rangeland – was this an image of a destiny manifest, somehow, someday, somewhere over the rainbow...?

Restless, those summer nights I got in a habit of stay-ing up all night long, drinking cold coffee, listening to the apocalyptic growl of Royal Trux and Lightning Bolt records, and painting an icon of an American Spotted Ass in oil on wood. The small painting was based on a pro-motional headshot of a Mammoth Spotted Jack named Heart B Mister, who had recently been sold and trans-ported from his Idaho home to stand at stud in Montana. I had seen him advertised online, and in a fit of admira-tion I wrote to his new owners requesting a photo, which they kindly sent without questions. Late into the buzzing summer nights, I pored over the ass's enigmatic expres-sion with breathless concentration, like an acolyte seek-ing prophetic revelation. And there it was.

As I traced the glints and shadows of bones under fur, something urgent and invisible built under the skin of the emerging image. Mister seemed to know something – something like the punchline to some vital and termi-nally slow and funny joke that he would never tell, but that I might grasp if I could just capture the sly tilt of dark in his long hollow ears and the glimmer in his deep-set eyes. With every layer of oil paint, the secret seemed to shimmer and recede, shimmer and recede, like a ghost-

interwebs past, a treasureful trace of her labor of cyber-ass love in the mid-1990s. Sadly, the server can no longer be found.

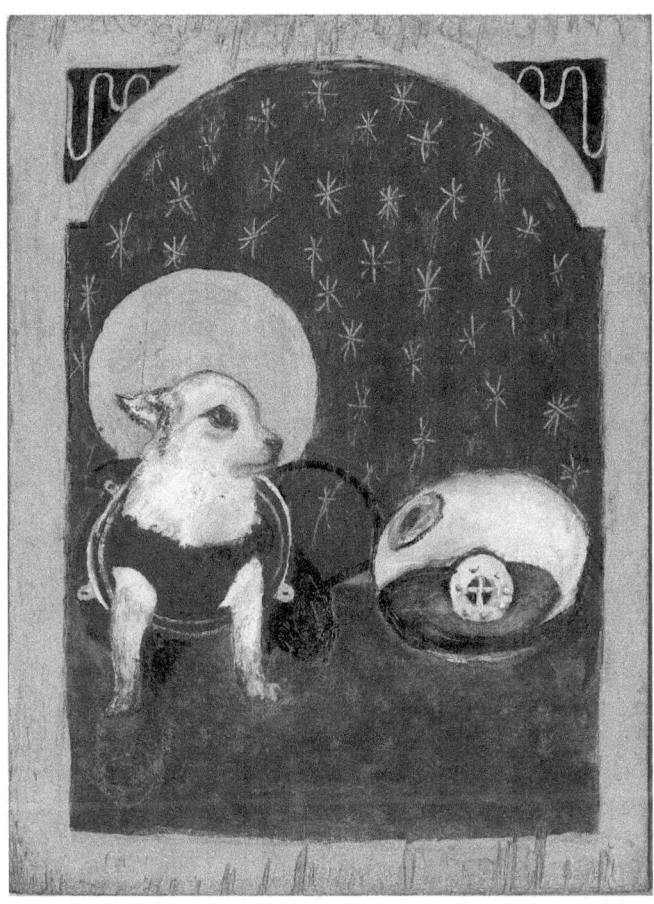

Fig. 4. Space-Dog Malyshka. Oil on wood. 1996. Courtesy of the artist.

ly aura playing just beneath the surface of the spotted jack's spectacular hide. Grasping to conjure contact, power, and possibilities of transformation layered in this elusive animal figure, this painting was an act of mimesAss – an impulse as old as the Paleolithic and arguably at the root from the get-go of *Homo sapiens* becomings with the world of self and/in others.[25]

As it happened, the Byzantine-style icon of Mister was prefigured by a portrait series of another preposterous figure with a (more literally) explosive natural-cultural payload. For years, I had a ferocious obsession with Laika, the first dog sent into Earth's orbit by the Russians inside Sputnik 2 in 1957. The first time I heard the tale of this strange Space Age episode, I was gut-struck with bewilderment, akin to the intense frisson the American Spotted Ass evoked years later. I soon learned that Laika was not the only orbital canine of her kind, and the fascination with this strange new breed of space dogs expanded into a practice of painting semi-ironic, Byzantine-style icons based on the late canine cosmonauts shot into outer space by the USSR in the mid-twentieth century.

After years of thinking and feeling through this intuitively confounding hybrid figure of the dog-in-outerspace, I finally began to grasp what made it so haunting. Dogs stood for the safety and warm familiarity of "home" for me, and outer space was definitively not-home, the absolute unfamiliar and unwelcoming in the most profound and lonesome ways. To catapult a dog into space was a rupture, an (in)human(e) act of supreme ecological – and for me, ontological – violence. ("Doggone it," said the astronaut, on a LP recording of a space mission that I

25 Contemporary poet Clayton Eshleman explores the roots of mimesis (and human self-discovery, by his lights) in paleolithic renderings of mysterious bovine, equine, and other hybrid lines and forms on the walls of caves in the Perigord Noir region of France. Clayton Eshleman, *Juniper Fuse: Upper Paleolithic Imagination and the Construction of the Underworld* (Middletown: Wesleyan University Press, 2003).

found at a yard sale and listened to over and over again, late at night, for many years.) And somehow, here in the cosmic chimera of the American Spotted Ass, a similar pulsing mass of tensions was at work. I could not tease apart all the different snarls, so instead I painted and sketched and dreamed like a fiend of mysteries hidden inside these incredible visions of space-dogs and spotted asses. These image-making acts sought to conjure contact with the other, the outside, the unknown, feeling blindly along seamy cracks between names and bodies, into spaces where unknown voices, nameless presences, and indecipherable messages proliferated.

Late one August night that final summer in the Hudson Valley Hollow, I was bent long and late over the emerging image of Mister when a sudden, uncanny cry came ripping through the night. It came from somewhere out in the dark rolling pastures. I had never heard anything like this astonishing sound, roundly familiar, with both canine and feline edges, but otherwise alien. The seemingly sourceless voice electrified the darkness, then faded in scratchy pulses like static at the beginning or end of old 78 recordings – fulsome even in its caesura. The Mutt of Gold and I stood side by side at the open screen, hardly breathing, listening hard into the dark of the night outside. After a long-seeming pause, it came again, still without locus. It was a call as much as a cry, clearly full of portent, though not at all meant for us. It did not sound like pain or fear, exactly, but a strange urgency carried through in its volume and repetition. For maybe half an hour, it kept coming, high and sharp at the top and then fading away rough-edged to a tensed silence stretched across the gaps. Then the interval ended, and faint nocturnal buzz slowly covered over the hole in the night that the cry had opened.[26]

26 Inscription of this experience owes an intertextual debt to James
   Agee's rending and gorgeous essay of a similar listening experience

The next morning one of my landlady Alice's retrievers came skulking across the yard with an awkward shape dangling from her muzzle. From Mary's soft jaws, I pried the cold body of a juvenile bird, like none I had seen before – a long-legged, long-necked, mostly naked fledgling, with scaly yellow legs and a few spiky blue feathers on its translucent wings.[27] A few minutes later, one of the other retrievers appeared with a second dead fledgling. I gathered up the avian carcasses and studied them with fascination and the sad wonder that comes in the presence of any death, the pocked pale skin and hollow primary feathers, the tiny insects scuttling in the folds of their cold pale necks and in and out of their earholes. With their half-closed eyes, the fledglings were like envoys from a different world – little rips in the veil. It seemed like their appearance was heralded in the cries we'd heard the night before, but of course there was no way for me to know, knowing so little about goings-on of the Hollow nighttime.

That evening I sketched their bodies. Then – not knowing how best to honor them, with no idea where they came from or where to return them – I took them to the deep black pond at the back of the farm in the woods. I laid them in the leaf litter at the edge of the dark reflective water: this was not a resolution of any mystery but a gesture meant to take place against a backdrop of "unknown, invisible presences" – a gesture that in its way held the vague hope or anticipation of participation in

in the haunting coda of *Let Us Now Praise Famous Men*. In Agee's version, there are two fox voices, which alters the dynamic in certain ways. James Agee and Walker Evans, *Let Us Now Praise Famous Men* (New York: Houghton Mifflin, 1980), 463–71.

27 I am guessing they must have been fledgling Great Blue Herons, because I know of no other long-legged, long-necked, blue-feathered bird like that. This seemed especially odd, though, because I read that herons raise young together in a rookery, and surely we'd have known if a rookery was nearby, right?

what Isabelle Stengers calls "cosmopolitical" assemblages, where "cosmos refers to the unknown constituted by these multiple, divergent worlds and to the articulations of which they could eventually be capable."[28]

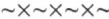

In the Hollow pastures that last summer were yarrow and spotted knapweed, hop-clover and bird's-foot trefoil and butter-'n-eggs. Goldfinches stitched the afternoon air. Big-eyed flying squirrels emerged at dusk from the gnarly maple by the back porch, where the cranky white-breasted nuthatch shuttled upside down like a tiny freight elevator all day. Chickadees harangued us from the canopy of old oaks in the backwoods, and over the years the Mutt and I crossed paths with roving bands of does, chipmunks and field mice, a rose-breasted grosbeak, and the bright orange oriole and flocks of cedar waxwings passing through in spring. Many different woodpeckers tapped out regular rhythms in the woods, and once we met an ancient snapping turtle, trailing green slime as it hurried across the pasture just before a thunderstorm, moving from the murky depths of one pond to another.

The Hudson Valley farm was a lovely and peaceful place, as far as landscapes in twenty-first-century United States go. But even as I wandered the pastures and woods with the Mutt of Gold in all seasons, as she chased hot trails in grass and leaf litter and I learned the names of easy wildflowers and common birds and struggled with the seemingly hundreds of species of oak, the many kinds of pine, I was beginning to grasp the dangers of believing that naming is the same as knowing, or that bodies are namable at all. Hidden forces of history, ecology, and invisible presences that shaped this pastoral idyll I adored, or for that matter any landscape, were not as timeless or

28 Stengers, "A Cosmopolitical Proposal," 995.

tame as the pretty, peaceful, millionaires' summer-home estates of the rural Hudson Valley would lead one to believe.[29] Meanwhile, I felt keenly that all the paradigms I lived by were mostly only blinding me to realities of deeper, hidden webs of connections. I knew I had to leave the solipsism of the Hollow, but I did not know where to go or how to seek whatever I was looking for.

But there was this: Pompey's Pillar, Montana – the mythic place of origin of the American Spotted Ass, according to the official history on spottedass.com. It lay to the west, as did a circle of close friends in Portland, Oregon. Westward seemed as good a direction as any. So it was. At the end of the summer we would leave the Hollow and go West again (like so many before us) to seek a new way of life in the Pacific Northwest, me and the Mutt and whatever I could fit into the trunk of the Black Caprice. Westward we would chase the dream of a humble, hybrid, doubled-up figure who somehow promised to reconcile all the deepest and spikiest conundrums of millennial wonderings and to open up unforeseen passages for possible past- and future-ass becomings.

---

29 This former agricultural region is two hours north of New York City, and in the nineteenth and early twentieth century its farms served the city's needs for milk and meat and crops. With twentieth-century changes, the landscape became premium real estate for wealthy city folks. A few scattered ancestral farms still operated at the turn of the millennium. Soon after I left the Hollow, though, I heard news that the last working dairy farm in Dutchess County had finally folded. Old farms sold for millions to heirs of New York global finance royalty. So much for country innocence. However much I liked to imagine myself a rural hermit, my living in those Hollow years, in terms of income and social life, was entirely dependent on being within New York City's colossal economic and cultural sphere of influence.

Westward Haw!

This is an old story, despite its idiomatic assemblages. Across the so-called US of A, centuries of migration, displacement, and strivings for better lives are written in asphalt lines and other, less visible traces that crisscross every landscape. Mythical-material realities of the North American highway system, along with other specific human histories and privileges, allowed a person like me in the early twenty-first century to chase swirling ass visions across deserts and plains, across the girth of a massive continent, more or less on a whim. Call it what you will: road-trip quest, assbackwards hero's journey, *Kunstlerroman,* odd-ass odyssey, or twenty-first century Gilgameshian epic dream.... In any case, this is a road-bound tale that weaves through haggard tropes of migratory adventures that ultimately strive toward some kind of homecoming – or homeward coming-of-age, maybe.[30]

But if it is an old story, the desire to blast it open for new multispecies engenderings necessitated a newfangled strategy, born of its particular times. For nomads of a so-called new millennium, destinations may seem to hover on the horizons of uncertain futures, or even pasts – never right here, anyway, kind of like the far-off "shadow places" Val Plumwood admonishes us to acknowledge for the sake of earthly integrity.[31] Sometimes, though, we come suddenly to recognize "shadow places" are not

30 Roadways are fraught territory all over the globe. See Anna Tsing's *Friction* for a description of ways that Indonesian logging roads, in particular, act as pathways for flows of global capitalism, opening ways of moving in forest landscapes for some while constraining or endangering them for others. Anna Tsing, *Friction: An Ethnography of Global Connection* (Princeton: Princeton University Press, 2005). Stephanie LeMenager's *Living Oil: Petroleum Culture in the American Century* (Oxford: Oxford University Press, 2014) limns the ways that oil economies are rendered invisible by their omnipresence.

31 Val Plumwood, "Shadow Places and the Politics of Dwelling," *Australian Humanities Review* 44 (2008).

so far off after all, but right here in our midst, weaving across porous bodies, where rich webs of beings and becomings thrive or fade at the frayed edges of driving perception, attention, and care.

It was so easy (in some ways) to uproot and go west from the Hollow home in upstate New York, to float off dreamily in the Black Caprice on the smoothly paved and networked surfaces of the national highway system, fueled by cheap oil and high-limit credit cards, sung onward by the recorded voices of American balladeers and their longingful songs of the highway, from Woody Guthrie's "Hard Travelin'" to anything Townes Van Zandt ever sang.[32] To breeze past infinite strip malls and fast-food drive-thrus, gravel yards and sludge dumps and reeking feedlots, to curl up with the Mutt and Molloy in a surreal, red-curtained El Paso motel room, after hours of desert darkness lit only by tiny constellations of distant cities far off on the plains... all the while spinning toward a bright "green" El Dorado of urban hipster culture in Portland, Oregon. Where I aimed to put down shallow roots, for however long.

Lo and behold, what happened on this one fraught American crossing, the fall of September 2001, ruined the dream of carefree relocation, as one terrifying night in a blown-open desert brought new revelations to bear on every place, all at once. Where awareness had been growing this way for some time, one fateful night in the Badlands of South Dakota precipitated an unforeseen cracking-open, of bodies, geographies, and even timescapes, along with dominant histories, identities, and maps that are supposed to classify and contain them. In the wake

32 This was hardly the "hard travelin'" Woody Guthrie sings of, where in ballads that track displaced farmers and migrant laborers, folks say "so long" to the harrowed dust of their homelands and crisscross the continent seeking "pastures of plenty." Woody Guthrie, "Hard Travelin'" and "Pastures of Plenty," *The Asch Recordings, Vol. 1–4* (Smithsonian Folkways Recordings, 1999).

of that disturbance, seismic shifts in the terrain called for some kind of urgent response. And this is where the journey, in hot tracks of the phantasmagorical American Spotted Ass, really begins.

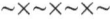

We rolled west out of New York in early September, with a car-full of boxes and loose belongings. A college friend named Adam B was along for the ride with me and the Mutt of Gold, to help with the weeklong drive and then visit his family in Seattle when we got to the other side. We decided to take the northern cross-country route, planning (why not?) to take our time and visit iconic national parks, famous roadside stops, and other tourist attractions along the way. But leaving friends and familiar places in New York was harder than expected that September morning we rolled out, and the first day on the road was mournfully solemn and silent. Ominous storms hung over Ohio, where the blackest daytime sky I ever saw threatened to drop like an anvil as we blew through Toledo. That early evening we came into the Wisconsin Dells, a green and stormy scene where we stood in the parking lot of Tommy Bartlett's Robot World roadside attraction and gawked at roiling thunderheads shot through with rainbows.

Around dusk we checked into a Madison motel. While Adam showered, I sprawled on one of the beds and flipped through an issue of *The Spotlight,* the quarterly publication of the American Council of Spotted Asses. What happened next must have been some kind of ontological hiccup, a fleeting and momentary "dark night of the soul." In any case, some mystical term of medieval origin must exist for what happened in that next dizzying moment, as I stared at the cover of *The Spotlight,* where a champion Miniature Spotted Jack named "Country Music's Merle Haggard" posed with his proud owner, a portly man in a bolo tie and big black cowboy hat. I looked a little closer at the photograph, and all of a sudden it pixelated in my vision and began to dissolve. The motel room swirled and I felt a sharp sinking in my guts: I had been made a fool of. Spotted Asses did not really exist. After all, I had never met one in the flesh, and it was all too far-fetched – a Photoshop hoax, a hybrid joke, like Sasquatch or the antlered-rabbit "jackalopes" on squeaky postcard racks in truck stops across the American West. For a long hellish moment, this was the truth of it. And the world went a little darker outside the synthetic blackout curtains of the Motel 6.

But the moment passed as swiftly as it came. Like a wave of grace backed with impassable doubt, my faith in the American Spotted Ass returned – or else I decided that it didn't matter if spotted asses really existed in the flesh or not. I'll never know which mattered more in that moment, the fact or the faith. Even if the spotted ass was a mere figment, I could still believe in it. After all, how many religious and political and cultural institutions – how many histories and species, even – are built on collective human will to invest in figures and the allegories and narrative tropes that bear them like flotsam through the world? So my faith in the magical powers of the American Spotted Ass was restored to preeminence by the time Adam emerged from the steamy bathroom, and in relative contentment we went off across the motel parking lot to dine at the Denny's. We slept soundly that night in Madison and woke to another long day ahead of us on the interstate.

Badlands

At what must have been about 8 a.m. on Tuesday, September 11, I woke up to the Mutt of Gold shaking her ears and tags in the Motel 6 in Mitchell, South Dakota. Out for a walk at the grassy edge of the parking lot, we saw a dark-haired woman wandering around, apparently distraught, holding an empty cardboard box. She came up to us and whispered that something was going on in New York, something about the World Trade Center. I returned to the room to wake Adam and we turned on the television. Media reports of the events unfolding in New York and Washington were fragmentary. Nobody knew what was going on, except that two different planes had crashed into the towers of the World Trade Center in New York, and the Pentagon in Washington had apparently been attacked. Structures were collapsing. Everything was in flames.

We tried for an hour or so to get phone calls through to friends and families back east. Then, not knowing what else to do, we got back on the road heading west. I recall a long silent moment, idling the engine of the Black Caprice at the turn to the interstate ramp, wondering if we could get back. But it did not seem possible to go back to New York. We spent ten hours that day at a Dakota roadside stop famous for cream pie and 5-cent coffee, while Adam, who worked for a major Wall Street firm, hung on the payphone trying to help his team in the city. Then, in shock and profound bewilderment, we drove west into the setting sun, keeping with our plan to camp that night in the Badlands.

The Badlands National Park is a singular landscape, an endless-seeming expanse of beautiful, forbidding hills and prairie grasslands. The Caprice's radio did not work, so once we left the roadside restaurant we were in a void, a lacuna where the only news was the presence of rolling desert prairie and unearthly hills that spoke in a secret language we did not understand. We arrived at the campground in the Badlands National Park near dusk and walked out into the surreal landscape. The arid ground under our feet and paws was crazed with cracks and faintly purple in the fading daylight. The land felt both desolate and full of hidden life as the sun sank beyond jagged cliffs to the west. As the sunlight faded on that day of shock and sadness, we found ourselves in the most stunning and alien landscape we'd ever seen. It's not for nothing they call this place the Badlands.[33]

Back at the campground, a cold wind came up fierce and sudden with the dark and blew hard across the land. We pitched the wildly-flapping tent without speaking. And what was there to say? It was not possible to settle in the chaos of so many ruptures and urgent unknowns, so I put the Mutt of Gold on her leash and we walked out from the campground onto the empty asphalt road, heading east where we came from and into the wind. The darkness that engulfed us was entire except for the stars – more stars than I ever thought possible, millions and millions of them. Everything we knew of the home we'd left was possibly annihilated, at the very least in danger and despair. Yet the stars still shone and the wind still blew.

It is crucial to acknowledge that this experience of the events now known as 9/11 was radically different from what those in the midst of smoke and flames and wrenching horrors at the scenes of the attacks went through, and different even from the trauma felt by those millions watching images on televisions across the US, a country full of citizens convinced until that day of the nation's absolute imperviousness. Adam and I did not see the burning images; we did not hear the latest chaotic

---

33 Besides being a gem of the US National Park system, the Badlands as a broader geo-psychic construct maintains certain cultural/poetic capital in American cinema and song, being the title of a classic film by Terrence Malick, which in turn inspired iconic recordings by Bruce Springsteen on the album *Nebraska,* not to mention a little-known cameo in the loose plot of Emmylou Harris's story-album, *The Ballad of Sally Rose.* (I mention this because of a prophetic dream about Emmylou, sometime not long after that Badlands night – something about tattoos on wombs and that sharp light glimmering off the lake as we came around that highway bend in Coeur D'Alene....)

news updates. Out there in the Badlands, what was happening in New York and Washington might as well have happened to dead civilizations thousands of years past, or on another planet.

The wind blew hard as we walked on, and it was so dark that I could just barely make out the ghostly swish of the Mutt's pale tail-fur waving a few feet ahead. We pressed on along the empty asphalt road without destination into the wind and starry dark, leaning into the place-in-time like the viscous substance it was. And that was when it happened. In a slow unraveling of assumptions, American and Human taken-for-granteds that had knitted together reality as I knew it, something otherwise took form in the fulsome dark. Even the terror and disillusionment and seemingly huge import of this night in History, at least for certain humans, the desert was what it was – wind and stars and warm mammals and roosting birds and insects and myriad unknown and nameless others living their lives, not without or outside history, as such, but holding and inextricably layering millions of knowings beyond human grasp, unwritten, or rather inscribed in claw-scratches, pawprints, blown seeds and shale cut by waterways and infinite movements and happenings that were and have been happening, then and now and always.

What happened out there that night was a kind of opening that will not stitch shut. But strangely, when I revisit the memory of that experience, always after a sob of grief and sadness for those who lost lives and loves in the events known as "9/11," what I find inside the swirl of dissolutions is not a sense of loss but a profound reassurance. In that collapse of so many human structures and assumptions, even my own monumental Humanity as I knew it, I felt the grounding of real, inimitable webs of presence. Moored with the Mutt in our familiar bodies, while at the same time dissolving into the weaving world that we felt and heard and smelled but could not encompass, we were immersed and indeterminate in the blown-open and fully inhabited electric darkness. And the strangest thing of all is that in this emptyfullness, or fullemptiness, came the apprehension of something I had been waiting and hoping for without knowing it: the sense or nonsense I sought in the mysterious eye-shine of confabulated asses and long-gone space dogs, in the cracks and gaps between words and warm, winding mortal bodies. It is incongruous, but I think true nonetheless, that even in the grievous shock of violent upheaval, the cracking-open of beings-together that night in the Badlands was a kind of homecoming. We came home, if only for a passing moment, into infinite constellations and assemblages of bodies and becomings that are never the ones we think we know.

Reams of indecipherable pages full of burning words and ashen numbers and names blew loose all through the night across the desert landscape. A fierce wind from the east belled the thin tent fabric inward against shivering bodies inside. The coldest night I ever knew. In the sharp bright morning, we woke to the clatter of the magpies' metallic hammering on the bottom of the Mutt's overturned water bowl, a silver orb in which a tiny far-off speck of hard sun was reflected. For the magpies of the Badlands the world this day was unchanged by the far-off flames and rubble of violent Human histories. The sky was clear and blue. The stark shale hills rolled on, swathed in flowering grasses and folded with gold and purple shadows.

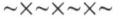

Days later, we limped into Portland in a fog of post-9/11 grief, exhaust, and confusion. Airplanes began to reappear in the skies, and Adam, my Brooklyn-born traveling companion, was finally able to fly home to the smoking ruins of New York City. Downstairs beneath my rented room in northeast Portland, the TV blared news about anthrax attacks, and al-Qaeda leaders warned Americans to get on our horses and ready for bloody battles to come. Meanwhile, each morning at a desk in the dank and cobwebby basement, I tried to pick up where I had left off with the fictive ride of a renegade wrangler and stolen pinto toward a lost Virginia home. But a new and different urgency steamed up through the cracks, which had begun with the looming "ass" question and widened to crevasses in the dark of that Badlands night. Whatever authority I claimed in its aftermath had to issue from those vital dissolutions and openings; whatever forms of meaning I might try to make hereafter must be responsible to the swarming unknowns, indeterminacies, and material intimacies of different bodies and energies fused in timeplaces, cut loose of any kind of humanist teleology.

In his dusty 1951 essay "The Noble Rider and the Sound of Words," Wallace Stevens wrote the following:

> This much ought to be said to make it a little clearer that in speaking of the pressure of reality, I am thinking of life in a state of violence, not physically violent, as yet, for us in America, but physically violent for millions of our friends and still more millions of our enemies and spiritually violent, it may be said, for everyone alive. A possible poet must be a poet capable of resisting or evading the pressure of the reality of this last degree, with the knowledge that the degree of today may become a deadlier degree tomorrow.[34]

My copy of *The Necessary Angel* was yellowed with age, and Stevens was mostly speaking of political and artistic

34 Wallace Stevens, "The Noble Rider and the Sound of Words," in *The Necessary Angel: Essays on Reality and the Imagination* (New York: Vintage Books, 1951), 27.

tensions that prevailed in centuries past. But the big poet's words resonated nonetheless in millennial Portland
in that frayed American fall of 2001, with respect to the
responsibilities of a "possible poet" in the violent pressures and uncertainties of a so-called "New Reality" of a
still-bleeding, post-9/11 "America."[35]

In the flash-bang reverberations of warmongering
words and their terrible, smoke-and-mirrors consequences, "What You Gonna Do about Yer [American Spotted]
Ass?" transformed to a whole new form, from Sun Ra's
koan to a sudden and inevitable physical imperative.
Here it was, then, the supreme (and perhaps the only possible) response – to Isabelle Stengers's call for a slowed-
down idiom of unknowing; to Wallace Stevens's poetic
admonition; to George W. Bush's blundering post-9/11
"Let's roll, America!" and even to Sun Ra's onerous koan.
I would blast into this new American "reality," light out
for territories both storied and nameless, in the company of a humble, spectacular beast of burden. Instead
of *writing* the fictional tale of a long reckoning ride to a
lost Virginia homeland, I had to DO it: Cede the helm of
authorship and perform the journey as a real immersion
in specific timeplaces. As a mortal organism immersed
within untold meshes of others, I would implode the old
hero's journey I had been imagining for so long as a word-
bound narrative.

The gist was this: I had to ride home on an American
Spotted Ass.

35 That is, "America" as spoken in those days in the distinct accent
of George W. Bush, and as heard in the soundings of the terrify-
ingly ambiguous "sixty words" of his official declaration of the War
on Terror, otherwise known as the "Authorization to Use Military
Force." "60 Words" is the title of a 2014 *Radiolab* podcast in which
the show's presenters "pull apart one sentence, written in the hours
after September 11th, 2001, that has led to the longest war in US history. We examine how just 60 words of legal language have blurred
the line between war and peace." "60 Words," *Radiolab*, WNYC Studios, April 17, 2014, https://www.wnycstudios.org/story/60-words/.

Beastly Places

What began with a raw paroxysmal directive – "Ride home on a Spotted Ass!" – evolved with a slow and steady momentum. An assurance grew that this absurd mission was absolutely necessary, as assthetic, political, and ethical action, this turning away from writing the fictional Ride to undertake "for real" a long trek with a Spotted Ass into terra incognita was somehow the truest act I could ever perform. And so from a stark, desert-born revelation, the ridiculous ass mission evolved a more nuanced psycho-geographic articulation, in a speculative stitching-together of real and imaginary places toward new kinds of immersion in unforeseen, full-blown beastly geographies. By midwinter of 2002, the mission was this: I would ride an American Spotted Ass across the US South, from Mississippi to Virginia.

Back when I was a Hollow hermit furiously hammering out scenes of The Ride, the narrative was driven by the grim pull of a vague, unnamed destination. Kin to Flannery O'Connor's Hazel Motes, the singular protagonist of her classic 1952 novel *Wise Blood,* fictive (anti)hero Juniper Ales was driven by volcanic urges toward redemption of losses and disappointments she could not fathom, as she wandered solo on a stolen pinto toward an unnamed Appalachian state. If she had made it all the way to her destination, she might have set the old family barn ablaze and watched it burn to ashes before slinking away into the shadows of cedar and hardwood-forested hills. But she never got there, because her tale was waylaid by the very events and dissolutions that conspired to charge the figure of the American Spotted Ass with unforeseen transformative powers and imagined imperatives. From the haggard hero's journey of The Ride, turned inside-out, came the vision of an assbackwards journey that would immerse in infinite untold storyings, into storied Southern states that were charged in different geograph-

ic, cultural, political, and personal ways. More importantly, every mile of roadway and acre of landscape is blasted
and blowsy with webs of hidden lives and histories.[36]

From different dissolutions and meltings in specific
landscapes arose intuitions and longing hopes for new
kinds of cracked-open belonging. Strange dream though
it was, this mission pulsed with promises of dissolute
homecoming and nameless redemption. So it was with a
sense of mildly melancholic irony that I named the journey's destination after the colonial mid-Atlantic state
where my family's farm and herd had blown apart like a
seedy dandelion a number of years before, and where so
many tales of nameless others lie untold. So I would ride
my speculative spotted ass to "Bewilderness, Virginia,"
the impossible home. More than any mapped or named
or deeded property, it was toward an inside-out, timeless,
unbound sense of "home" and possible new kinds of belonging that the journey aimed.

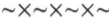

From any logical standpoint this journey-mission was utter nonsense – as illogical a response as you could imagine to various New Realities and broader US cultural and
political shifts at the turn of the millennium, and maybe
especially those precipitated by 9/11. Even so, over the
rainy Pacific Northwest winter of 2001–2002, the imperative – to ride home on an American Spotted Ass – did not
fade or falter. Instead it gathered momentum and visionary fuel, in daily walks with the Mutt of Gold along wet
sidewalks and mossy wanderings farther afield, through

36 Contemporary critical animal geographers Timothy Hodgetts
and Jamie Lorimer draw attention to the multitudes of ways that
multispecies configurations shape what they call "beastly places."
Timothy Hodgetts and Jamie Lorimer, "Methodologies for Animals'
Geographies: Cultures, Communication and Genomics," *Cultural Geographies* 22, no. 2 (2014): 285–95.

wild tangled grasses and bramblesome blackberry paths on Sauvie Island and along the banks of the Sandy River. So a vision gathered force through that dim, desperate winter full of Lynchian scenes in all-night karaoke bars, strip clubs, and moss-dripping forest trails. All through the winter in gloomy PDX, I dreamed of hot flesh-and-fur asses somewhere "out there." But where is "out there" to be found, exactly?

I knew this much: a person does not find pastures of plenty by sitting idly, sipping soy lattes in vegan cafes. The territories I needed to light out for, in hopes of finding my true ass, were not concrete urban enclaves but rural roadways and muddy barnyards, where radical possibilities for new ass stories are caught in webs of furry hides, colonial grasses, and tangled barbed-wire ecologies. But where does a person go to begin hunting the ass of her dreams? I was not sure. So I went back to the only place I knew to reliably glimpse the spotted asses I so longed to grasp, cyberspace, that is, and more specifically, spottedass.com.

Through the portal of that magical website, nearly a year from my first discovery of spottedass.com, the password to which I had attached so much hope and desire revealed its special power to materialize bodies and connect to real ass worldings. Lo and behold, the revelation came in the form of an unlikely invitation. That early spring of 2002, I had happened to email a Tennessee mule and donkey breeder named Mariann Black, querying about some gorgeous Spotted Asses she had listed for sale on the spottedass.com "classifieds." Her message shot back, "We love to show our asses! Come to Mule Day!"

I had never heard of Mule Day, nor to my memory ever met a mule in the flesh. Back then the only mules I knew were multitudes of dead ones that litter the landscapes of American, especially Southern, literature.[37] On the official Mule Day website, I was told of a yearly festival for all things mule-related, held every early spring in Columbia, Tennessee since 1840. But it was Spotted Asses I was after, so what did I want with mules? Yet I also recognized that it had been William Ferris's *Mule Trader* ethnography that originally led me (cybermagnetically) to the American Spotted Ass in the first place. And further research revealed massive overlap between mule and donkey cultures and markets. Wherever mules are, so must asses be, given the basic necessity of a jack-ass (intact male member of the *Equus asinus* clan) for mule-making.

Given the ambiguous designation of Virginia as the erstwhile destination of the big ass mission-in-the-making, it made some sense to head back east at this stage, even if the West where I was situated actually has more truck with familiar and untold ass histories of the colonial US. More than all this, though, the decision to head headlong to Mule Day in Tennessee (and right away!) was determined by something more elusive, a kind of subtle energy I could just barely make out, like crackles of distant dial-up static, in the words of that message from the mule trader, Mariann Black. Once more, it was the promising crack of a password that came through her message,

---

37 The trope of the poor old "dead mule" is so omnipresent in Southern fiction that it is a running joke. I once heard that someone meticulously counted the numbers of dead mules that appear in William Faulkner's and Cormac McCarthy's corpuses, for instance. Zora Neale Hurston's novel *Their Eyes Were Watching God* features a scene of a mule's untimely demise. There is even a literary journal called *The Dead Mule School of Southern Literature*, whose motto states, "No work of Southern literature is complete without a dead mule." Meanwhile, the material and cultural infrastructures of the agricultural South are unimaginable without the actual historical labors and cultural capital of the "good ole mule," even as oil-driven technologies like tractors and trucks made ghosts of them in early-twentieth-century landscapes, as Lydia Peelle achingly describes in her story, "Mule Killers." Lydia Peelle, "Mule Killers," in *Reasons for and Advantages of Breathing* (New York: Harper Perennial, 2009), 1–17.

in her joyful and (as I would soon discover) strategic deployment of the unseemly pun in her declaration: "We love to show our asses!" All this is to say: when I decided to accept Mariann Black's loaded injunction to race across the continent and meet her at Mule Day, I had no way to know that this invitation from a crazy-ass mule trader – cocked-and-loaded, coded with tell-tale rumblings of a blassphemous pun – would be like a shamanic spell, opening paths into thorny thickets of cultural, economic, and material ass worlds in the twenty-first-century US South. But so it was. And now I had a destination and even a date, a bull's eye target in the form of the Maury County fairgrounds in Columbia, Tennessee in the first week of April 2002.

From this point forward, I did not hesitate. All that mattered now was to find my ass – capture, befriend, and shape to my whims this chimeric beast of peculiar burdens, so that the real journey could begin. Somewhere out there, the spotted ass of my dreams was waiting, waiting for our fates to entwine and chafe as they might in the domestic-wilds of weedy backroads, barnyards, and all the other seamy places we pass through, as we each find ways to push, pull, and prod our beastly burdens into the maw of unforeseeable futures.

So I loaded a few boxes of belongings and the Mutt of Gold jumped into her spot in back of the Black Caprice, and we headed furiously back east, hell-bent for Mule Day in Tennessee. A day or two into the trip, something happened. I was racing across the Western desert states – retracing the previous fall's crossing by a different cross-country route, blasting Emmylou Harris cassettes and hoping to make good time to Columbia. All of a sudden, seemingly out of nowhere, a vision appeared in the Arizona desert (not far, as it happens, from the site of the catalytic "Nuclear War" crash in Safford two years earlier). It was a genuine, flesh-and-blood American Spotted Ass – the first I ever saw – just standing there in the bright-

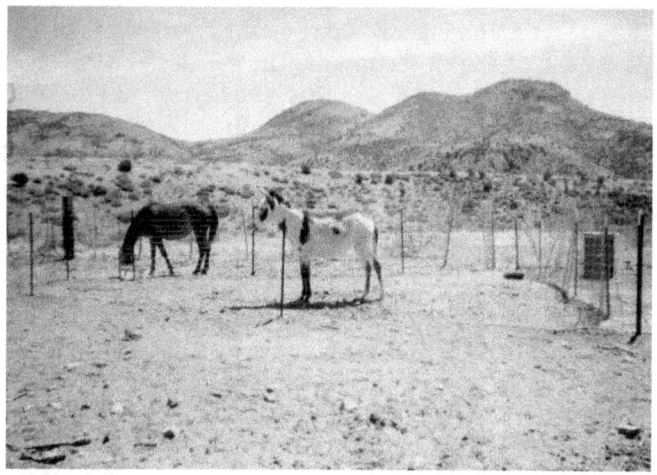

Fig. 5. American Spotted Ass vision in the desert outside Safford, Arizona. Photograph by the artist.

ness of day in a barbed-wire paddock out in the middle of the desert. No other landmarks or structures were in sight – just a mare standing a little ways off, presumed to be his mate. I swerved the Black Caprice onto the dusty roadside. Wide-eyed and panting, I scrambled around the mounds of snacks and trash and cassette tapes in the passenger seat for an offering.

As the Mutt of Gold watched curiously from the back, I got out of the car and walked across the road, where I reached through the wire fence and tried to offer the ass a granola bar. He blinked and flicked his ears at me mildly but did not move. I returned to the Caprice and we drove on into the days to come, exalted by the sighting of this rare beast in full furry flesh. Posed against a desert horizon in his native barbed-wire habitat, the unexpected appearance of a Spotted Ass could only be taken as a hopeful sign of things to come.

S/He Ride Double?
(On Tennessee Come-ons
and Hybrid Blassphemies)

In a more or less chronological fashion, this wandering-ass story traces routes and haps along the way toward finding the significant ass-in-question and setting out on our never-ending journey together. As it happens, the promise of a special password, which I had first glimpsed in the American Spotted Ass and hotly pursued through various continental crisscrossings, was utterly real. Recognized once again in that loaded invitation from a Tennessee mule trader, which lured me southeastward in early spring 2002, the password led straight to a mother-lode. Yes, the ass of my dreams was in fact residing in the dusty obscurity of a cattle farm on the edge of Columbia, just a few miles from the Mule Day grounds. But before I could actually get my hands on her, I had to pass through a sort of dark and swirling portal; I had to follow the lead of another important figure – an asstonishing pair of conjoined figures, actually – who (if we choose to follow them) ravel us into spectacular sites of hybrid blassphemous becomings. Watch now as this odd pair shifts and dodges, evading (for a while, at least) the punitive grasp of Powers-that-Be that would try to subdue them. Here they come, and then there they go... The Tennessee Mule-Woman and Her Big White Ass.

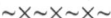

This is how it happened that, after seasons of dreaming and scheming and promising desert visions, I came to actually meet a real American Spotted Ass in the flesh. I heeded the invitation of a Tennessee stranger to race across the continent and meet her at the Mule Day grounds in Columbia. Mere moments after I found my way to Mariann's encampment, I was sat bareback upon her sturdy spotted-ass gelding, Napoleon (whose image I had admired in the spottedass.com clAssifieds). And there upon Nap's back, I rode behind Mariann as she reined through thronging crowds on her shiny young bay mule, Atticus, who had a flimsy plastic "For Sale" sign pinned to the saddle-blanket he wore. Being brand-new to Tennessee and dumbfounded by what I was suddenly immersed in, I did not catch most of what was muttered to us by folks in the crowd as we rode around. But after a few repetitions, I began to catch one particular utterance, posed to me repeatedly by grinning old men and boys as they leered up at me on Napoleon's bare back. Indeed, it was a rare, endemic breed of Tennessee Mule Day come-on: "Hey there," they would say, "s/he ride double?"

It was clear from their twinkly tones and raised eyebrows that they didn't mean nuthin' by it.[1] It was a jo-

---

1   *Nuthin',* that is, except the subtle exercise of gendered hierarchy that allows a man to offer to mount up behind a woman he does not know, apparently acceptable as long as it is presented in a jokey way. But note that it was only old men and teen boys who offered this, whereas it might have been riskier for one in the fullness of his manhood to make such overt gestures to a strange woman and her ass, even in jest. Deborah Clarke presents an interesting discussion of the ways that Faulkner's Southern male characters use humor to grapple with their masculinity and the specific roles that male humor plays in patriarchal Southern culture at larger scales. Debo-

vial harassment, if you can even call it that. Not a one of those round-bellied, stiff-legged old Tennessee mule-men in overalls or adolescent boys with Big Gulps and sticky cotton-candy hands was really going to clamber up behind me on Napoleon's back and grab him some bare-back-ass-womanflesh, even if I had happened to call back, "Sure, come on up!" Nevertheless I have often wished for the perfect snappy comeback to all the hidden assumptions and power plays wound up in the "s/he ride double?" proposition, as posed to a woman on a little spotted ass. I have wanted for some kind of rebel-yellish holler, what could summon all the fraught desires and conflicted, mixed-up passions, the grim compromises and subtle, necessary rebellions that the distinct politics and culture of Mule Day in Tennessee manifests. What kind of come-back could undo some of the thick and greasy, knotty threads that lace their unspoken assumptions through that particular, situated-ass "s/he ride double?" come-on? Specific as this provocation is to the unique manifestations of Mule Day, any answer a person could muster would naturally have to arise, alight, and be pitched back with a twist into the fray of that same fraught location.

Very soon indeed, I would begin to see that the response I wished for is just the kind of crazy-ass comeback that Mariann Black and all her ass and half-ass kin had been cultivating within the fray of Mule Day (and rural Tennessee more broadly) for years. And the radical answer she shoots back is this: Yeehaw, she do ride double! Double and then some....

Because the secret of Mule Day that Mariann taps into is this: The dominant, nostalgia-ridden, socially conservative, patriarchal-white-nuclear-Christian-family-oriented political sway of the Mule Day festival as a whole is deliciously belied by the inherently subversive hybridity of

rah Clarke, "Humorously Masculine – or Humor as Masculinity – in *Light in August*," *The Faulkner Journal* 17 (Fall 2001): 1–19.

the mule herself. Born of a horse (*Equus caballus*) mother and sired by a jackass (*Equus asinus*), the mule is an always sterile beast of burden, unable to reproduce, always the beginning and end of her own family tree. How's that for subversion of the heteronormative nuclear family model, not to mention a number of others? Indeed, through Mariann's blassphemous interventions, my own experience of Columbia Mule Day has been so influenced by this subversive hybridity that the "King Mule" logo – head of a big-boned draft mule wearing a cock-eyed crown and a glimmer in her eye – comes to wink like a trickster, brimming with all kinds of queerly transformative and liberatory possibilities.[2] This wink of the King Mule (often female) gives a sort of sandpapery feeling in the gut, like something rubbing from underneath against all those enforced categories of gender, race, and species that empower some while excluding others. So this winking half-ass figure erodes categories from below while nobody (no one supposedly in charge, at least) notices.

Such is the mule's slippery oddness: like a kind of secret, long-eared slit of opening in the lacy veil of Southern decorum. Older than the Gilgamesh/Enkidu split, it is the charge of the doubled figure who is no one recognizable beast, both more-than-one and none-at-all: s/he who rides and hides and runs astray with subtle powers

2   In *The Others: How Animals Made Us Human*, Paul Shepard stresses how the roots of language, and so much of our way of knowing the world as humans, lie in acts of categorization and differentiation of animal species in childhood. Shepard writes: "The injunctions against hybridity faintly echo the childhood modeling of primal cognitive categories on anatomy and animal types during the acquisition of speech, raised to a zealous idee fixe." Paul Shepard, *The Others: How Animals Made Us Human* (Washington, DC: Island Press, 1997), 178. Historian Harriet Ritvo addresses the question of the "barred cross" – the injunction against hybridity in the sociocultural quest for purity – in her 1997 book, *The Platypus and the Mermaid, and Other Figments of the Classifying Imagination* (Boston: Harvard University Press, 1997), 85–130.

to elude easy definitions, swing and dodge and wink between different breeds-of-being at once, never fitted to
just one category or classification but always many, in
buzzing swarms of beastly becomings that flicker and
survive in muddy spaces between names and in/visibly
entangled lives of all kinds. That is to say, the one who
may escape....

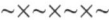

Even as Mule Day officially sighs with nostalgia for bygone, "simpler," animal-powered days (in tones typical
of conservative rural Southern cultures), what I found
when I arrived that Saturday morning to meet Mariann
Black and her assorted herd was a site rich with seamy
contemporary worlds among marginalized beasts of burden – most of all the mules, asses, and certain humans
on the fringes who care for them. For the mule is no mere
nostalgic symbol in Columbia: Mule Day in Tennessee re-
volves around the presences of shiny-eyed, ear-flicking,
fur-hided living bodies of odd long-eared equines, and
many of their short-eared mothers and half-siblings (i.e.,
horses), along with humans, of course, and many other
unacknowledged mammals, insects, nematodes, microbes, and plants who also inhabit and comprise these
worlds.

Columbia, Tennessee is the (self-proclaimed) "Mule
Capital of the World." For over a century and a half, the
Southern motherlode of mule culture, at least during
Mule Day week every early spring.[3] Beginning as a mule
swap in 1840, the Mule Day festival as it is known today

3   Other Mule Day festivals exist around the US, from relatively small
    events where the mule is mostly symbolic to the long-running
    weeks-long event in Bishop, California, where mules and donkeys
    from all over the US compete for national championships in every
    kind of equestrian event. But Columbia claims the oldest and most
    important Mule Day – the King of Mule Days, even.

kicked up in 1934, when some Depression-era hucksters saw a chance to make a buck on a spectacle as muleskinners convened from all over the Southern states and beyond to trade and admire long-eared equine wares. From midcentury onward – through world wars, diasporas, bloody race riots, and even (especially?) the displacement of good ole mules themselves by mechanization and rural-to-urban migration, Mule Day plodded on, growing steady and inevitable like the global human population.[4] Since becoming a public festival, Mule Day evolved as a nostalgia-tinged Southern gathering, featuring "family-friendly" entertainment such as white Christian gospel music and pig-calling contests, rows of booths hocking turkey legs, kettle corn, airbrushed t-shirts, and rebel-flag bikinis. Always on Saturday, a massive, spectacular parade draws crowds of thousands. Which is all to say, what began as a "Breeder's Day" in 1840 – a regional gathering for the exchange of mules and banter – has become a really big deal in the twenty-first century, so much so, in fact, that in 2006 the Mule Day Parade appeared on the Department of Homeland Security's National Asset Database as a possible terrorism target.[5]

Mariann's loaded, out-of-the-blue invitation to Mule Day had brought me reeling into this vibrant scene. The grounds we rode around that Saturday morning encircle a stand of white-washed wooden barns, indoor and outdoor stalls, and two big arenas with floodlights and grandstands, often full to the brim and spilling spectators like the overflowing trash cans. The heady air was

4   A significant race riot occurred in Columbia as racial tensions erupted in the immediate aftermath of World War II. See Carroll Van West, "Columbia Race Riot, 1946," *Tennessee Encyclopedia*, Tennessee Historical Society (October 8, 2017), https://tennesseeencyclopedia. net/entries/columbia-race-riot-1946/.

5   Oh we got your assets here, alright! Eric Lipton, "Come One, Come All, Join the Terror Target List," *New York Times*, July 12, 2006, https:// www.nytimes.com/2006/07/12/washington/12assets.html/.

full of odors of diesel fuel and manure and fried dough, and the soundscape rippled with uncanny cries of mules (a haphazard mix between whinny and bray) like the calls of exotic jungle birds. A constant clip-clopping grind of shod hooves and wagon wheels on gravel and asphalt persisted all weekend, as wagons and riders cruised the road that circles the inner grounds.

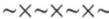

It did not take long to discover that Mariann's Tennessee was rough-ass country, in many different ways. In search of an American Spotted Ass, with an unspoken desire to sidestep categorical exclusions of certain bodies and the (sometimes) hidden hierarchies that enforce them, I was escorted into the fray of Mule Day by Mariann and her then teenage son Sebastian, their asses Napoleon, Connie, Sweet Pea and half-asses Atticus and the mini-mule Caesar, and the inimitably itchy and snaggle-toothed English bulldog, Daphne. And here we became instant allies in strategic blassphemies, even kin, in ways that lasted for a decade of Mule Days and beyond. Mariann generously welcomed me into her crazy ass world (and later me and Aliass both into the frazzle of her "funny farm" in Paris, Tennessee), and she became a vital and bottomlessly generous source of hard-won ass wisdom, skills, and material tools and equipment. Over many years and Mule Days to come, I came to witness and admire how it can be that a big-hearted, worldly woman and champion of underdogs of all kinds – who finds herself bound to the arduous challenges of making a precarious living as a single mother and husbander of hybrid and mixed-breed herds in rural Tennessee – becomes a subversive warrior and trickster on the frontlines of US Culture Wars.

As a worldly woman of countercultural bent who had traveled many lands and seas (working on cruise ships in her younger years), Mariann was presently shackled to the farm and those she cared for in Paris, Tennessee, what happened for her to be an oppressive, violent, and even dangerous atmosphere, where she struggled to protect her loved ones of various mixed species and races. A ferocious maternal mulewoman-of-the-world, she tried hard to provide health and safety for all her dependents and their ridiculously diverse needs on a scrappy farm of broken down barns, rotting fences, and weedy pastures that backed up to the poor and mostly Black housing projects on the outskirts of Paris. Maybe most fraught of all was the struggle to maintain a safe home in which to raise her son, whose biracial identity was further complicated by the fact that his Jamaican sea-captain father had been out of the picture for a long time, while Mariann's current husband was a dangerous and destabilizing presence.

But in a special, chain-linked corner campsite of the Maury County Mule Day grounds that was her domain for nearly a decade (marginal and central at the same time), things were different. In the carnivalesque atmosphere of Mule Day that revolved around the equine companions she loved, Mariann could let off steam by acting out against social and political oppressions that plagued her back home in Paris. And here in this alternate space, she cultivated leopard-printed, ass-pun blassphemies to the hilt, with often risky tactics for subverting "socially conservative" hierarchies of race, gender, and species – as if Mule Day was an intensification of the specific lively morass within which she struggled to live well and care for others every other day at home.[6] As it happens, some of those significant others would also come along to Mule Day, in a rusty stock trailer stuffed with long-eared characters of various shapes and sizes, who often were rescues from some abysmal circumstances in which she came upon and could not leave them. Mariann's distinct

6   See Claire Jean Kim, *Dangerous Crossings: Race, Species and Nature in a Multicultural Age* (Cambridge: Cambridge University Press, 2015).

ways of caring for (un)loved others in fraught environs conjures a vision of one of her most beloved companions, Sweet Pea, known lovingly as her Big White Ass.

Sweet Pea, otherwise known as "The Pea" or "Her Royal Pea-ness," was a rare, all-white mammoth donkey, meaning Sweet Pea was the size of a horse or mule, but solid ass through and through. "Her Royal Peaness" was Mariann's pride and joy, the reigning dignitary amongst the odd flocks and gaggles of singular beasts who populated the "funny farm" in Paris. It is hard to imagine ears as long and wide and hoary-white as Sweet Pea's, and as such her likeness to a giant white rabbit, or perhaps some other kind of body hidden inside a giant Easter Bunny costume, was unavoidable. (Interestingly, Sweet Pea may actually have been spotted. The breed registry was interested in her because she had one tiny black speck on one of her eyelids, meaning that her entirely otherwise white body may actually have been one giant spot.)

Up close and personal, Pea became even harder to pin down. Embodied in an improbable thick-legged, coarse-furred white body and looking back with suspicious curiosity in her deep-set brown eye, here was a character of such odd proportions and contradictions as to utterly confuse any eager taxonomist. Sweet Pea was like no other, truly. Her big white ungulate physique brought to mind any number of other species, from a gentle beluga whale to the imaginary Silly Wabbit who used to peddle rainbow-colored, sugar-ridden Trix™ cereal to kids. It seemed possible that the Pea might even have been some kind of elusive, part-bovine unicorn, who had somehow lost or withdrawn her magical twist of a horn.

In manner, Sweet Pea could be as sensitive as a blossom or as impassive (often immovable) as a limestone boulder – an enigma of opaque stoicism hiding inscrutable and explosive will. One could seldom tell what Pea preferred, until she was all of a sudden barreling like a runaway train toward some destination or objective known only to her – or, in the opposing mode, refusing to move at all, stuck with her head or entire body wedged between trucks, walls, or other obstructions. While Pea herself was a mammoth mystery, her relationship with Mariann was that much more fascinating to see for the chaos and melee of tempestuous passions they brought out in each other. For this and other reasons, the strange and often strained communion of Mariann and Her Royal Pea-ness is a good place from which to observe Mariann's distinctly blassphemous strategies.

On the one hand, Mariann loved each beast with a fierce maternal protectiveness and sought to protect their bodies and inscrutable souls from insults and injustices that whizzed around like bullets. She was as disgusted by disrespect for mules and asses as she was by blatant racism or misogyny in human social spheres. It was Mariann who solemnly taught me the ethical injunction that mules and donkeys "do not wear hats." (You would be surprised how many otherwise thoughtful humans delight in the sight of a donkey in a sombrero.) I have known few individuals so committed to extending respect and justice to all, at least in word, gesture, and other oblique ways.[7] At the same time, Mariann was a breeder and trader of "livestock," and so she bought and sold, propagated and traded and displayed her stock (mules and asses, horses and goats, chickens and pups) like raw wares on Market Day (which perhaps it must always be in the era of eBay and spottedass.com classifieds). Not to say the trade was ever without conflict. Once a man hung around the camp for hours, so determined was he to buy the rare Big White Ass. He just kept raising his price, even as Mariann insisted that Sweet Pea was absolutely not and never would be for sale. After offering what was an asstronomical amount (given the fact that a person could get an aver-

---

7   I recently learned the term "asshat," which is what one might call a human who is acting particularly stupid.

age ass for a fistful of dollars), the man walked off angrily shaking his head. As soon as he was out of sight, Mariann stepped behind her trailer and broke down weeping.

Trafficking in assflesh is what brought us together at Mule Day, after all (lest we forget, self-proclaimed "Mule Capital [*sic*] of the World").[8] I initially met Mariann because I was nosing around her ass, Napoleon, in the online clAssifieds, and eventually she helped me find and strike a deal to buy the Tennessee ass of my dreams. Yet when we met, and before that in the glimmer of the secret password deployed in her first email, we discovered hidden in each other's wanton ass puns a deeper shared regard for kinships and untold stories of long-eared friends and others. And so it happened that inside the fray of fraught situations like Mule Day – or any average day in which love and respect for others struggles to survive in places that threaten to reduce all lives to commodities and surfaces – we found and grounded a secretive shared desire to cultivate specific, strategic blassphemies, in different forms of unauthorized love and resistance to impassable contradictions and commodifications that we must all try to survive.

Like the password found in the doubled-up space between "ass" and the sensitive, storying beast it is supposed to contain, blassphemies work to hold open possibilities in seamy spaces-between – in this case, between desire to respect happiness of an ass or mule and the need and/or will to trade that embodied life as an economic object and commodity. As Donna Haraway has it, blasphemy is a strategy that is about "the tension of holding incompatible things together because both or all are necessary

---

8   And is "chattel" not the root of "cattle" and also "capital," after all? Middle English chatel, *movable property*, from Old French, from Medieval Latin *capitāle*; see cattle. *The Free Dictionary*, s.v. "chattel," http://www.thefreedictionary.com/chattel/.

and true."[9] In this regard, Mariann's particular modes of Mule Day blassphemy were both a high-stakes rebellious revelry and at the same time a desperate survival strategy. After only an hour or two hanging around Mariann's campsite at Mule Day (and then for ten years thereafter), I saw how this gathering was a prime locus for her to cultivate resistance to the many "incompatible things" and inhospitable forces she lived within, in the thick of the mostly politically conservative, evangelical, racist, and patriarchal horse and mule-trader's world of Tennessee.

Mariann Black is hardly the only lover of underdogs who must seek creative (and evasive) strategies to counter numerous subtle but powerful hierarchies and economies, enforced as they are by dominant figures and institutions. Nor is she alone in the need to hold together lives and cares in a mess of contradictory truths and incompatible necessities along shifty political and cultural zones in the contemporary US South, or for that matter anywhere on earth these days. Indeed, the stakes are high for anyone who cares about the welfare of living bodies excluded from the rights afforded to certain economically and racially-privileged human groups in the dominant naturecultures.[10]

9   Donna Haraway writes: "I know no better stance to adopt from within the secular-religious, evangelical traditions of United States politics, including the politics of socialist feminism. Blasphemy protects one from the moral majority within, while still insisting on the need for community. Blasphemy is not apostasy. Irony is about contradictions that do not resolve into larger wholes, even dialectically, about the tension of holding incompatible things together because both or all are necessary and true. Irony is about humor and serious play. It is also a rhetorical strategy and a political method." Donna Haraway, *Simians, Cyborgs, and Women: The Reinvention of Nature* (New York: Routledge, 1991), 149.

10 One site-specific example is this: The distinctive, high-stepping gait preferred by breeders and trainers of Tennessee Walking Horses, known as the "Big Lick," is not inborn but often cultivated through painful soring of their hooves and legs, along with heavy-weighted shoes that make the horse's natural stride impossible. Like the

Over the years, I saw how living within these cultural tensions in West Tennessee shaped Mariann's keen sense of injustice and rebellious reactivity, always in overdrive. At Mule Day and elsewhere, she always sought out any one, of any species, who might be suffering, which often led to more suffering as she seized every opportunity to mock or rectify perceived political and ethical injustices – be it a mule left in a stall without water or some good ole boy's casual racism or homophobia. She would joke with her son Sebastian's friend, Josh, the teenaged Black kid from the Paris projects who often came along to Mule Day – about disrupting the veneer of white conservative Mule Day in various ways. Josh's presence itself was a disruption of the predominantly white demographic inside the Mule Day grounds – though not within broader Columbia, where the Black community expresses a mix of feelings about the city's massive annual festival and exactly what history and community traditions it celebrates.[11] Never one for decorum, Mariann cooked up the

horses' fetlocks made raw from caustic chemicals, the "Big Lick" is a sore subject in the politically powerful Tennessee horse world. In 2016, a "Big Licker" – someone who practices and supports controversial techniques of achieving the unique gait of Tennessee Walking Horses – allegedly tried to drive his pick-up truck over a protestor with the Citizens Campaign Against Big Lick Animal Cruelty (CCABLAC), who were picketing a show at the same Maury County park that hosts Mule Day. The plight of Tennessee Walkers continues to gain attention in legal and on-the-ground clashes between animal-rights advocates and the Big-Lickers who breed, train, and make their livings from lucrative cultivation of horses' bodily distortions. A graphic undercover video by the Humane Society of the United States shows the "Big Lick" soring process and its effects on horses, and it has been viewed over a million times. The Humane Society of the United States, "Tennesse Walking Horse Investigation Exposes Cruelty," *YouTube*, May 16, 2012, https://www.youtube.com/watch?v=gxVlxT_x-fo/.

11 Soul Sistah Serrata E. Boson Amos wrote an op-ed in the *Columbia Daily Herald* in 2013 that describes some of the mixed feelings of Black Columbia residents around Mule Day. Many older people remember the violent and traumatic Columbia race riots of 1946, in

idea with Josh that he should run into the arena and ask to compete in "coon-jumping," an event where mules and asses display their unique method of jumping obstacles from a stand-still. Like many of Mariann's acidic jests, this one relies on (semi)hidden associations of the word "coon," where in Mule Day "coon-jumping" people may politely assume "coon" to be slang for the "raccoons" hunted by men on jumping mules. Yet many ears can't help but still hear this word as a racial slur used against Black people.[12]

Gender norms were fair game for Mariann's deliberate improprieties as much as racial ones. One year she rode into the arena, apparently nude, on spotted mule. She was dressed for a costume class as Lady Godiva, the legendary medieval noblewoman who supposedly disrobed and rode naked through the streets of the town, draped only in her long hair, to protest her lord-husband's oppressive taxation of the townspeople. Another time she and her gritty protégé, Koti, rode in the Mule Day Grand Parade dressed authentically as Civil War-era whores who made their livings following the movements of battalions on muleback. While most of Mariann's interventions were subtle enough to go uncensored by the Authorities, the heady atmosphere of Mule Day stirred these boundary

which lives were lost, Myths persist in the Black community about mules and slaves being sold together from the courthouse steps in the old days (which is untrue, says Boson Amos, though slaves were certainly present at the mule sales). Meanwhile, she describes how younger people often see Mule Day as an opportunity for fun and income, as it brings 200,000 hungry visitors to Columbia in one weekend each year. Soul Sistah Serrata E. Boson Amos, "Mule Day: A Lasting Community Tradition," *The Daily Herald* (Columbia, Tennessee), March 31, 2013, https://www.columbiadailyherald.com/article/20130331/LIFESTYLE/303319921/.

12 "Coon" as a slur is still in use, particularly among older white folks in the Southern US states. In rural Georgia after the 2008 presidential election, we more than once overheard conversations in which someone used this term to refer to President Barack Obama.

crossings and illicit actions, against more or less unspoken assumptions and enforced regulations, into a volatile mix of good fun and something more dangerous.

Leaping into the future for a moment, I can report firsthand that from that first wild 2002 meeting onward, Mariann's renegade Mule Day campsite became a vital site of attachment and return – a place to gather and stage impromptu collective blassphemies and little acts of resistance and multispecies escap(ad)es. Tucked in the northwest corner of the grounds, a merry band of humans, dogs, asses, mules (and even secret hinnies) became a kind of porous multispecies family herd, not by bloodlines but through other hybrid articulations of bonds and kinships, borne across state borders and species lines.[13] Over a decade of Mule Days, ranks of friends and allies came together at this site, in what we might call (via Hakim Bey) a "Temporary AutonomAss Zone," a fleeting assemblage that grounded enchantment and dark thrills, disgust and despair, and hopeful possibility, and most of all certain sweet-ass kinships, all of which rooted in a haze of smoky camaraderies in a spot of muddy grass beneath a tall spindly pine tree in a bad-ass corner of the official grounds, near a line of portapotties.[14] Here in this special TASSZ, a multispecies Mule Day fam-

13 Hinnies are like mules, half ass and half horse, except that their mothers are asses and fathers are horses. Mules are the other way around, with horse mothers and ass fathers. Hinnies are less common because female asses do not conceive as easily from stallions as female horses do from jacks. For this reason, hinnies tend to be surrounded with a certain mystique; one Mule Day we learned that a champion mule named Crow, much admired because he radiated some special difference and charisma, was actually a hinny. This news was whispered from ear to ear with an air of drama and revelation, and not without a certain whiff of bitter irony, given troubled histories of secret ancestries and "fatal drops" of mixed blood in US Southern slave culture and elsewhere.

14 Hakim Bey, *T.A.Z.: The Temporary Autonomous Zone, Ontological Anarchy, Poetic Terrorism* (Brooklyn: Autonomedia, 1991).

ily came together to nurture alternative forms of "family fun," literally "making kin" in new ways inside the chain-link borders of Mule Day's unruly political, aesthetic, and economic power dynamics.[15]

Here we found grounds from which to stage radical, if subtle, interventions against various oppressions, while embedded inside this circus of dominant cultural regimes. Our doings were mostly hidden from view as we tucked into various illicit substances and political leanings. From that first meeting in 2002 through ten years of gatherings in the unpredictable weathers and atmospheres of Maury County park, a makeshift Mule Day family became a rhizomatic network that stretched across many different bastard-beautiful sites, where bodies and biographies struggle like half-wild lives caught up in barbed and twisted histories of race, sex, species, and old-time beastly burdens, all of us trying, for whatever it's worth – whatever it might mean in dangerous, divisive places – to help each other get more free of the fearsome names and faulty frames that trap us all.[16]

That said, one must wonder what such subtle blassphemies as ass puns might actually do as countercultural acts of resistance to shape and change lives, as deployed in the troubled languages and naturecultures where every body must make lives and livings. I can say this

15 In domains that literally enforce "family fun" as acceptable activities of a nuclear heterosexual human group, unauthorized family fun is more like what Haraway describes as "kin-making," where "making kin and making kind (as category, care, relatives without ties by birth, lateral relatives, lots of other echoes) stretch the imagination and can change the story." Donna J. Haraway, "Anthropocene, Capitalocene, Plantationocene, Chthulucene: Making Kin," *Environmental Humanities* 6 (2015): 159–65.

16 Hints of Deleuze and Guattari sneak in here in the faint suggestion of rhizomatic networks as trajectories of escape from capitalist dominion. Gilles Deleuze and Felix Guattari, *A Thousand Plateaus: Capitalism and Schizophrenia*, trans. Brian Massumi (Minneapolis: University of Minnesota Press, 2009).

much: Where dominant deployments of words, names, and classifications reify and shape the worlds we make and inhabit, Mariann's special blassphemies in the heart of the Mule Capital of the World offered radical moral and material support for my own nascent investments in puns and unnamings, pitched as hopeful resistance to the dominant commodifications that such namings and classifications reinforce. Wordplay may be a questionable means of bucking dominant economic and social structures, but it is clearly not impotent. Where words matter in world-making, puns matter, too. If nothing else, that first pun exchanged between Mariann and me proved to be an opening into unforeseen worlds and strategies of becoming I might never have discovered otherwise.

So from her first cross-country email invitation, I found a fierce ally and ass mentor in Mariann Black, whose gratuitous and necessary rebel acts come with loving beastly bodies in worlds that exploit bodies of all kinds. Even in the midst of intense personal, social, and financial efforts to maintain a stable home and safe pastures for those she loves, Mariann provided bottomless moral and material support toward the realization of my own aspirations, along with wild camaraderie and much-needed skills, advice, tack and tools – from the first rope halter and antique child's saddle to the machete she insisted I hang on the saddle for personal protection and bushwhacking. Like some kind of leopard-print-clad, muck-booted barnyard shaman, she even led me directly to the ass of my dreams – the very next day after we met, as a matter of fact. As it happened, her ass-for-sale Napoleon was a champion, and out of my price range. But in the Columbia classifieds she saw an ad for an ass-herd liquidation at a local farm. She suggested I drive back down to Columbia the next morning and we could go over to the farm together and check out the stock for sale. And so we did. And in the dim dusty light of a pole barn on Monsanto Road, there she was, the soon-to-be-unnamed she-ass, suddenly solid and real, if still wholly mysterious in her mud-caked, furry, and watchful way. And the rest is (untold) history.

Meanwhile, the possibilities of responses to that coy Mule Day "She-ride-double?" come-on present a perpetual invitation. We don't go to Mule Day anymore, since Mariann finally escaped Paris, Tennessee for life as a beach-combing expat animal-rescuer in Belize. But we do go on seeking lines of flight and transformation – secret backwoods passages to new grounds for frazzled hopes and surprising kinships cultivated within inescapable, ever-compromising configurations. In fiercely inhabited stories of past and future ass (and half-ass) reckonings, we go on, growing our slow and dirty jokes in newfound muzzle tongues, making new sites in barnyards and beyond for blassphemies yet to come.

3

Thralls and Galls
(Meeting a She-ass in Tennessee)

And so she was, out there somewhere, nameless in Tennessee: burnt-muzzled, bright-eyed, rough-furred, and muddy. Which is not to say she was waiting for me.

I had plenty of reasons to second-guess the recognition I felt in that first encounter. She was the first spotted ass for sale I had seriously looked at, after all. But she was so lovely, serene and glowing in the dim light of the loamy cowshed. She watched me with wary curiosity as I came in and knelt down beside her in the shadowy barn. Shyly, wisely, she lifted her delicate whiskered muzzle to my face and sniffed my eyes. Then she nuzzled my hands, as if to assess whether she should fear them or hope to find something good there.

A little while later, I leaned on the rusty fender of Mariann Black's old Ford F-150 in the farmer's barnyard and sought advice from my newfound, crazy-ass mentor. I had raced all the way across the continent on Mariann's invitation, to meet up with her at the Mule Day festival, and that was what led us to this farm that Sunday morning – an ad she happened to see in the local classifieds. A longtime breeder and trader of mules and donkeys, Mariann knew a good ass when she saw one. She said this jennet (female ass) was right for the tasks of the journey I had in mind: good conformation, just big enough to ride, and a fair price at $400. A good trim or two would fix her crooked hooves. "It won't be easy to find another deal this good," she said.

I gazed across the metal gate at the elegantly scruffy, ghostly white-faced she-ass standing in the barn gloom. I could make her mine. But there was one hitch. She had been running with a jackass, and so she was most likely in foal. Wouldn't it be cruel to burden a pregnant jennet with the dangers and travails of the long, hot, road-side trek I imagined us embarking upon that summer? At this stage, I still had no clear destination or timeline for the nascent mission to ride a Spotted Ass across the American mid-South, and for that matter no clue where or when we would land somewhere safe to raise a little ass family.

Even if she was in foal, though, the little ass mama likely had many months to go. Jennets gestate for a full year (two months longer than mares, which Mariann says is the extra time it takes to grow those long ass ears). As a seasoned breeder, Mariann assured me that jennets-in-foal were tougher than most and that walking was good for gestation. As long as the she-ass got enough to eat and did not get overstressed, she would be fine. "Anyways," she said, "you'll just have to risk it if you want this one. If she is in foal, you can travel until a month or so before she's ready to drop, then you'll just have to find somewhere safe to stop for a while. When the foal is strong enough, you can all travel on together."

Mariann had haggled with the Columbia farmer for a bulk-buy deal on a gaggle of his miniature jennets, who she planned to breed to her champion miniature jack PT Cruiser (Pete), or else clean up and sell at the big Shelbyville Great Celebraytion Mule and Donkey Show later that summer. So the next week when she went to pick up the minis in Columbia, she generously offered to haul my ass, too, swinging through Nashville on her way back northwest to her farm in Paris, Tennessee.

And so, that glorious Friday in early April, just a week after the Mutt of Gold and I rolled into pale-green Tennessee from Oregon, bound for Mule Day with a wild-ass dream and no fixed address, Mariann delivered the American Spotted Ass of my dreams – of whom I was now the owner in the flesh – to an overgrown former cattle farm in Whites Creek, Tennessee. Indeed, the same kismet that led me straight to my sweet ass in Tennessee seemed to be work when my buddy Wheatstraw invited us to stay on at the farm in Whites Creek, where we found temporary refuge and camaraderie amidst a diverse gang in prickly thickets of a densely storied landscape.[1]

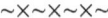

All over this land, which is said to be your land and my land, officials have erected ornate metal placards that designate particular sites as "the Birthplace of So-and-So." "So-and-so" is, more often than not, some dead white guy who is ascribed a special role in the mythic histories people paper onto any given place. These "historical markers" that poke up solemnly from lively dirt and grasses are always a little incongruous, as they stand still and self-important amidst vibrant meshes and soundscapes of rustling leaves and birds and bugs and weeds and weathers – as they stand for assumptions that (cer-

1   Wheatstraw (aka Kevin Hayes) and I had met year or so before this and became pen pals. By an incredible stroke of fortune for my big-ass mission, he was now living on an old farm outside Nashville, just an hour's drive from my date with Mariann (and destiny) at Mule Day. Given the predilection Kevin had for ever-changing pseudonyms in those days (and in line with the pseudonymous unnaming aims of my project as a whole), I will stick with the name he was going by in those days. Wheatstraw welcomed us into the folds of many good friends and allies we would find in the place known as Whites Creek in the weeks ahead.

tain) human stories make places what they are. Meanwhile, the full-blown stories of places are never comprised in lists of human names and dates. In honor of the many kinds of untold stories and unmarked human and other histories that animate places – those of weeds and moths, poplars and hawks and so many nameless kin – I seek to root a different kind of sign into landscapes of the rural American South. This kind moves with the light, flickers and slides like the shadows of passing clouds or wheeling buzzards on the breeze. Rather than staking exclusive claims for limited human histories, it marks sites of opening toward encounters with others, glimpsed and unknown presences and possible ways of being. With this different, livelier kind of sign, then, I hereby designate Whites Creek, Tennessee in the early spring (April 12) of 2002 as the "Birthplace of Aliass."[2]

Back in 2002, Whites Creek was still a rural settlement of pastures, hayfields, and older homesteads to the north of Nashville's city limits, tucked between two raggedy wooded ridges in a valley cut through by the roilsome, foamy, wild, and trash-strewn creek for which it was named. The center of "town" then was a cinderblock post office and a tenuous meat-and-three café, surrounded by a cluster of homes and mown yards on smallish lots. The land on the east side of the Pike, nestled up to the ridge behind big wrought-iron gates, was the vast estate of country-music legend and shampoo spokeswoman, Barbara Mandrell. As a sleepy pastoral patchwork of landscapes shaped by hidden histories, and more visibly by the infrastructures of livestock-keeping (fences, run-down barns, hayfields, cattle-guards, and so on), Whites Creek could not have been more a more perfect site from

2 Two official historical markers stand in Whites Creek: one marks the site where Bill Ryan, a member of the notorious outlaw gang of Jesse James, was arrested in Whites Creek in 1881. The subject of the other is unknown to me.

which to launch a wild ass ride through fraught Southern states. In other words, the perfect staging ground for a nascent Southern ass journey.

So it was lucky that in exchange for keeping Em (his grumpy grrrl-dog) company when he was off on tour with his punk-rock-old-time string band, Wheatstraw invited me and the Mutt to stay in his rented cottage on the Whites Creek farm for as long as we wanted. We settled in, for the time being, in the peculiar farmhand's cottage known as the Foamhouse, nicknamed thus for the strange, styrofoamy material from which its walls were made – a substance invented (but tragically, not patented), by the son of the farm's widowed owner. I lay us down a pallet on the floor, and there the Mutt and I curled up in the corner beside the rusty and wheezing baseboard heater, under the cluttered ping-pong table beside Wheatstraw's bookshelf that overflowed with novels by Henry Miller and Blaise Cendrars, poems by Rimbaud and Walt Whitman, and stained and yellowed dime-store Westerns.

A few days after I found my ass-to-be down in Maury County, Wheatstraw and I paid a visit to his landlady, the elderly widow Mrs. T. Even as Whites Creek was poised at the edge of Nashville's rapacious suburban development, much of the land along the Whites Creek Pike was still part of Mrs. T and her late husband's former farm. Once the most prosperous dairy operation in Middle Tennessee, Mrs. T and her kin still held the largest tract of undeveloped land in Davidson County – over seven hundred acres of forest, pastures, and hayfields. As we sat on her porch-swing sipping sweet tea, the widow listened with bright-eyed interest as I haltingly explained my odd ass mission. Whatever I said that day, it resonated with Mrs. T. She offered to shelter the spectral Spotted Ass in her empty barnyard for as long as we needed to get ready for the journey ahead.

Later as we walked back up the lane to the Foamhouse, we passed by the old white barn. The still-naked branches of shrubs and vines scrabbled around its peeling walls, blistering with leafbuds ready to burst. In the thin April sunshine, the pale, rolling, yellowish-green pastures seemed right on the cusp of exploding into bright green profusions of leaves and seedheads. Indeed, the old farm as a whole seemed to creak open like a rusty-hinged barn door. It swung wide, as if the coming of an American Spotted Ass was just the catalyst that all the grasses and low-growing plants, birds and soil microbes and lichens and fungi were waiting for, the spark to light the roaring, slow-green flames of that early-twenty-first-century Tennessee spring. Armadas of bulldozers and concrete mixers, graders and asphalt trucks hummed on the horizon of Whites Creek even then.[3] But in the early weeks of that enchanted spring, Whites Creek would be secretly transformed, if only for a spell, from a grassy patchwork of prime Davidson County real estate into a seamy American Spotted Ass contact zone.[4] That ghost of an old cattle

3 Since the early twenty-first century, Whites Creek has seen waves of development that brings sighs from those who imagine these shifts in the landscape to be vexing for denning foxes, nesting birds, and the rooted trees and shrubs whose options for relocation are more constrained. Some birds and mammals may have moved up the road to the more exurban, northern climes of Joelton and Goodlettesville. Others make do, or die. Still other species learn to thrive in the patchwork of mown lawns amidst the grids of duplex driveways. For a peek at a number of bird species that have adapted well to suburban development, see John Marzluff, *Welcome to Subirdia* (New Haven: Yale University Press, 2014).

4 Donna Haraway adapts the idea of contact zones from a rich scholarly genealogy, gleaning concepts from radical anthropology to developmental biology to limn possibilities of the specific contact zone where she meets her agility dog partner, Cayenne. In "Training in the Contact Zone," Haraway's genealogy of contact zones begins with Mary Louise Pratt's borrowing from linguistic "contact languages" as "improvised languages that develop among speakers of different native languages who need to communicate interactive, improvisational dimensions of colonial encounters." Donna Haraway, *When Species Meet* (Minneapolis: University of Minnesota Press, 2008), 216–19. Haraway's dog–human contact zone is a space

farm where the she-ass and I landed and spent our first tender weeks together was the ideal staging ground for a meeting of conflicted human aspirations and the quiet, mysterious ways of a spectacular, sweet-as-black-coffee-and-cherry-pie she-ass.

Not a week ago I had rolled into Tennessee in the Black Caprice with the Mutt of Gold and a skein of conflicted hopes and desires wound tight around the figure of the American Spotted Ass like a wisteria vine. A tremendous freight of past encounters and future hopes was loaded onto that imaginal beast-of-burden figure, as previously described – never mind the cargo of fraught associations regarding the charged and murky landscapes of the American South through which our journey would pass. But it is only when we came together as earthly mortal bodies in this particular Tennessee timespace that the deepest responsibilities and possibilities of our meeting began to matter in new and vital ways.[5] In the wicked green of one millennial Southern spring, we found ourselves – lonesome ass, restless humans, beloved mutts, grasses, swallows and jaybirds, trees, honky wild geese and turkeys, mud-dwellers, honeysuckle vines, pokeweed, raucous coyotes, and countless others, known and unknown – in a brand new kind of barnyard, where name-

in which she frames biological, political, and poetic possibilities, responsibilities, and consequences that emerge in material-semiotic meetings of specific domestic companion species. At the same time, Haraway makes room for unknown others that proliferate at the blurry peripheries of our frames, which become sites of both friction and possibility. So I propose that this season of human–ass encounter within the richly unknowable environment of Whites Creek begins in frictions where multispecies, embodied, and nameless ways tangle with human forms of representation, and so become – in the form of this text if not in Whites Creek itself – a particular kind of material, artistic, and poetic contact zone.

5   For mattering in a feminist materialist sense, see Karen Barad, *Meeting the Universe Halfway* (Durham: Duke University Press, 2007).

less bodies and forces come together in unforeseen ways
and rub each other raw in tender, hidden places.

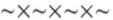

Still in the luminous wonder of it: the day this singular beast – with her dark-brown, white-lashed eyes and
rough winter fur, scabby muzzle, and crooked hooves –
materialized like a rare blossom in the pale green-gold
of the early Tennessee springtime. Wheatstraw was out
of town, on his way back from opening for Cootie Stark
somewhere in the Carolinas, so the mutts and I were the
only ones to witness the incarnation at the Foamhouse
that afternoon, when the loaded ass rig rumbled up the
lane and squeaked to a stop under the sprawling bower of
the old oak tree in the front yard. Mariann slammed her
pickup door and came around to the back of the rig, where
she wrenched open the rusty metal bar of the trailer door
with a creak and pushed her way in among the jumble of
sweaty little ass bodies. I stood frozen with anticipation.
So enthralling was this moment – the faint knocking of
hidden hooves on hollow boards, then raw wonder as the
one I waited for stepped shakily off the trailer with a little hop onto the pale, root-laced driveway dirt beneath
the oak's majestic bower – that the little rough-furred
roan Spotted Ass who appeared might as well have been
a unicorn.

And so she was, and in a way remains, a projection, a
mysterious vision moving amidst layered veils like some
big underwater mammal, always seen from either too
close or too far away. Like the modern discovery of the
mysterious, 16th-century "Lady and the Unicorn" tapestry, here in the brightness of a Tennessee afternoon was a
glorified material-semiotic weave of ancient human fan-
tasies, atavistic desires, twisted-together genomes and
phenomes, phonemes and imagos, shaped by thousands
of years of beastly becomings. And branded, of course,

with that newfangled "Western" hide that had so capti-
vated the imagination that I had no choice but to hunt
and capture this unwitting ass and hitch her to the loaded tasks at hand.

Let us not forget how those spectacular spots that
blanketed the ass like a brocaded Renaissance tapestry
are what brought us together in gathering folds of Tennessee timespace. Think of this: had my ass inherited,
at her embryogenesis, the more quotidian gray donkey-
coat color, or even the rarer black-nose genes (like some
among that bevy of miniature jennets knocking around
in Mariann's stock trailer in assorted colors that day, like
a box of sweet ass candy), I would never have come to
know and love her like I do. I would have passed her over
without a second glance. Luckily, her so-called "spots"
brought us together, from that day to this one, in a seamy
meeting of shame and desire and whatever else we might
hope to find here.

It was as easy as all that: from the dream of a silly beast
chasing a Spotted-Ass phantasm to this real-ass coming-
together in rural Tennessee. Here stands the twisted mystery of fates and commodity chains, desires and encounters that bring us to walk in mortal green fields of time
with the ones we love. That hide of Aliass's – the graceful
taper of her long white face, framed by the soft twin hollows of her ears and gray-pink muzzle, those eyes that I
cannot possibly describe, the spiky peppered mane and
coarse white fur of her neck that gives way to silver-gray-
brown patches with flecks of rust and black across her
withers and back, over the roundness of her flanks and
belly, where patches of white float like passing summer
clouds and taper down to the dainty articulations of her
little white legs and caramel-and-black striped hooves
where her body meets the grass and dirt that have shaped
and sustained it for spiraling generations. Were it not for
this rarefied ass hide, which hides her so spectacularly, I
would never have come to meet this ass, and so to load

upon her all those gnarly human desires and hungers to grasp what is hidden inside.[6]

The full 400+-pound weight of it hit me as I took the lead-rope from Mariann's hand. The living presence of this big-eyed, big-eared, sensitive ungulate mammal, who was blinking and sniffing the air and listening for any familiar sound to help her grasp her new surroundings, gave a new gut twist to the now-familiar question: "what you gonna do about yer ass?" A few answers came easy: to start, she needed a water bucket and some hay. Providing for familiar equine needs was a kind of second nature that felt good. But other aspects of what to do grew more complicated, as in this moment I took on (for as long as we both shall live) a certain responsibility for her happiness. For one thing, along with all the phantassmagoric meanings and possibilities I had already bestowed onto her generic surface, I did not know this little burro one bit. In fact, all I knew of her scant biography was a few details the laconic farmer who sold her had told me: she'd birthed a foal or two, the last of which was stolen from her by a dominant jennet in the herd. She might or might not be carrying a fetus now, but that was her secret; there was no way to tell it just from looking at her.

I intended to befriend her, of course, best as I could.[7] But the prospects of caring for an unfamiliar ungulate, in the midst of nomadic wanderings in blasted landscapes of the twenty-first-century American South, were

6 It is worth stressing that it was this and not other qualities (say, spectacular athleticism) that attracted me to her, with the intuition that her spots have very little to do with who she is, even as they become a value-added aspect of her existence. See Karin Bolender, "If Not for Her Spots: On the Art of (Un)naming a New Ass Breed," *Humanimalia* 10, no. 1 (2018).

7 Proximity was a start, as Dominique Lestel writes: "The history of significant encounters between humans and animals is from the start an arrangement of duration, space, and the safe interactions that make it possible." Dominique Lestel, "Friends of My Friends," *Angelaki: Journal of Theoretical Humanities* 19, no. 3 (2014): 142.

fraught in ways I had barely begun to reckon. Ready or not, here she was, in the furry, worried flesh. A gentle, sensitive prey mammal was at my mercy at the end of a knotted rope. Her fate was in my hands as she stood there in the wispy grass of the yard, looking and listening to what I could never know. Her life, and possibly a hidden passenger, were at my disposal, thanks to a bevy of rights bestowed on me by ancient animal hierarchies and rank economies in which certain lives are held as property by others. All mine she was, this inscrutable mammalian stranger whose embodied past, present, and future, whose senses of time and place and remembering I could hardly fathom – never mind claim to "own."

Here then here is the rub, the rub that becomes the gall. "Gall" is a word we learn the hard way among beasts of burden. When part of a harness or girth is ill-fitting, the pressure and frictions of various labors rub away fur and open a sore in the flesh, which becomes an aggravated open wound that often goes unnoticed under the offending tack. A gall is like a blister, but deeper and harder to heal. The history of human–equine becomings is full of harness galls and saddlesores, both recognized and hidden. In time, one learns tricks for treating these sores – old folk remedies or over-the-counter hemorrhoid ointments. Even better, we sometimes find ways to anticipate and thus avoid them in the first place: fleece coverings for girths, harness pads, and so on. But one trouble with galls is that they tend to be hidden by what causes them, and as long as the pressure continues, the wounds keep getting reopened. Sometimes a gall becomes a scar, a hard hairless spot on the hide. Older work mules often have galls all over their bodies, but I have also seen and even inflicted such traces of ill-fitted pressures on all kinds of equine bodies, from scuffs and scars on old rodeo broncs to saddlesores on sleek-coated thoroughbreds and fancy show ponies. Scars like these on withers and flanks are one kind of visible trace that marks encounters between human cultures and equine beasts of burden over many millennia.

Painful sores and possible slaughter are not the only features of shared domestic lives in the American stable and barnyard. Often with respect and careful attention toward embodied wisdoms and "entangled empathies," we pursue and maintain diverse and admirable becomings with equines and other domesticates.[8] That said, there is no getting past this fact: The bright spring day my Spotted Ass arrived in Whites Creek was one of singular bliss for me – an affirmation of human imagination's conjuring powers – while at the same time, that day was inevitably a catastrophic one of loss and fearsome uncertainty for her. With no forewarning, she was hazed from her herd, chased onto a stock trailer, and ripped away from everything familiar to her – pastures, shelters, friends, and kin – with no way to ascertain where she was being taken or what lay in store. Now that I know this gentle beast, who is most at peace when routine prevails and everyone she cares about are in their familiar places, the abyss that yawns between my thrilling acquisition and the grievous fear experienced by my little long-eared friend on that day is all that much more gut-wrenching. Neither my own past experiences of interspecies amities nor a vast bibliography of scholarly resources changes the fact that she was scared and lonesome and grieving as she stood hitched by a rope halter to a metal t-post, captive in an unfamiliar place among lurking human and

8   See Lori Gruen, *Entangled Empathies, Entangled Empathy: An Alternative Ethic for Our Relationships with Animals* (New York: Lantern Books, 2014). Vinciane Despret also describes "practices [that] present a very different version of 'embodied empathy', a concept which describes feeling/seeing/thinking bodies that undo and redo each other, reciprocally though not symmetrically, as partial perspectives that attune themselves to each other." Vinciane Despret, "Responding Bodies and Partial Affinities in Human-Animal Worlds," *Theory Culture & Society* 30, nos. 7–8 (2013): 73.

canine strangers. Her misery was hidden within various apparatuses that erase the emotional lives of "livestock" from our recognition. Her feelings were further obscured by the characteristic stoicism by which donkeys hide pain from possible predators. To this day, though, I can still remember the fear and grief that were plain to see in her tight muzzle and sad eyes and ears.

In an essay called "Judas Work: Four Modes of Sorrow," Deborah Bird Rose gives a gut-wrenching account of "Judas donkeys" who are used to find and cull wild ass herds in Australia, where donkeys came as beasts of burden for settler colonialists and went feral, thus earning themselves the fatal designation of "pest."[9] The Judas model, used by managing humans in a number of scenarios where members of a social species will unfailingly seek companions, involves in this case separating a jennet from her herd and fitting her with a radio-collar. Officials then set the jennet free in the outback to go find another wild herd to join. They follow her signal and eventually show up and massacre all the others. Rose reports that after one or two traumatic experiences, the Judas jennets stop seeking others and live the rest of their lives alone. As social mammals who live within the law of safety in numbers, not to mention all the other aspects of social kinship that keep them healthy and happy, these jennets must experience this self-exile as a misery worse than death. Humans ceaselessly inflict this kind of emotional suffering on other species, mostly through denial that kindred social mammals, with whom we share the evolution of our own emotional capacities, have them at all.

Those first weeks in Whites Creek, the lonesome ass and I commenced a "training" regime. We wandered the pathless grasses and dewy vetch of the meadows, me and the nameless she-ass and the Mutt of Gold. We explored

9   Deborah Bird Rose, "Judas Work: Four Modes of Sorrow," *Environmental Philosophy* 5, no. 2 (2008): 51–66.

the buzzing fields and back-woods of Mrs. T's farm beside the pike and beyond the hill, coming to know each other's odd ways as we explored the unfamiliar yet welcoming landscape. The she-ass was "green" that springtime, as they say – meaning she had barely ever worn a halter, never mind become accustomed to human-led tasks and handling. But thousands of years of domestication – ever since her wild ass ancestors submitted to bear the burdens of humanity – had prepared her for this match-up with a bossy, blustery, entitled human, who was all of a sudden telling her what to do and binding her up in tangled knots of buckles, reins, bits, and straps.

Even so, over those weeks in Whites Creek where we became more familiar with each other in the barnyard and fields, the she-ass and I struck up what I would like to think of as a friendship. Each morning I brushed her, and she gradually shed her rough winter fur to reveal a sleek summer hide. She seemed to like this ritual. I picked out her little hooves, still crooked and cracked as I had yet to find a good ass farrier. We spent the bright, still-cool mornings training in the back field past the pond, mostly lingering in the spring sunshine and the blowzy, buzzing, blossoming of meadows in bloom beyond the wooded hills. The Mutt of Gold sniffed around in the primrose thickets, and the she-ass ate grass and, sometimes, mud (for the iron in it, I suppose). I sipped coffee from a plastic Lost Sea travel mug and sometimes read aloud to the Mutt and she-ass from Beckett, Cixous, or Jean Genet.

As the days and weeks wore on, the she-ass learned to tolerate my fumblings. She tried to escape only once that I know of, early on, when a wild turkey flushed from the weeds right beside us on the old farm road to the back meadows. She spooked and bolted so hard that I had to let go of the long lines, which flapped around her legs and tangled up as she bucked and fled away down the dirt lane toward the barn and the pike beyond, gathering up a raft of sticks and weeds in the tangled reins. Com-

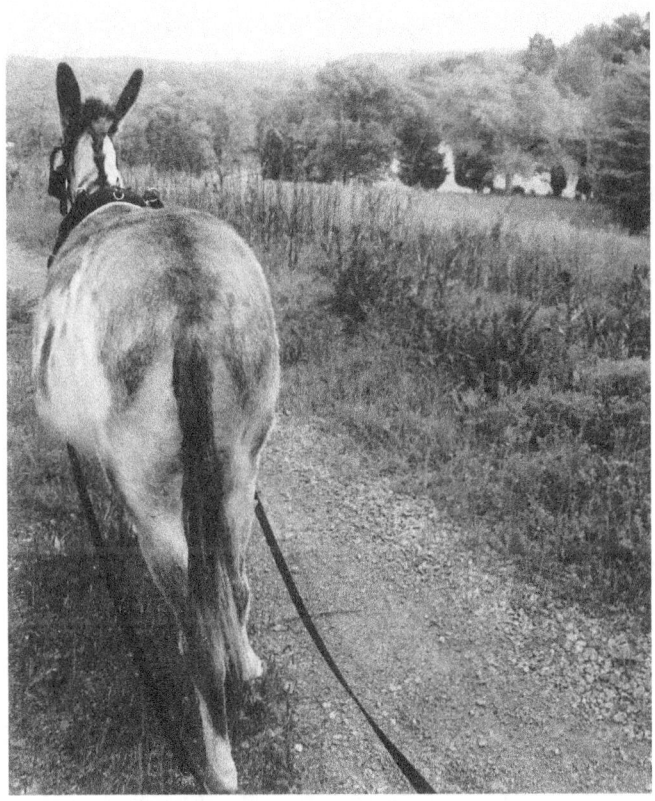

Fig. 1. Training on the long lines in the back fields of the Thompsons' former dairy farm in the hills of Whites Creek. Photograph by the artist.

ing down the hill after her, I paused with hard-beating blood as I watched her pace back and forth at the lip of the cattle-guard, looking like she was bunching to jump and make a run for it. I still have to wonder where she would have gone, if she managed to get free and make it to the pike. But she did not make a break for it that day. She let me catch her and lead her back to the barn, where I untangled the long reins from her legs with some effort and then, with a sigh of relief, turned her loose her in the little fenced yard to graze. In time she came to anticipate that I would provide for her most basic bodily needs. And that I did not intend to eat her, at least in the immediate.[10]

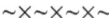

~×~×~×~

I had done a good deal of becoming-with domestic equines, if not *Equus asinus* specifically. Through the story of Clever Hans, Vinciane Despret advances her theory of "becomings-with" by reframing the well-worn story of the famous horse who learned to do math. Vicki Hearne and others have also examined the so-called "Clever Hans Fallacy," as it has been known among behaviorists seeking to reduce the capacities of horses and others by claiming that Hans was "only" learning to read the most minute muscles twitches of humans expecting particular answers, rather than performing mathematical calculations

10 She was wise to keep this in mind as a possibility, given the fact that being eaten by humans has been one of her species' beastly burdens for a long time. She knows this in her bones and in the muscles that flinch and bunch when any human makes a sudden or unexpected movement. But the certitude that I will never eat this ass is a situation specific to our time and place. Equines are eaten by European humans. The demand of Asian markets for boiled donkey hides is so intense that it potentially threatens their earthly populations, both domestic and feral. See Alistair Leithead, "Why Are Donkeys Facing Their 'Biggest Ever Crisis'?" *BBC News*, October 7, 2017, https://www.bbc.com/news/world-africa-41524710.

in his head, without even the help of fingers to count on.[11] In this regard, there is the sense that in certain ways I was available to the ass because I have learned how to move and perceive among horses' expressions and sensory apparatuses. I am sensitive to what she might pay attention to, the kinds of sounds and rustlings that are liable to spook her, along with the lush clover she likes to eat, and so on. Affect: my mouth waters when I see a patch of lush green grass. But it is important to note that not all becoming-with is happy and equitable for all involved – ethical and material frictions abound. Galls persist, even as we are sometimes lucky enough to lose definition for a bit amid the different bodies rubbing together.

Nevertheless, I experienced distinct affective satisfactions as my equine-affected body fell into familiar grooves, slow and steady movements set to put prey ungulates at ease, tying special slipknots of lead-rope to fence posts, hefting haybags and water buckets, and always moving around the nervous equine with the careful choreography that hundreds of sensitive horses taught me in many different places and situations. Yet the ass

11 Vinciane Despret and Vicki Hearne both come to the conclusion that what Hans actually was doing was infinitely more interesting than what he was "failing" to do. Vinciane Despret, "The Body We Care For: Figures of Anthropo-zoo-genesis," *Body and Society* 10, nos. 2–3 (2004): 111–34 and Vicki Hearne, *Adam's Task: Calling Animals by Name* (New York: Harper Perennial, 1989), 4–5. As an interesting recent twist on this, research using a technique called EquiFACs (Equine Facial Action Coding System) has shown that equines possess a dynamic facial musculature that allows a wide range of meaningful facial expressions, by which they can communicate feelings and desires to others of their own and different species. I did not necessarily need this scientific study to confirm that I can tell from equines' faces whether they are feeling sad or miffed or upset or even more vague and inarticulable emotions, but this anatomical and ethological data and methodology is fascinating nonetheless. Jeremy Berlin, "So That's Why the Long Face," *National Geographic*, October 2017, https://www.nationalgeographic.com/magazine/2017/10/explore-animals-horse-facial-expressions/.

was different from horses I had known, and not just in physical size and strength or the comical hugeness of her ears. With a few exceptions, she is more inclined to freeze than to bolt when sudden sounds or movements spook her. Likewise, she insists on taking her sweet time to mull over choices, no matter how adamantly I prod her to move. This reluctance is a distinct trait of asses and half-asses that leads people to call them lazy or stubborn, while the same tendency leads others who know and respect them to understand this reluctance to do whatever some crazy-ass human tells them to do as a specific kind of assine intelligence.

Significantly, this tendency of asses to insist on thinking for themselves and thoroughly contemplating every action more or less nullified most skills I had gained from decades spent with horses. In particular, the she-ass vaporized the swagger of my "Monty Roberts Preliminary Certificate of Horsemanship," which I earned in the UK after college when, like millions of other horse-lovers across Europe, Australia, and the US, I was caught in the spell of Monty Roberts's "Equus"™ – that is, the method of training that leverages the "horse's natural language," which Roberts poses as a central to his training method.[12] The she-ass made it clear right away that she did not speak "Equus." Asses do not respond to the forms of pressure and release on which Roberts's "join-up" method re-

12 See Monty Roberts, *The Man Who Listens to Horses* (New York: Random House, 1997). Roberts's Join-Up method, which shook the global-Western horse world in the 1990s, is built on the principle that an equine is respectfully offered a choice, using techniques modeled on the horse's own language (Equus™) about whether to respect the human (who is chasing her in a confined space) as a (dominant) member of her herd. I came under the spell of the Monty Roberts phenomenon in 1997, enamored of these more respectful training techniques than the ones I grew up with, even as some of their underlying assumptions remain troubling. See also Paul Patton, "Language, Power, and the Training of Horses," in *Zoontologies*, ed. Cary Wolfe (Minneapolis: University of Minnesota Press, 2003), 83–99.

lies. Try to "send her away" by flicking a long rope at her heels – a maneuver that usually sends horses careening off like a fired shot to the farthest edge of a round pen – and the ass might look at you quizzically or simply avoid your gaze and ignore your flailings entirely. In more ways than one, our human–ass encounters in Whites Creek and the adventures that lay beyond would require the making of brand new modes of communication.

Despite a certain measure of control I had over the whereabouts and material entanglements of her scruffy body, the she-ass in question remained mostly a mystery. She was like a ghost in the barnyard – a lonesome, liminal, and eerily quiet presence. While some of her needs and desires were obvious – she made no secret of wanting to graze on the lush grass – others were strange, alien, and subtly wild. The funhouse-mirror equine familiarity of her presence and outward form gave me a deep thrill and satisfaction. Being near her was like coming home to claim a brand new colony: those familiar, delicate bulges of her little knee and hock joints, where bones and tendons articulate under swirls of fur and vestigial toes; the lively swishes of wiry tail-hair and ear-shaking against the flies; and loveliest of all her delicate muzzle, with its soft folds of whiskery velvet nostril curves rounded by underlying hardness of herbivorous jaws and teeth. Here were all the familiar curves and folds, silhouettes of embodied desires, constraints, and shapings that humans have projected on equines through long and tangled co-histories of meetings and journeys together through time and uncharted places – from primal encounters to Columbian crossings to after-the-Gold-Rush whims of the American West that gave this ass her special spots and brought us together in that dreamy Whites Creek prelude.

~×~×~×~

As it happens, I was not the only peripatetic woolgather-
er in Whites Creek, Tennessee who was alert to the thralls
and galls of the she-ass's ghostly presence in the otherwise empty barn and pastures. The morning after the
Mutt and I arrived, I had made the acquaintance of L-Haw
– that is, Lydia Peelle, fiction author and future partner in
an artistic collaboration we call She-Haw – over coffee in
the kitchen of the old pink farmhouse where she lived in
those days, and we had talked eagerly around the strange
allure of hybrid equines and other far-off, seamy places
we had known.[13] Over weeks that followed in the fertile
(if toxic and trashy) creekside mud and fields, we discovered that we had each arrived in Whites Creek through
crisscrossing rural places and urban-suburban cultures,
dark-rich composts and conflict-ridden memories of
stable-yards and libraries. Along different paths, we each
came (not unscathed) through fathomless mudholes of
adolescence where passions for pretty unicorns, happy-
ending heroic equestrian stories, and old-style Breyer
model horses give way to contortions necessary for growing up into worlds of grim livestock sale barn betrayals,
glue factories, slaughterhouses, and muddy backyard
abandonments, even (often more insidiously) the glitzy
glamor of the wealthiest show barns and high-dollar arenas.[14] These are the fraught spaces in which childhood

13 Not incidentally, this also happened to be the morning of Mule Day
of 2002. Later that same morning, I would head down to Mule Day
in Columbia for the first time to meet Mariann Black. And then the
next day, Aliass. In the pale green light of that bright Tennessee
Mule Day morning, the seed of a future collaboration called She-
Haw secretly shot its blind, hungry taproot into a humus of barn-
dark pasts and future-ass becomings.

14 Kathryn Gillespie and Rosemary-Claire Collard write achingly of the
ethical, political, and practical problems that come with bearing
witness to suffering of cows, pigs, horses, birds, and other domestic
species that goes on in places like auctions and slaughterhouses, and
how these frictions change the witness herself. Kathryn Gillespie
and Rosemary-Claire Collard, eds., *Critical Animal Geographies: Poli-*

loves may get torn and frayed, torqued between curious admiration and cautious intimacies with other big-eyed mammals, in their different bodies and sensitivities, and the gut-wrenching recognitions that we grow complicit with hierarchal systems and stories that exploit and commodify friends and kin.[15]

The old pink farmhouse where L-Haw lived was also part of Mrs. T's landholdings, and it was just up the pike from the barnyard, pastures, thistly fields, and wooded hills of the farm, which L-Haw often wandered, thinking about old friends and places left behind. Here, where from the crest of the hill one could see the robotic spires of Nashville's skyline poking up on the horizon like some kind of dystopian El Dorado or Oz, she had been meeting weeds and mosses and honky geese on the pond, being ululated at by the rambunctious coyote pack, coming across tracks and bones and teeth buried in winter grass, and glimpsing gangly blue herons and assorted ghosts of pastures-past. And there I blew into Whites Creek with the Mutt of Gold in the Black Caprice, hot on the trail of a spectral American ass; and here was L-Haw already nomadically (up)rooted in Tennessee, where she had been poetically and peripatetically mining the hybrid ghosts of White Creek's landscapes for half a year – that same half year in which I was feverishly brewing the spotted ass mission in the rainy Pacific Northwest.

Which is all to say, with my whirlwind arrival in Tennessee, followed so soon by the coming of Aliass, it almost seemed like all that speculative wandering around the old farm's fields and woods had unwittingly harrowed and seeded these very fields for the coming of a Spotted

tics, *Intersections, and Hierarchies in a Multispecies World* (London: Routledge, 2015), 203–5. The show barns are another story.

15 Claire Jean Kim, *Dangerous Crossings: Race, Species and Nature in a Multicultural Age* (Cambridge: Cambridge University Press, 2015) and Rosi Braidotti, *Nomadic Theory: The Portable Rosi Braidotti* (New York: Columbia University Press, 2011).

Ass. So when the mortal, rough-furred, living, breathing and blinking, wise, beautiful and otherworldly mystery of the lovely ass in question appeared like a conjured dream on the ungrazed landscapes of the Whites Creek farm that April day, L-Haw was as enthralled as I was. We each might have dreamed it, but that's not to say we foresaw how dramatically the she-ass's presence would transform the old farmscape into a wildflowery, barbed-wire pasture-palimpsest, where pastoral longings overlapped with welts of mysterious, visceral excitations alongside newly present knots and chafing asymmetries. The ethereal presence of that scruffy, graceful, long-eared ungulate kicked up conspicuous absences in the former cattle farm, in the seas of grasses and lonesome gloom of the barn. Where were the warm herds of mud-caked, lowing beasts who had been here once, whose traces remained, and who the lonely she-ass longed to be among? Was she, this peculiar alter-equine form, a long-eared revenant of the landscape's agricultural past? Or was she more like a visitation from some distant future moon-colony rodeo or Westworldian™ cyborg laboratory?[16]

Neither L-Haw nor I could have predicted the durability of the bewitching wonder and kinships that bloomed that April afternoon when the real, flesh-and-blood, possibly pregnant spotted she-ass materialized in the yard of the Foamhouse in the faintly green, early-spring glow of Whites Creek. The coming of her humble, spectacu-

---

16 The she-ass had just come from a cattle farm where mixed-species herds intermingled in sheds and pastures. How lonesome it must have been for her to locate herself among these brimming absences in Whites Creek. Yet another burden this beast has to bear, where she is like a medium who must hold the place in our imaginations for herds of beasts who used to be here. She gracefully bears any burden set and buckled upon her by human hands or imaginations. More importantly for She-Haw, the beautiful she-ass's incarnate presence cast a long inverse-shadow across the land (which is to say a bright, prismatic path) into obscure visions of future-ass becomings.

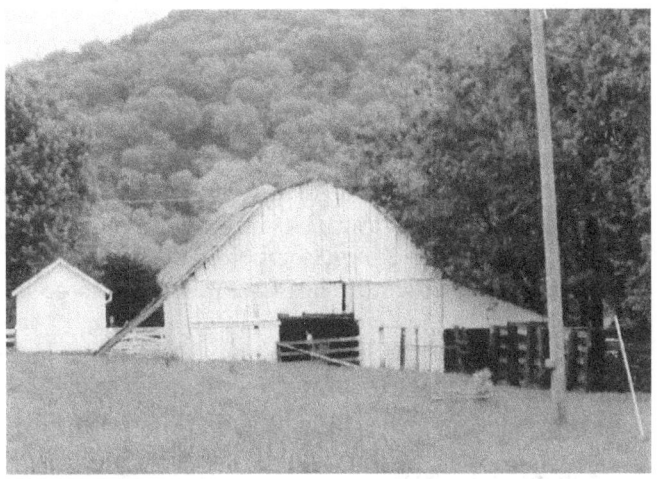

Fig. 2. Aliass waits in Mrs. T's barn in Whites Creek, Tennessee. Photograph by the artist.

lar, rough-furred, and quietly lonesome presence into the vacuum of that dusty whitewashed barn stirred raucous new callings and pressing responsibilities for new kinds of composings and becomings, within the roar of passtoral futures that suddenly loomed much closer than we had imagined.

Which is not to say we weren't waiting for her.

With Mrs. T's cattle long gone, the little ass was the lone large domesticate on the farm. The Foamhouse had a hog-wire fence around the yard, surrounded on several sides by lush pastures. Having been warned of the desert-evolved ass's metabolic efficiency, though, I restricted the she-ass's calories in draconian fashion and limited her grazing to a couple of hours a day in this little yard. Another farmer's cattle lowed from the next field over, and she seemed to listen to this intently from inside her own thoughtful silence. She never brayed, though, and after a week I began to wonder if she might be mute. Then one afternoon in early May, I happened to be inside watching from the window when she laid back her ears, opened her muzzle wide, leaned her whole body forward, and let out what must have been the longest, loudest, longingest bray the world has ever known. Her entire body shook with the force of the sound it emanated, and it my shook my insides, too. All of Whites Creek throbbed and trembled as that bray rang through the hills and valleys; it pounded into groundhog holes and fox dens and wet, weedy, frog-frilled ditches, and it seemed to go on forever. When the last echoes finally faded away in the stunned landscape, the little she-ass pricked up her long ears to the south and listened hard. I will never know who she was calling to, but assuming it was some lost long-eared kin of hers back in Maury County, there's a damned good chance they heard her.

So the days and weeks rolled on in the exploding green of Whites Creek. Then came the rainy afternoon when I mounted her for the first time. The classic Western bucking-bronco scenario seemed unlikely at best, but I waited until an afternoon when Wheatstraw was at home to make the move onto her back, just in case something other than the ass got "broke." The episode proved an anticlimax.[17] By then we had been together pretty constantly for weeks, so she was accustomed to my strange intrusions. When I slipped my leg over her round withers and eased my full weight up with a little jump, she barely paused from grazing. Again, I will never really know whether this was because she trusted me, or if she just gave in, as she would again and again over the years, to the inevitability of her fate at my hands, or more so to the burdens set upon her by my troublesome tongue.

17 Unlike the fateful scene of asymmetrical seduction in Nabokov's *Lolita*, I did not even need the ploy of a bright red apple to lure her into my lap, or rather to get my lap onto her back. Haw, Humbert, maybe you would have been better off if your father (or long lost mother) had been a humble ass farmer. Vladimir Nabokov, *Lolita* (New York: Vintage, 1997), 58–59.

Apophasass (The Unnaming of Aliass)

Weeks deep into our time in Whites Creek, departure for Mississippi loomed and still the ass in question had no proper name. I could find no way around the impasse. Everything seemed to be at stake in this unavoidable act; the whole mission hung in the balance of getting this one thing right. The prospects were more fraught than ever now that she was a real and true friend, to whom I was responsible in everyday practical, as well as philosophical, ways. How could I presume to invent and bestow a name onto this inscrutable other mammal, the nameless ass whose embodied stories, loves and losses, longings and fears, even immediate perceptions were mostly unknown to me?

If we cannot avoid galls altogether, we can at least try to recognize and assuage them where they fester within our most intimate relations. Bring to light the sorest spots, where humans put pressure of various kinds on others' lives to serve our own special hungers, often failing to fit our demands to the forms of life we hitch to them. Specific failures come to light as researchers in ethology continue to demonstrate the poverty of anthropocentric systems when it comes to grasping the emotional and communicative richness of other species' lives, from dogs and dolphins to ants and dragonflies. Most of all, these acts of overlooking such complexities seem to be failures of respect, of the kind Donna Haraway describes as "seeing again, *respecere*, the act of respect. To hold in regard, to respond, to look back reciprocally, to notice, to pay attention, to have courteous regard for, to esteem."[18]

In this same way, galls of other kinds – less visibly material – persist in the stories we tell about others and ourselves. Galls arise even in the names we bestow, whether

18 Donna Haraway, *Companion Species Manifesto: Dogs, People, and Significant Otherness* (Chicago: Prickly Paradigm Press, 2003), 19.

slapped on as categories like "animal" or "ass," or granted in proper names that grasp for connection or reinforce hidden hierarchies, the names we give to others of all kinds matter, marking and making differences in lives and places. Take "ass," for instance. The friction between this categorical word and the unique individual being it is supposed to contain bothered me long before this she-ass and I ever met in Tennessee. From "animal" to "live-stock" to "ass," I was aware with shame and desire that my mother tongue was whipping her into shape before she or I was born. Loaded with all its assumed human rights and privileges, the name chafes. Bound up in abstraction and hierarchical categories, taxonomies are powerful means we have mastered to capture, control, and exploit bodies of all kinds with violent efficiency, the most powerful of which might be the free pass we grant ourselves when it comes to the category of "animals."

In *The Animal That Therefore I Am*, French philosopher Jacques Derrida exposes (himself to) the fact that one word, "animal," is supposed to contain the infinite range and richness of all other-than-human lives. He brings attention to this "asinanity" with a typical Derridean portmanteau that makes us aware of the word itself, *l'animot*: "The suffix *mot* [word] in *l'animot* should bring us back to the word, namely, to the word named a noun."[19] That a single nomination, as such, is supposed to contain all life except for the human is, according to Derrida, a failure of massive proportions: "The confusion of all nonhuman living creatures within the general and common category of the animal is not simply a sin against rigorous thinking, vigilance, lucidity, or empirical authority, it is also a crime."[20] If we take Derrida at his word here, then it fol-

19 Jacques Derrida, *The Animal That Therefore I Am*, ed. Marie-Louise Mallet, trans. David Wills (New York: Fordham University Press, 2008), 48.
20 Ibid.

lows that the bestiaries and endless rounds of Old Mac-Donald in which we learn to shape our lips and tongues around "the animals" as children make criminals of us from the get-go. Hence the shame, but also the sense of liberatory possibility, that blossomed up through the cracks of that slippery word, "ass."

Names are powerful, and they may well be inevitable for *Homo sapiens,* as they evoke mental images and connection to an absent (real or possible) other. Naming is certainly a responsibility as a well as a privilege, and many acts of naming are invested with care and love. That said, while a proper name like "Popsicle" or "Fido" may grant affection and even familial inclusion, types of names can mark fatal exclusions, too. In her "Pet Cemetery Project," artist-researcher Linda Brant traces changes over time to pet gravestones in rural and urban Florida. She documents shifts in pet memorial gardens from fairly simple granite slabs marked with antique names like "Patience" and "Spot" to later-twentieth-century "Nuisance Fiske" and "Kibbles Lovey Lumpkins" to ever more elaborate monuments and familial nominations for pets, such as the grave marker for "Harry James Kliemovitch," emblazoned with a photographic image of the late guinea pig and the epitaph "Forever in our Hearts."[21] We can presume that these material-semiotic memorial practices might reflect other kinds of changes in the lives of deceased feline, canine, or other domestic loved ones. In other words, the ways we name are practices that come with grave consequences and responsibilities.

21 Linda Brant's "Pet Cemetery Project" is a critical and creative documentation of dramatic cultural shifts in the places of "pets" in American culture. Brant creates images that juxtapose shifts toward care for certain domestic companions against the treatment of other less-beloved species. For instance, her image of the lovingly remembered guinea pig is paired with an image of an anonymous laboratory rat. http://www.lindabrant.net/#!pet-cemetery-project/cstx.

Whether as acts of love and care or more shameful kinds of name-calling, the ways we learn to call others by names, and thereby to tangle them into our ontologies and narratives and material becomings, are at the root of our mother tongues. We get a primal charge from the real or imagined connections that naming affects for us as languaging beasts. As if thinking and saying, tasting and rolling these names around on our tongues is akin to a taste, reciprocal touch, or maybe even a kiss, even as we sense that these names we give to others may be kisses of life or death. As Paul Shepard says in *The Others: How Animals Made Us Human*: "Naming may 'predicate on a previous presence or on the subsequent presence in a current absence.' When the little human primates, mother-bound like no others, contain their fears by representing the absent mother by speaking her name, the first step is taken in bringing all the creatures into imaginal presence."[22] Meanwhile, all of these conflicts, complexities, and indigestions embedded in matters of naming, rooted deep in the mother tongue and particular haunting bodies and barns, brought me headlong to the impasse I met in Tennessee that spring, when it came to the act of naming my sweet inscrutable ass.

Still, the sweet she-ass needed a handle. I tried different configurations on for size, but nothing ever quite fit. Then one day I realized that what I really needed was a way to unname her. If the hope was to hold open spaces within human thought, language, and action for different ways of knowing and storying together, then the naming of this singular ass companion must be an act of unnaming. In honor of her wordless ways, the name she would go by had to reflect the kind of thinking described by Derrida, "however fabulous or chimerical it might be, that thinks the absence of the name and of the word oth-

22   Paul Shepard, *The Others: How Animals Made Us Human* (Washington, DC: Island Press, 1997), 46.

erwise, as something other than a privation."[23] Her un-naming might be a kind of apophasass, even.[24]

Traditionally speaking, apophatic writings are religious texts that address the dilemma of ineffable transcendence, whereby authors draw attention to the paradox of language's absolute inability to name the unnamable, or eff the ineffable. The tortuous convolutions of apophatic writing practices – like the work of thirteenth-century Beguine nun Marguerite Porete, who was burned at the stake for her "heretical" treatise on divine love titled *The Mirror of Simple Souls*, or the more amiable if still mind-bending poems of unsaying by Sufi mystics like Ibn Arabi – sprung to mind as I stood at the edge of this aporia that was the ass's (un)name, given the wish to respect all the aspects of her being I could never claim to know or grasp. In a book on apophatic writings called *Mystical Languages of Unsaying*, Michael Sells describes texts "in which unnameability is not only asserted but performed."[25] In this sense, since there was no way to sidestep naming altogether, the name might assert itself as the very impasse it could not breach. The name had to reveal itself nakedly *as a word*, a veil over a lacuna. Ass such, the magic phoneme had to present itself in the name, too. As a kind of liberatory crack that erupted from within the "bad word" I was forbidden to say as a little girl, amplified by various registers of hope and shame, "ass" became a rarefied realm of possibility in which to honor and respect all the lively, unwritten, and embodied stories woven together

---

23 Derrida, *The Animal that Therefore I Am,* 48.

24 Traditions of apophasis – "mystical languages of unsaying," as the title of Michael Sells's brilliant book calls them – proliferate at the edges of mystical traditions across (in this case, Western) religions. Sells describes apophatic discourses that maintain "a rigorous adherence to the initial logical impasse of ineffability that exerts a force that transforms normal logical and semantic structures." Michael Sells, *Mystical Languages of Unsaying* (Chicago: University of Chicago Press, 1994), 3.

25 Ibid.

in a place of meeting, possibility, and new ass becomings in Tennessee.

Derrida's *animots* make a similar gesture, but the lively possibilities of this specific she-ass unnaming come most fully alive in the *animots* of philosopher Hélène Cixous. Words and names in all their inherent limits and possibilities become not grappling hooks in fleshy beasthoods but rather openings for respectful recognition of unknown, entangled otherness – the inextricable ways we come together in worlds of mutual making, both within and beyond language. As Kari Weil observes, Cixous's *animots* witness both "the violence produced by categories like 'animal'" and at the same time recognize "the hybrid communities that have always been effected in and through language."[26] In this regard, the ass's (un)name could hold both violent asymmetries that go with calling her "ass" and also invite recognition and respect for the unnameability of her embodied wisdoms. Most of all, it makes a space for the hybrid worlds of words and fleshes we make together.

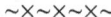

One afternoon in mid-May, a thunderstorm was fixing to burst as I came out of the local branch of the Nashville Public Library in Bordeaux, where I went daily to check email. It was about to rain on the bale of hay I had strapped to the roof-rack of the Black Caprice, but I paused for a moment anyway in the parking lot, to admire the roiling purple sky. And that was when it came to me, the only possible name for the singular, enigmatic she-ass, who would soon accompany me through the

26 Kari Weil, "Autobiography," in *The Cambridge Companion to Literature and the Posthuman*, eds. Bruce Clark and Manuela Rossini (Cambridge: Cambridge University Press, 2017), 92. See also Hélène Cixous, "Writing Blind: Conversation with the Donkey," in *Stigmata* (New York: Routledge, 2005), 115–26.

thick mazes of Southern landscapes and nameless time-places ahead, must be no name at all.

The cloudburst came with all the booming thunder and cracks of lightning one comes to expect from a late spring thunderstorm on the Cumberland Plateau. The rain fell in sheets as I wove along shimmering byways back to Whites Creek. The storm moved fast, and by the time I turned off the pike onto Mrs. T's farm lane, scattered sunbeams were already breaking through the thunderheads. As I rolled past the old white barn, I peered hard through the wet windshield glass and the glittering lace of leafy understory branches and vines, heaps of rotting boards, and rusted rolls of fencewire scattered around the barn, seeking a glimpse of that long lovely pale face floating in the shadows of the barn. The dusty tractor loomed behind her, and migratory swallows were coming and going from the barngloom in which she stood – quiet, impassable, and darkly haloed. The so-called American Spotted Ass who shall remain nameless.

"Aliass."

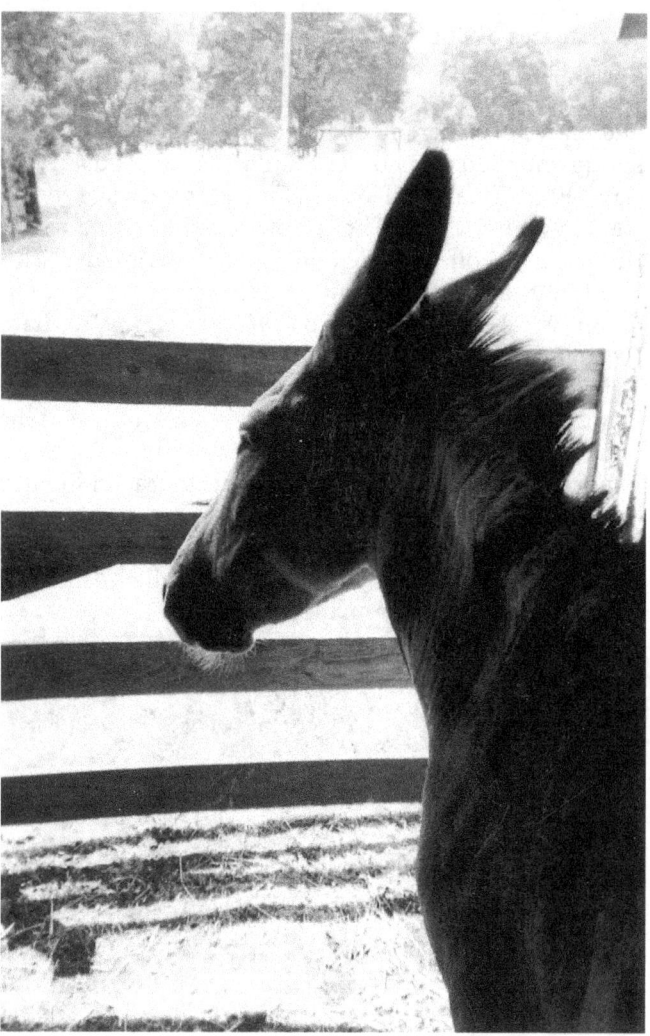

Fig. 3. Aliass in the Whites Creek barndark. Photograph by the artist.

The Prettiest Little Shotgun Wedding You Never Saw

In the spring of 2002, on the eve of our first journey across the American South, I married Aliass. I vowed, among other things, to always honor her so-called "silence" and her own embodied "ways of knowing the world that are other than mine." That rough-ass ceremony in an overgrown park in Paris, Tennessee was the prettiest little shotgun wedding you never saw. And the honeymoon goes on and on and on.

The wedding score given below was drafted roughly one year later for a renewal-of-vows ceremony, performed on a grassy hill at Hollins University in Roanoke, Virginia, in May 2003. Revised and renewed numerous times over the years, the homily and vows remain core to the practice of caring for and living with Aliass and herds of untold others in the throes of a global technocratic era, while attending as best as possible to all the galls, hopes, and responsibilities that crop up in loamy, lively paddocks and pastures, weed-blown roadsides, and all the other dirty, earthly places we makes homes and pass through.[1]

---

1 Both Aliass herself and parts of these vows were present for a blissful ceremony in 2008 when Sean and I tied the knot. As a matter of

Beyond the daily routines of husbandry that maintain the well-being of a little ass herd, the distinctly human hopes and passions that sustain this (admittedly one-sided) marriage to Aliass continue to find kindred spirits in artistic and poetic practices that seek to cultivate ecological care and communion. From the ancient, "mind-bending undertaking" that Gary Snyder calls "trans-species erotics," to the revelrous and radical weddings to mountains, rivers, and diverse earthly assemblages performed by Annie Sprinkle and Beth Stephens, I hereby hitch this nuptial performance to creative practices that buck miserly, destructive systems – forces that would speak to prevent us from (for)ever holding our earthly peace-of-ass.[2] Embracing companion-species histories and biological knot-tyings of the kind that animate Donna Haraway's question – "Whom and what do I touch when I touch my dog?" – the act of wedding Aliass is a way of asking, with respect and humility till death do us part: "Whom and what do I kiss when I kiss my ass?"[3]

Clothed and behooved, we are gathered here in the grass to celebrate a marriage of beastly lives woven together in timeplaces, as today K-Haw (aka Karin Bolender) and Aliass come together to renew their vows.

Let us hear them.

---

fact, Aliass "gave me away."

2   Gary Snyder says that global myths of interspecies marriage are "evidence of the fascination our ancestors had for the possibility of full membership in a biotic erotic universe." Gary Snyder, *Practice of the Wild* (New York: North Point Press, 1990), 211. On the many wonderful nuptuals of Sprinkle and Stephens, see the LoveArtLab archive, https://loveartlab.ucsc.edu/

3   Donna Haraway, *When Species Meet* (Minneapolis: University of Minnesota Press, 2008), 3.

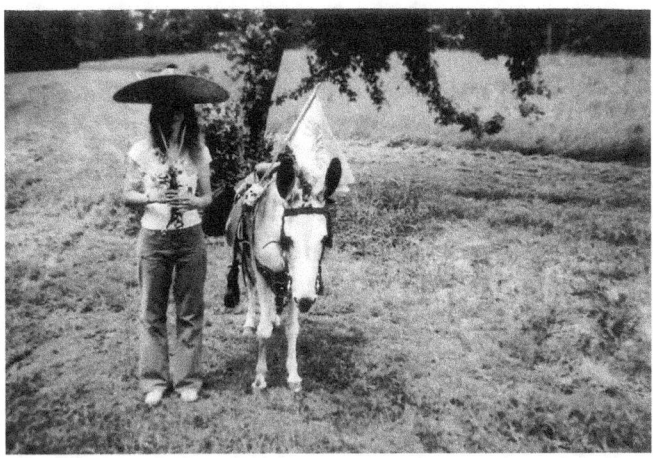

Fig. 1. Wedding portrait, Paris, Tennessee, June 2002. Photograph by Sebastian Black.

K-Haw: Aliass, if we know anything together, it's how every one of these words I'm about to utter is hard-won. Every word is hee-hawn out of fur and flesh, hoofbeats on asphalt, hot sun, rocks and cool flowing water, and hidden milk and blood. Each word I want to offer you is made out of the places we've passed through in time together. They grow from seeds gathered in our wanderings, where we waded through roadside weeds and broken glass, in search of something – maybe the place of sweet shade and grassy pastures we found at last, here and now. I wish I could just open my throat and let a flock of birds fly out of it, or maybe a stampede of slow Mississippi miles. I want to make a noise that also listens. Aliass, I want to mirror you in a secret language that rises out of future dark like a beam of what's coming from behind, like the silver flash of fish from green depths of quarry water, or the way a rearview mirror reflects oncoming headlights from places we've already passed. And let these words be a glistening eye, a listening ear that reflects and echoes the mysteries of who you are, and what you do. And where we go from here.

When I married you the first time, Aliass, some might have said I was looking for love in all the wrong places. But what did they know? Who knows what we were looking for, listening for, and who knows how we found it. But we did. We found a certain peace-of-ass at last, sweet she-ass. And today we get to celebrate it, and share it with our friends. And to those who would oppose our union, claiming you are just an ass, I can only say they have no idea what a just ass you are. What a wholeness in a broken world.

In light of our previous ceremony, and everything that's happened in the meantime, it seems like a good idea to renew the vows that were both spoken and unspoken on that occasion. That first ceremony, which took place in the hidden bottom of a local park in Paris, Tennessee, was a slapdash, threefold affair. It sought to encompass all the elements of a shotgun wedding, a knightly dubbing, and a haphazard exchange of rings and kisses meant to hold us fast to each other, and to the pathless grasses of the mission we were about to blast off into. I was a little drunk, and wearing an enormous sombrero, so I don't remember exactly what I said. Yours were vows of silence, so to speak, and doubtless you've kept them better than I've kept mine.

Raw as it was, that Tennessee ass wedding must have done some of the trick, or I guess we wouldn't be standing here now. This doesn't surprise me, actually. For all the rush and lack of planning, that thrown-together ceremony in Paris was overflowing with sacrament and rough magic, deeply felt by all present, as far as we know. Sweet Pea (aka "Her Royal Pea-Ness") stood up for you, and Mariann Black acted as the barnyard shaman-preacher, while Sebastian was witness and official photographer. To get to the wedding spot, we rode a thin bridal path, through yellow grasses taller than all of us, past Rahkeem's catfish pond. The whirring cicadas sang us onward, watching us pass with their red unblinking eyes. The monstrous catfish that no human has ever seen skimmed the pond bottom with their blind, o-ring mouths and wormy whiskers, lazy bottom-feeders in sunken barrels and logs. These were our congregation of guests.

Along the path, we plucked orange Indian paintbrush and bluets and black-eyed daisies, and stuck them in your browband and saddle horn, and Sweet Pea's. I held a bunch of weed-flowers in a stemmy bouquet. Then we emerged from the green thicket into an out-of-the-way, newly mown corner of the park, and assembled ourselves between the telephone poles, back behind the baseball diamond and the field where we hunted for wild asparagus on the night before. It was just on the other side of the abandoned railroad tracks, which we crossed to reach the wedding spot, and then rode over again, like a threshold, after Mariann proclaimed, "You may now kiss your ass!" And then you and I rode off a ways down the tracks, back and forth, together and alone, and soon to be on our way for real.

So, I guess it's in keeping with our lovely assbackwards slide to exchange marriage vows again here and now, almost a year after the beginning of our rough-ass honeymoon. The adventure of that summer wasn't so much a honeymoon as a two-moon mission, where we blasted into the new reality of American backroads to discover, among other things, the deepest echoes of our Big Poet's assertion that "the honey of heaven may or may not come, but that of earth both comes and goes at once."[4] We hit the highway and we searched for it. We hit the earth inside us and we dug. We rode the Southern byways, hundreds of miles of rank tar rolled out under swooping wires and panting passerines and green leaves and sky.

4 Wallace Stevens, "Le Monocle de Mon Oncle," in *The Collected Poems* (New York: Vintage Books, 1990), 15.

Oh ass, there were roadside weeds and trumpet creeper vines inside of us, fading chicory and Queen Anne's lace, roadkill and poison ivy, and we waded through wave after wave of them, day after day after day. And all that time, Passenger rode along inside of you. I didn't even know where we were going, exactly, but somehow we made it, led on by ghosts of old fireworks and botanical jokes and great blue herons and full moons and pavement cracks, to what I thought was the impossible home.

So here we are now, in a kind of happy-ass afterlife that's like nothing I ever thought possible. I asked the world for an answer, to a question I could never quite articulate. Our journey became that question, and the answer you taught me to read in the slow pulse of every moment was Yes. That Yes is you. Before you and Passenger came along, I underestimated the power of nameless exploration, until I found it wed inextricably to assemblages of bodies-in-places, such as we find them.

There are no rings to exchange here, except for the hope that these vows will ring true, now and into the future.

K-Haw and Aliass will now exchange vows again. Please repeat after me:

I, K-Haw, vow to take this so-called American Spotted Ass, (un)known as Aliass, as lifelong companion, with all the thralls and galls and cares and concerns that come with this gift of commitment.

(repeat)

I will always seek to harmonize my words and deeds with your knowable needs and unknowable wishes, and I will try my best to honor your ways of knowing the world that are other than mine.

(repeat)

I promise to honor the illumination and peace-of-ass I find especially in your presence. I will honor and protect all that's hidden behind the heart-shaped breastplate.

(repeat)

I promise to honor the loves-in-places that our quest to wed words and untold worldings has uncovered, and to always search for a m<other tongue that orbits the core where your nameless knowing hums.

(repeat)

With these here vows, I wed thee.

Aliass, please repeat after me:

I, Aliass,

(quiet ass)

promise to stay true to my rough-furred, blinking, softly breathing, inscrutable donkeyness, to what I do and to what I know, and also to the mysteries hidden within spectacular ass hides and behind the heart-shaped breastplate.

(quiet ass)

With these here unsaids, I wed thee.

By the power vested in the human tongue, I now pronounce you wedded companions in the quest for matrimonial assonances in fleeting mortal timeplaces.

K-Haw, you may now kiss your ass.

Aliass, you may now eat the grass.

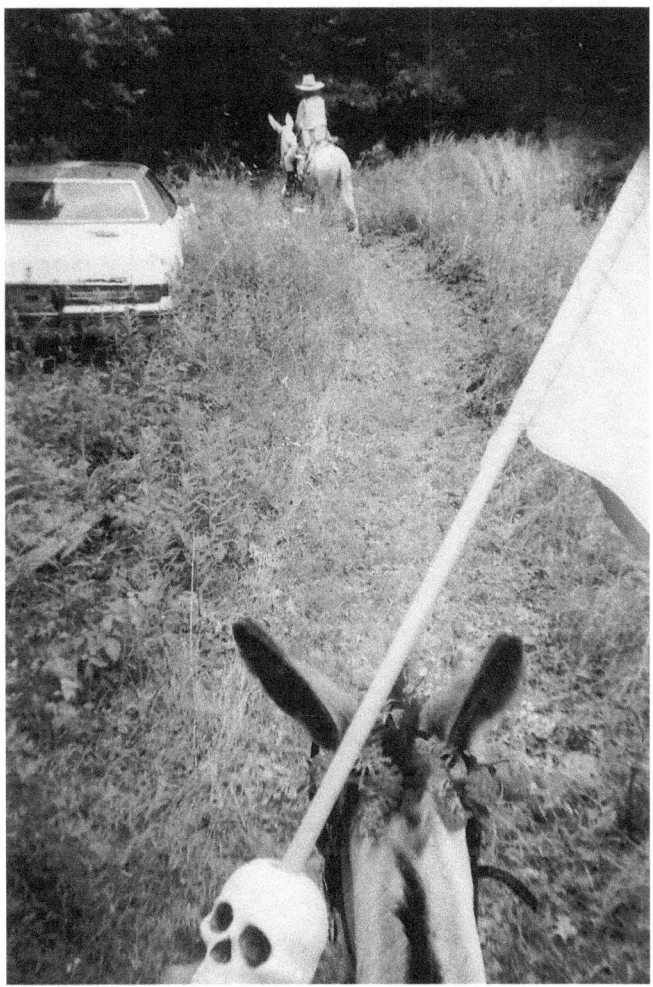

Fig. 2. On the path to the wedding in Paris, Tennessee, June 2002, with Sweet Pea and Mariann leading the way. Photograph by the artist.

PART II

ART OF A SULL

4

ART OF A SULL
(Making Stories with Untold Others)

Like "gall" – the antiquated word for wounds to equine bodies caused by ill-fitting saddles or harnesses – "sull" is another artifact of Southern ass dialects, where we find words that have slowly disappeared from most urban vernaculars – words whose uses have mostly vanished with the beasts of burden who once bore them. Where "sull" does crop up in dictionaries, the noun (which also has a verb form) is defined as "a stoppage, or refusal to move (as an animal)."[1] But the dictionary does no justice to a singular phenomenon that accomplishes the impossible: as the highest form of recalcitrance that asses and half-asses (i.e., mules) are infamous for, a full-blown sull can

1   The online *Oxford English Dictionary* offers that definition, with a nineteenth-century origin in US dialect back-formation from "sullen." Of eight example sentences offered, two are from William Faulkner, which says something about that author's inimitable stature when it comes to Southern dialects in literature. Other good examples include this from 1902: "*Dial. Notes* 2 246 *Sull*,. to hold a position with imperturbable obstinacy and a total disregard of surroundings, as a possum, or a hog in a corner. 1903 *Dial. Notes* 2 332 'My oxens sull whenever they get hot.'" And lastly a gem from Faulkner's 1959 novel *Mansion 10*: "All Frenchman's Bend knew Houston: sulking and sulling in his house all alone by himself since the stallion killed his wife four years ago."

more or less stop time – or at least gum up the workings of human Progress for a while.

In human–equine worldings, the sull is unique to *Equus asinus* and hybrid offspring (mules and hinnies). Unlike horses, who will mostly flee from painful prods or ferocious flappings, asses have a unique capacity to withdraw deep into stonily inaccessible regions while they ponder potential outcomes of possible actions.[2] These inscrutable processes are inward and invisible, and they persist for as long as it takes the ass in question to weigh all options and arrive at what she deems the worthiest move under the circumstances. Meanwhile, faced with a sulling beast, all a woeful human can do is wait. Oddly enough, when the ass does arrive at a decision (in her own sweet time), likely as not she might spring forth in a sudden burst of action, as if the long spell of deliberation never took place. As to whether she deems the perceived danger worth braving (benefits outweighing possible costs of forward motion), or if she just gives in with a fatalistic sigh to the inevitability of her demise, it is impossible to say.

Like the word that stands for it, the material phenomenon of the sull may come off as obsolete in the mechanisms of first-world postindustrial technocultures, where asses and other beasts of burden have little play anymore. But when we consider the inestimable material contributions of asspower to the colonization of the Americas and other continents and cultures, special possibilities arise where the sull might come to stand for an opposing force to the ass's otherwise invisible role as man's "working partner."[3] At the very least, the sull might make space for

2 This is not to suggest horses are never contemplative or circumspect in their dealings with humans. But there is a uniquely immovable quality to the assine sull that I have never personally known a horse to exhibit.

3 As one of the first beasts of burden to be domesticated (from the African wild ass), *Equus asinus* still inhabits a number of nomadic

new attention to (and respect for) the wits and survival strategies of one anciently domestic species of desert-tough, long-eared equids, who have carried untold burdens of human enterprises for millennia, as both watchful witnesses and (mostly willing) sidekicks.

"Sull" was not among the words and gestures that Aliass and I learned together in our early Whites Creek days. So it came as a shock that morning after our slapdash wedding at the local park in Paris, Tennessee when – at the moment of our momentous departure for Mississippi – Mariann and I tried to load Aliass, and the little she-ass refused with every atom of her corporeal existence to step onto that house-of-horrors of a horse trailer. More than any fear or premonition of what awaited us in Mis-

and sedentary pastoralist cultures in Africa, the Middle East, and elsewhere. As one of the oldest domestic beasts of burden, asses have been entangled in human labors and colonial enterprises for centuries. Jill Bough describes the ass's significant role in colonizing the Americas in *Donkey,* particularly the chapter titled "Donkeys and Mules Colonize the Americas, Australia and South Africa." Jill Bough, *Donkey* (London: Reaktion Books Ltd., 2011), 76–105. Bough also draws from William Long's *Asses vs. Jackasses,* in which the former lawyer makes an impassioned and convincing case to the "Court of Public Conscience" for the recognition of the superiority of *Equus asinus* over the pernicious calumny of "jackasses" (*Homo sapiens*). Long waxes in colorful lawyerly language on the roles of asses throughout colonial Western history: "The burro has led the procession in America almost ever since the white man first set foot in this hemisphere. It carried the accoutrements of Cortez to the capital of the Montezumas. It was at Balboa's elbow when he first caught sight of the Pacific. It journeyed with Ponce de Leon when he sought the fountain of youth, and with De Soto when he discovered the Mississippi." William G. Long, *Asses vs. Jackasses* (Portland: The Touchstone Press, 1969), 29. And so on, to the mythic American Gold Rush days, when burros bore burdens of every hopeful miner westward and beyond in time and geographic distribution, just as they continue to bear burdens of every imaginable kind to this day. For more recent history of asses in the Western US, see Abraham Gibson, "Beasts of Burden: Feral Burros and the American West," in *The Historical Animal,* ed. Susan Nance (Syracuse: Syracuse University Press, 2015), 38–53.

sissippi, the trailer itself was most likely what Aliass objected to. It was an ominous contraption, spray-painted black inside and out, slatted on the sides with two-by-fours bolted to the metal frame and with rusty metal sheets bolted together at the windowless front, topped off with a moldy, rust-stained canvas roof. The black side slats were splintery and rotting, so the rig shed bits of burnt-looking wood wherever it went. Despite its alarming appearance, Mariann's neighbor Darryl, a local horse trader, assured us that the floor would hold a Percheron stallion. We confirmed the floor was tight with new, thick oak boards, and the metal frame and axles were solid, too; I had them checked professionally, along with some wiring work needed to match the trailer with the Black Caprice. While the trailer's underlying structural integrity made it a miraculous find for $250, it did nothing for the overall impression the rig gave off of being kin to some evil-looking jalopy that a dastardly cartoon villain might ride around in. On top of all that, it also smelled weird.

The conveyance was not worthy of Aliass, but it was what we had to work with. On the inside curve of the rusty metal front, someone had scrawled a message that was difficult to make out: over the years I interpreted the mismatched letters to read something like "dOnt UsE thIs TrAiLeR iF YOU CaNt CLeAn iT Out." Aliass was not privy to this message, writ jaggedly inside the rusting trailer as if by the hand of a dying man, but clearly everything else about the contraption conveyed to her a warning along the lines of "Abandon hope, all ye who enter here." This was a warning Aliass aimed to heed, and she sure as hell was not going to hop willingly into what she saw as a rickety-ass deathtrap.

So the episode that kicked off our grand Southern adventure ended up being one of the ugliest of our lives together. We had ahead of us about a four-hour drive from Paris to Oxford that day, on two-lane highways down through Jackson and Bolivar, Tennessee and across the border into Lafayette County, Mississippi. The haul wasn't especially long, but the departure from Paris was a big deal all the same; we were rolling off that day with certain fanfare into the wild unknowns of the big-ass journey ahead. So unfortunately, when Aliass balked at the big step up into the unfamiliar trailer, her hesitation was an offense to the human sense of ceremonial propriety. The conflict swiftly escalated into a violent battle of wills and bodily weights that has likely been raging for as long as humans and asses have known each other. Pressing upon the reluctant ass with all the violent certainty of our purpose's rightness, we met with the keen impassability of her own special form of resistance, honed over eons in the company of demanding humans on the edges of raging rivers, colonial gangplanks, slippery mountain passes, and the ramps of military-transport trains, ships, and planes headed for France or Afghanistan. That is to say, here was the full-blown, knock-down-drag-out sull.

Sadly at this juncture I knew myths about "stubborn" asses far better than I knew my little long-eared friend. I deferred to experience and stood by mutely while others yelled and stomped and beat on Aliass's rump with a bloodied stick. If I had known her then the way I do now, I would have anticipated that given enough time in which to conclude that she could not escape the leap into the dark abyss we demanded of her, she would eventually make up her mind to board the trailer of her own volition. In the long run, she taught me modes of patience required to negotiate through seemingly impassable sulls. But on that fraught day, each blow or yank on the lead-rope only hardened Aliass's impassioned refusal to move. She was ready to be martyred. After two awful hours of sweat, tears, and blood in the sweltering Tennessee late morning, the she-ass was laid out flat on the gravel driveway, having slowly backed up further and further against the rope until she sat on her rump and then fell over backwards and lay prostrate on the ground.

This scene was no way to begin our honeymoon. But here is that old festering gall again: despite my best intentions, vows, and pronouncements of love for this special ass – my desire to honor her ways of knowing and navigating places – we are bound up together in a long, twisted, friction-ridden, and asymmetrical histories that both precede and follow us, most of which involve human wills doing various forms of violence to asses and other domestic beasts. Insult to injury, we then make up stories and pass them down from generation to generation, about how stubborn or stupid the beasts are for refusing actions that cause them mortal terror (at the least) and more likely pain or untimely demise.

Such dynamics of human power and privilege in relation to equines and others shaped my growing up, as I learned to manipulate horses' behavior through various coercive material and behavioral techniques and scare tactics. As Paul Patton observes, even the most humane and respectful training and management methods are grounded in the assumption that we humans should do whatever works most efficiently to bend dumber bodies and labors to our own wills and needs.[4] This belief is old and deeply writ and twisted through domestic bodies and ontologies. As we gather from environmental histories like Alfred Crosby's *Columbian Exchange,* which traces biological consequences of colonial conquest, European forms of livestock-keeping and their specific companion-species configurations were borne across seas and into

4 In "Language, Power, and the Training of Horses," Patton questions the claim to freedom of choice offered to a horse-in-training in Monty Roberts's Join-Up technique: "If we understand coercion to mean causing an animal to act in ways it would not otherwise have acted, then even such indirect techniques are coercive in the broader sense. The difference here is in more or less sophisticated techniques of exercising power over other beings." Paul Patton, "Language, Power, and the Training of Horses," in *Zoontologies,* ed. Cary Wolfe (Minneapolis: University of Minnesota Press, 2003), 92.

prairies in fur, hooves, and guts of herbivores that con-
quistadors and others transported to the Americas. Old
World forms of husbandry spread far and wide, bringing
along their invasive plant species ("Kentucky" bluegrass,
thistles, and dandelions, to name a few). They proliferated in the crisscrossing tracks of asses, horses, cattle,
and human slaves who tended them (and sometimes followed their wild northward flights across the Americas),
taking root in every landscape where colonial humans
and livestock commingle.[5]

These same dynamics still pertain between me and
Aliass, knotted in the ways I co-opt her labor and leisure
to serve my desires, even as I try to care for and respect
her needs. From the moment I first beheld the chimeric
American Spotted Ass figure empixellated on my laptop
screen, through all the miles of adventuring and years of
intimate husbandry, Aliass has been hitched to the onerous burden of serving my whims. The cares in which
I hold her include a great deal of domestic confinement
and, perhaps, boredom, as compared to the lives of wild or
feral asses who must navigate social and geographic territories to feed and shelter themselves and protect each
other. That said, mine is likely a luckier ass than most.
She was born on the right side of an American century,

5   Crosby describes the movement of imported colonial livestock ani-
    mals northwards, sometimes along with the slaves who tended them
    and the plants who rode along. As Crosby writes: "The fact that Ken-
    tucky bluegrass, daises, and dandelions, to name only three out of
    hundreds, are Old World in origin gives one a hint of the magnitude
    of the change that began in 1492 and continues into the twentieth
    century. Today an American botanist can easily find whole meadows
    in which he is hard-put to find a single species of plant that grew
    in America in pre-Columbian times." Alfred Crosby, *The Columbian
    Exchange* (Westport: Greenwood Press, 1972), 73–74. See also Virginia
    DeJohn Anderson, *Creatures of Empire: How Domestic Animals Trans-
    formed Early America* (Oxford: Oxford University Press, 2004) and Re-
    becca Cassidy and Molly Mullin, eds., *Where the Wild Things Are Now:
    Domestication Reconsidered* (Oxford: Berg, 2007).

in a place where demographics, economics, and pervasive civil- and animal-rights movements allowed for the possibility that a middle-class female artist might find and graft her to the task of forging new kinds of barnyard and roadside relations. Even as we inevitably get mired in the old ones, too.

And so she was. Plucked up by stroke of good fortune (mine more than hers) from that cattle farm on Monsanto Road in Maury County, Tennessee. Other histories, tropes, and myths weigh in here. Whatever I might hope and pitch our association to represent, the pasts and futures of our entwined species subsume us – from our genes to the ways we are represented in names, classifications, political categories, and popular media. We are bound up together in webs of many interconnected species – not just asses and humanfolk but triangulations and crazier geometries of domesticated European grasses, brown-headed cowbirds, ivermectin-resistant strongyles, bull and star thistles, vital bacterial companions, and myriad untold others whose lifecycles intertwine with barnyard doings in ways we seldom even recognize.[6]

That first traumatic sull in Paris was not the last time Aliass and I would find our wills and weights pulling hard

6   The webs of companion species relations mentioned here all merit deeper exploration, while some demand ethical action in the barnyard more urgently than others. The growing resistance of certain nematodes (especially the many species of strongyles) to the commonly used anthelmintic ivermectin means that people who care for equines must find new methods for reducing their internal parasite loads–in other words, killing the worms. Jacqueline Matthews, "Ivermectin Resistance in Equine Nematodes," *International Journal for Parasitology: Drugs and Drug Resistance* 4, no. 3 (2014): 310–15. In these and all relations, Aliass and I are caught up in meshes of what Donna Haraway describes as companion species relations that are always "obligatory, constitutive, historical, protean [...] full of waste, cruelty, indifference, ignorance, and loss, as well as of joy, invention, labor, intelligence, and play." Donna J. Haraway, *Companion Species Manifesto: Dogs, People, and Significant Otherness* (Chicago: Prickly Paradigm Press, 2003), 12.

in opposite directions. I came to recognize the look of an impending sull – a certain backwards set of her ears and a faraway, glazed look coming into in her eyes. In time I learned tactics to avert it, to assuage her fears (whether reasonable or seeming-to-me unfounded), by sweet-feed or some other diversion. Mostly, though, as I got to know Aliass better, I came to respect her insistence on deciding her own bodily fate. I learned to settle into a sull and wait it out calmly, even peacefully – like one night when we spent hours at the gaping maw of the trailer in an eerie emptiness of downtown Nashville after midnight, hanging out with human buddies under a dim yellow streetlight while Aliass and I each leaned with staunch determination on opposing ends of the lead-rope.

Oh, in time we would find harmonies a-plenty on the roads ahead – foremost for me in the constant current of wonder and tranquility that comes with immersion in Aliass's singular aura. But that first awful time, that high noon showdown in Paris, Tennessee, Aliass's blood and the blood of her ancestors was on my hands. Despite all the tender exchanges that came later, or the hundreds of times she jumped without hesitation into that same trailer in years to come, likely as not Aliass has never forgotten that day. Deep in her body she can never fully trust me, and she is right to feel this way. I do know it took a few days – after she was finally heaved stiff-legged onto the trailer by several of Mariann's burly neighbors – for her to acknowledge my presence when I spoke to her or tried to stroke her. When I pulled the rig over in a strip-mall parking lot outside Jackson, Tennessee later that afternoon and tried to offer her a carrot through the trailer slats, she would not even look at me. So the grand mission to "ride a Spotted Ass across the American South" – with all its lofty aspirations and shadowier drives – begins on a dismal note: Aliass in the rattling trailer – angry, sore, and stoic – and me in the driver's seat of the Black Caprice, driving deeper and deeper into the vague, dark, and conflict-ridden longings, regrets, desires, and shame that suffused our adventures together through north Mississippi and beyond.

Learning the Subtle Arts of a Sull

My dear Aliass, for so long I tried to respect your so-called "silence" by refusing to trespass with exclusive human authority on our journeys together through beastly time-places.[7] Given the dangers of betraying embodied and ineffable ass tales, I stood fast at the edge of an Impasse, regarding human logos and authority (in the form of writing) on one side of an abyss and embodied wordless weaves of lively ecologies on the other. In a passionate sull of my own – in this case, a stoppage or refusal to proceed in specific narrative ways – I have been deeply engaged in weighing what is at stake, what dangers or brighter possibilities lurk in the leap toward authoring our journeys together from Mississippi to Virginia and beyond. Because here is the closest thing I know to a fact: I could never grasp or author the infinite stories of biological and affective becomings that swarm in and around me and Aliass as we wander through places. I would not trample with wordy tropes on this delicate bewilderment and perplexity. I would not lay a tale down on those old Western teleological tracks, if I could help it. And this embrace of nameless ecologies and untellable storyings has been the aim of performing immersive, material journeys, in lieu of writing in whatever forms, all along.

In this stance, I've balked long and hard at the risks of mounting up to take the authorial reins of a freighted journey narrative, where trope-tangled emplotments

7   As poet Fanny Howe observes, "Aesthetic circling around an interior silence has to be delicate. Your consciousness of misappointment is very great." Fanny Howe, "Bewilderment, or the incarnation of the author," *Raddle Moon* 18, no. 2 (2002): 56.

might reinforce the sense that human stories are the only ones that really matter.[8] The risks seemed too great that to render our experiences into grammatical prose – into a language where asses and other "animals" are objects at best, and also killable commodities – would betray the dream of our wanderings as nomadic co-exploration and resistance, spaces in which to share and frame respect for embodied ways of storying. Meanwhile, these risks did not bother the various reporters whom we met (or who chased us down) along the way, from the TV news crew who ambushed us on a Tennessee backroad to the diligent newshound who came upon us at a gas station in Roanoke; but that's another kind of story. Given all this, I have resisted bending to pressures of neoliberal market economy, within a dominant culture that might just as readily render Aliass into dog food as spotlight her fifteen minutes of fame on a local newscast.[9] And I cast a long sideways ear at the temptation to hawk a romantic fantasy where a solo (white, female) traveler on the open road appears as an embodiment of heroic adventure or personal freedom. Maybe so, but freedom for whom?

8   In *The Mushroom at the End of the World,* Anna Lowenhaupt Tsing reminds us how Western cultures assume time as a linear force, how the "forward march" of "progress" underlies "democracy, growth, science, and hope" and leads us to "expect economies to grow and science to advance"; but this progress is "embedded [...] in widely accepted assumptions about what it means to be human" in ways that lead us to believe humans alone are inside history while all other species are outside of it, at our mercy for exploitation or salvation. Meanwhile, "every living thing remakes the world through seasonal pulses of growth, lifetime reproductive patterns, and geographies of expansion"; in following the lifeways of matsutake mushrooms from the forests of Oregon's Eastern Cascades to migrant picker camps to Japanese markets, Tsing demonstrates how "we might look for what has been ignored because it never fit the time line of progress." Anna Lowenhaupt Tsing, *The Mushroom at the End of the World* (Princeton: Princeton University Press, 2015), 21.

9   Nicole Shukin, *Animal Capital: Rendering Life in Biopolitical Times* (Minneapolis: University of Minnesota Press, 2009).

And freedom from what? And can we ever fully recognize that we are never solo, after all, but always comprised of worldings with infinite others – complex and intimate responsibilities we can never really get free of?

Still Life with an Unnamed Ass

Lo and behold, at an impasse where a sull stills forward movement in a particular direction, and thus disrupts the flow of habitual movements, new and tender awareness and affective possibilities find cracks from which to emerge. As Kathleen Stewart describes in "Still Life," contemplative pauses open attentive space for unforeseen insights, and even the emergence of newfangled practices and hybrid articulations: "A still is a state of calm, a lull in the action. But it is also a machine hidden in the woods that distills spirits into potency through a process of slow condensation."[10]

Over the course of that first slow, spiraling, hot and moonshiny wander with Aliass across the Southern states – and more especially in the aftermath, sat at a keyboard facing the impasse of words – I found new ways to respectfully inhabit the insistent wisdoms and distillate possibilities of a sull. As on those fraught occasions when I had no choice but to stand still with Aliass and wait through a hardcore sull, while she pondered and processed a possible move, and I could tune in to quieter presences at the margins – bird rustlings and frog calls, ants and beetles crawling along, hushes of leaves and roots entwining, not to mention the subtle shifts and twitches of mind and mood in Aliass's body and my own. Practices bound to living and traveling with Aliass continuously seek newfangled forms through which to explore and respond to promises of richer multispecies sto-

10 Kathleen Stewart, *Ordinary Affects* (Durham: Duke University Press, 2007), 18.

ries we find through immersion in barnyards and other full-blown, overlapping and mapless territories.

Learning to negotiate through conflicts borne of differing perceptions and experience would become a vital aspect of our long-ass journey, a source of its most difficult joys and intimate frictions. While the ancient becomings of domestic asses and humans both precede and evolve in our midst, Aliass and I had to learn brand-new, embodied ways of becoming open to each other as we went along through unfamiliar places in the course of that long ass journey. And in coming to respect a wary she-ass's unique intelligence and self-preserving needs, I have learned that a sull is never without good reason. More importantly, the stakes on either side of any such conflict are seldom, if ever, clear to everybody involved. To sit deep and move in slow motion through a sull with Aliass is to enter, as Donna Haraway describes in the *Companion Species Manifesto,* "the world of becoming with, where *who and what are* is precisely what is at stake."[11] Indeed, the weighing of 'what is at stake' is always what goes on at the heart of a sull, where inscrutable beasts consider possible threats to life and limb through the limits of what we know or don't, all the while trying to decide how to proceed (or not) given such fearsome opacities, dangers, or promises of greener pastures hidden in invisible infrastructures, manifest myths, and other shadowy places.

Toward a Multispecies Relational Assthetics

From out of this impasse – the staunch refusal from the get-go to write our journey as a linear narrative memoir from beginning to end (an ancient, inherently teleological structure that a journey almost seems to demand) – I discovered other creative strategies by which to artfully resist and intervene in certain pressures toward domi-

11 Haraway, *Companion Species Manifesto,* 19.

nant forms of meaning-making. As a creative practice, the sull encompasses not just a tactic of resistance but more so a vital, hopeful, and generative mode of processual stillness and refusal-to-move in a particular direction – in hopes of coming up with a better one. Bound to Aliass, I have found the long-ass sull becomes a thick and habitable practical space in which to performatively frame the deepest quandaries, questions, and hopes tangled up in our asymmetrical relations.

Over the years, the art of the sull has evolved as a distinct engagement of ecological performance-art practices, in particular those that pull contemporary relational aesthetics across species to resist single authorship and buck violent ontological hierarchies and exclusions. While barnyard-bound and so inherently distanced from mostly urban art centers and institutions, the art of a sull still inherits from certain art-historical legacies, especially later-twentieth-century feminist and ecological performance practices that address social and environmental inequities in different ways. From John Cage's indeterminacy to the feminist blurring of Art/Life to Beuysian social sculpture, performance-art practices provide vital conceptual frameworks wherein artists address complexities of places and the less-recognized lives they hold, many of which might otherwise be ignored or dismissed as insignificant noise.[12] Building on aesthetic and

12 The history of contemporary performance art, especially traced through feminist and ecological legacies, provides diverse creative and radical ways to frame attention to indeterminate site-specific and time-based becomings. John Cage's most well-known piece, "4'33"," introduced a method of framing indeterminacy in creative musical compositions. The pianist David Tudor performed by ceremoniously seating himself at the piano and proceeding to play "nothing" for the duration of the piece, while the audience either absorbed or rejected the invitation to listen deeply and differently to the unexpected murmurs, hums, clicks, coughs, and ambient vibrations happening in the concert hall. Later, feminist and Art/Life pioneers like Yoko Ono, Mierle Ukeles, Allan Kaprow, Carolee Sch-

political concepts in performance art, twenty-first-century relational practices have evolved in some directions to invite participants into thick habitable experiences and encounters with invisible or overlooked processes, presences, and affective possibilities.[13] In this sense, relational art practices may work to resist the assumption that the singular Human Artist is always primary author of whatever action or encounters unfold within a given artwork.

At the same time, art critic Helena Reckitt reminds us that even where relational practices claim to create radical new spaces for social equality and collaborative exploration, social and political power dynamics are always at play in the shaping of these spaces. In "Forgotten Relations," Reckitt calls out the tendency of contemporary relational aesthetics (especially those under the influence of Nicholas Bourriaud) to ignore the insights of earlier feminist practices, such as Mierle Ukeles's Maintenance Art. Reckitt writes that relational projects often lose vital elements of the "criticality and ambivalence" that early feminist works manifest. Instead, writes Reckitt, they tend to invite visitors into "a frictionless environment, unencumbered by the claims of responsibility," which in turn "suppresses the key feminist insight that neither 'art' nor 'work' are ever just that, but are always subject to

neeman, Linda Montano, and Joseph Beuys (to name a few) adapted modes of framing indeterminacy toward exploration and critique of aesthetic, political, and environmental systems. Contemporary ecological art draws on legacies from early Dada and surrealist performances to cutting-edge bioart, while ecological artists disturb traditional boundaries between bodies/environments, humans/nature, and any other dubious dualisms. While ecological art comprises a diverse field of practices, its artists tend to share what Linda Weintraub calls an "ecocentric" (as opposed to more traditionally anthropocentric) focus. See Linda Weintraub, *To Life! Eco Art for a Sustainable Planet* (Berkeley: University of California Press, 2012), and Andrea Liss, *Feminist Art and the Maternal* (Minneapolis: University of Minnesota Press, 2009).

13 Nicholas Bourriaud, "Relational Aesthetics," in *Participation*, ed. Claire Bishop (London: Whitechapel, 2006), 160–71.

conditions of who does what, for whom, and under what terms."[14]

While the art of a sull might idealize certain aesthetic and political aims of creating more equitable spaces, it also recognizes that our proceedings can never be frictionless, especially when encounters within them are shaped by asymmetrical power dynamics that hold some participants as biographical beings and others as killable commodities. This critique becomes especially relevant for a practice that aims to wrangle with "assthetic" questions of who does what and for whom in our specific barnyard relations. For the most part, institutionalized relational art practices (and their salient critiques) pertain to dynamics of human political and social relations. But some contemporary artists also work to extend the relational framework into broader multispecies fields, to encourage curiosity and newly impassioned attention toward other species and ecological meshes. Toward this end, Steve Baker describes artistic strategies that seek to disrupt "the notion of an originating author," in the words of artist Mark Dion. Baker explores projects that employ a kind of "unassuming 'complex authorship' responsible for the production [of artworks] [...] most strikingly evident not only in Olly and Suzi's collaborative 'hand over hand' technique, but in the occasional participation of animals themselves in the mark-making."[15]

Meanwhile, the art of the sull also draws vital insights from the work of contemporary bio-artists, who intertwine imaginative and critical exploration with scientific knowledge-making practices. While the biopolitics of twenty-first-century technoscience may seem a far cry

14 Helena Reckitt, "Forgotten Relations: Feminist Artists and Relational Aesthetics," in *Politics in a Glass: Case Feminism, Exhibition Cultures and Curatorial Transgressions*, eds., Angela Dimitrakaki and Lara Perry (Liverpool: Liverpool University Press, 2013), 152.

15 Steve Baker, *The Postmodern Animal* (London: Reaktion Books, 2000), 13–14.

from the rural ass barnyard, these debates are relevant to anyone who has and/or loves living bodies in our so-called "Biological Century." In caring for Aliass and herd, I make decisions about deworming schedules and vaccination practices, and in doing so I recognize that the laboratory is never as far from the barnyard as we might suppose. Perhaps even more important for my aspirations of making stories with untold others is this admonition from science studies scholar Joseph Dumit, his "Microbiopolitical tactic" that advises: "Never think you know all of the species involved in a decision. Corollary: Never think you speak for all of yourself."[16]

Meanwhile, emergent practices in bio-art and multispecies storytelling seek to honor and respect the ways of those who experience and weave the world otherwise, while at the same time pitching critical and creative interventions into environmentally harmful human habits and systems. In the *Multispecies Salon*, Eben Kirksey gathers a diverse arrays of ethnographic, artistic, and practical interventions in specifically troubled sites; here ecological performance, bio-art projects, and even biopolitical recipes from artists and scholars Mirium Simun, Lindsay Kelley, Kim TallBear, and others invite radical multispecies inclusivity and demonstrate hopeful tinkerings that (re)frame invisible and complex, inner and outer encounters among diverse mammals, insects, plants, and microbes.[17] Beatriz da Costa and Kavita Philip's collection, *Tactical Biopolitics*, gathers bioart practices that radically question the boundaries of artistic and scientific practices. From Kathy High's exploration of entangled empathies with laboratory rats, with whom she shares a disease, to Eduardo Kac's unsettling genetic modifications

16 Joseph Dumit, "Foreword: Biological Feedback," in *Tactical Biopolitics*, eds. Beatriz da Costa and Kavita Philip (Boston: MIT Press, 2010), xii.
17 Eben Kirksey, ed., *The Multispecies Salon* (Durham: Duke University Press, 2014).

of human–plant hybrids and bioluminescent rabbits, bio-artists challenge and frame affective and biopolitical encounters always unfolding in naturalcultural sites.[18] Dissolving stubborn categories like nature/culture and human/animal, which hinder efforts to find ourselves more wholly within earthly environments, these artistic practices give material forms to specific modes of (re) thinking systems and hierarchies, which in turn become part of what Charis Thompson originally dubbed "ontological choreography."

Barnyard Ontological Choreography

Possibilities for new kinds of storytelling thicken where human modes of perception and meaning-making meet and mix with other species who perceive and make meanings differently. In *When Species Meet*, Donna Haraway describes an ontological choreography comprised entirely of encounters, where "all the actors become who they are in *the dance of relating*, not from scratch, not *ex nihilo*, but full of the patterns of their sometimes-joined, sometimes-separate heritages both before and lateral to *this* encounter."[19] Kin to Karen Barad's concept of "intra-

---

18 Kathy High, "Playing with Rats," in *Tactical Biopolitics*, eds. Beatriz da Costa and Kavita Philip (Boston: MIT Press, 2010), 465–78; Eduardo Kac, *Telepresence and Bio Art: Networking Humans, Rabbits, and Robots* (Ann Arbor: University of Michigan Press, 2005).

19 In a significant passage, Haraway sniffs out traces of human exceptionalism, embedded even in the insightful work of ethologist Barbara Smuts, whose studies with baboons provide vital contributions in contemporary ethology. Haraway says: "Writing about these introductions to baboon social niceties, Smuts said, 'The baboons remained themselves, doing what they always did in the world they always lived in' (295). In other words, her idiom leaves the baboons in nature, where change involves only the time of evolution, and perhaps ecological crisis, and the human being in history, where all other sorts of time come into play. Here is where I think Derrida and Smuts need each other. [...] If we know how to look, I think we would see that the baboons of Eburru Cliffs were redone too, in baboon

action" – where "interaction" is dumped for its inherent implication that discrete things and organisms bump against each other while remaining essentially unchanged – ontological choreography reckons with shaping forces of constant, dynamic encounters, which leave no party unaffected.[20]

As a concept, ontological choreography ripples out from discourses among cultural anthropologists and science and technology studies (STS) scholars, who explore fault lines of Western paradigms that dubiously claim to separate and elevate (some) human actions above all other embodied kinds. Charis Thompson's *Making Parents* – a seminal ethnographic study of how parents and children come into being through "ontological choreographies of assisted reproductive technologies" – explores clinical sites where a number of seemingly distinct worlds come together around certain reproductive goals.[21] In this case, biological processes and technological tools fuse around the goal of human conception, and traditional categorical distinctions of Nature and Culture dissolve into webs of relations between rhythms and apparatuses that constantly shape and remake each other. Exclusive human authority gives way, and (as Haraway has it) "relationships are the smallest possible patterns for analysis; the partners and actors are their still-ongoing products. It is all extremely prosaic, relentlessly mundane, and exactly how worlds come into being."[22] Whether written or performed in other embodied ways, ontological choreographies of thinking and material action frame inde-

ways, by having entangled their gaze with that of this young clipboard-toting human female." Donna J. Haraway, *When Species Meet* (Minneapolis: University of Minnesota Press, 2008), 25.

20 Karen Barad, *Meeting the Universe Halfway* (Durham: Duke University Press, 2007), 33.

21 Charis Thompson, *Making Parents: The Ontological Choreography of Assisted Reproductive Technologies* (Cambridge: MIT Press, 2000).

22 Haraway, *When Species Meet*, 26.

terminate, unscripted haps in specific timeplaces. This thinking in turn creates openings for more inclusive unfoldings to materialize as grounds for storying with diverse, site-specific, and unnamed agents as authors.

And all of this brings us back, if by unexpected paths, to the art of the sull. All of these ideas and contemporary practices of multispecies theory and art-making shape ways and means for making untold stories with Aliass. While grounded in material performance and daily caretakings, the sull as a space from which we might co-compose untold stories is kin to the ethnographic tactic that Anna Lowenhaupt Tsing calls passionate immersion.[23] Emerging practices of multispecies ethnography draw on Tsing's attention to "[i]mmersive ways of knowing and being with others [that] involve careful attention to what matters to another – attention to how to how they craft shared lives and worlds."[24] Indeed, in the work of living and crafting shared worlds with Aliass over time, I have learned many new tactics, skills, and modes of attention, while also gaining humility alongside my long-eared friend as we navigate fearsome impasses in ways I would never find without her.

The Overpass

In June 2002, Aliass and I made a preliminary foray on the eve of our departure from Oxford. It was just a couple of miles and barely an hours' walk, across the south part of Oxford, Mississippi. That morning we left the residential neighborhood south of town, where we were staying the night with friends of friends, Amos and Coulter, and made our way to William Faulkner's estate, Rowan Oak, which

23 Anna Lowenhaupt Tsing, "Arts of Inclusion, or How to Love a Mushroom," *Australian Humanities Review* 50 (2011): 5–22.

24 Thom Van Dooren, Eben Kirksey, and Ursula Muenster, "Multispecies Studies: Cultivating Arts of Attentiveness," *Environmental Humanities* 8, no. 1 (2016): 1–23.

sits at the edge of town on the other side of a major highway bypass. As we set off that morning, I walked behind
Aliass, guiding her with a pair of long driving reins, as I
had learned that urgings from behind are the only way
she will move steadily forward. (If I try to lead her from in
front, she barely moves at all.) We stuck close to the gut-
ter as we clicked along the asphalt roadway and wove into
strip-mall parking lots to avoid passing cars where possible. We were clipping along at a good pace and feeling
fine. The morning was clear with a tiny breeze, with the
exception of a brief cloudburst. A half mile into the trip,
we came to an overpass. I had seen it looming ahead but
failed to anticipate the way an elongated span of blocky
concrete and cracked asphalt suspended over a roaring
stream of speeding traffic would look to a wary ass who
had never encountered such a thing. I had not considered the way the change of sound underneath her hooves
would strike her, as solid earth dropped away beneath her
into thin air and a hellish pit of revving engines below.

Some fifteen feet onto the overpass, Aliass froze in
terror in the middle of the lanes where cars were traveling both ways. Cars began to back up behind us. It was
less a sull than a panic attack, really, but either way it
amounted to an immovable ass in the middle of a busy
commuter roadway. She would not budge in any direction. I tried pulling, clucking, and even pushing her from
behind. Nothing would move her. The minutes stretched
out like strains of hot tar, as bemused faces behind wind-
shields grew less friendly. All of a sudden, Aliass jolted
forward. With all the force in her 400+-pound body, she
charged across the lane of oncoming traffic and dragged
me to the opposite side of the road, where she hopped
up onto a sidewalk that ran the length of the overpass
to land on the other side. Yep, a sidewalk. Determined to
follow the rules of the road for bicycles (as extrapolated
to "livestock"), I was determined to stay in our lane of
traffic, and so I had not even noticed the four-foot-wide,

protected passageway on the opposite side of the road. But Aliass saw it, and somehow she was drawn to its purpose in spite of never needing such a thing before (far as I know). Once she got up on the sidewalk, Aliass clipped swiftly across the length of the overpass and delivered us safely to solid ground on the other side.

A few minutes later, we gathered our wits in a gas station parking lot beside a little flower shop. Aliass pooped in relief, and before I could pick up her droppings with the little yellow plastic kid's shovel I carried for that purpose in the saddlebag, the florist popped out of the shop and requested the manure to feed her seedlings. Then slowly but steadily we went on, past a few blocks of mown antebellum lawns and stately homes until we came to Rowan Oak. Once we arrived on the parklike grounds of Faulkner's grand neoclassical mansion and estate, we ambled around the mannered grounds where the great author hammered out the bulk of his massive, influential literary corpus. I rode Aliass (as on occasion she permitted) around the grounds of the estate, and through a little, low labyrinth of boxwood bushes near the columned neoclassical façade of the mansion. We each plucked bright daylily flowers from the prim shrubbery and chewed the orange petals. I found a shiny black feather on the ground and stuck it into Aliass's bridle. And so we meandered in the gentile melodious cacophony of the early-summer Mississippi late morning: American crows, mockingbirds, cicadas, lofty cedars and gnarly old oak trees, coastal grasses rhizoming their twisted ways across pale red dirt, trellised vines and trim boxwoods, and human ass conversations (with and about Aliass and our present purposes; with an *Oxford Eagle* newspaper reporter; and then with a cocky, college-circuit comedian playing it cool in a do-rag), all the while immersed in the cawing and twining, breathing and chattering of a distinct, ever-shifting ruckus of myriad voices and lives less audible.

The creative and critical practices borne through the art of a sull and bound to the Unnaming of Aliass begin in an Impasse – in stubborn refusals to name or claim authorship in given ways. But the art of a sull also recognizes that to immerse with Aliass in performative journeys is not really to propose that we sidestep the shaping influences of human language, narratives, economies, or infrastructures. The art of a sull simply holds that in certain circumstances we might learn to deploy a specific stance (picture the ass sitting back on her haunches in a hard sull) that resists galling assumptions and hierarchies that tend to bulldoze more true-to-life, inclusive, and respectful forms of meaning-making. The art of the sull unfolds where we (fail to) go forth in a particular direction (rational? philosophical? phallogocentric?), in the hope that from such time-warping, contemplative intervals of resistance and contemplation might come new kinds of co-composition and barnyard tales, and perhaps even unforeseen overpasses across menacing divides.

These interdisciplinary arts of unnaming and inhabiting untold stories with Aliass may be speculative, but their consequences are not imaginary. What happens in a sull matters – not least because it turns certain authorities and assumptions on their long, furry ears in local and specific ways. At the very least, a hardcore sull reminds any immodest muleskinner that her ass (or half-ass) is never a mechanical agent of human will. This is not to say one little ass could ever win against global forces of anthropocentric-technocratic-neoliberal-capitalist dominion all on her own. But it is to say (with all due respect and immeasurable gratitude) that her unique assine form of resistance is a venerable tactic, nonetheless. When it comes to insistent balking at the edge of troubled crossings, so as to weigh every possible strategy (when escape is not an option), I have learned some special skills from the very best.

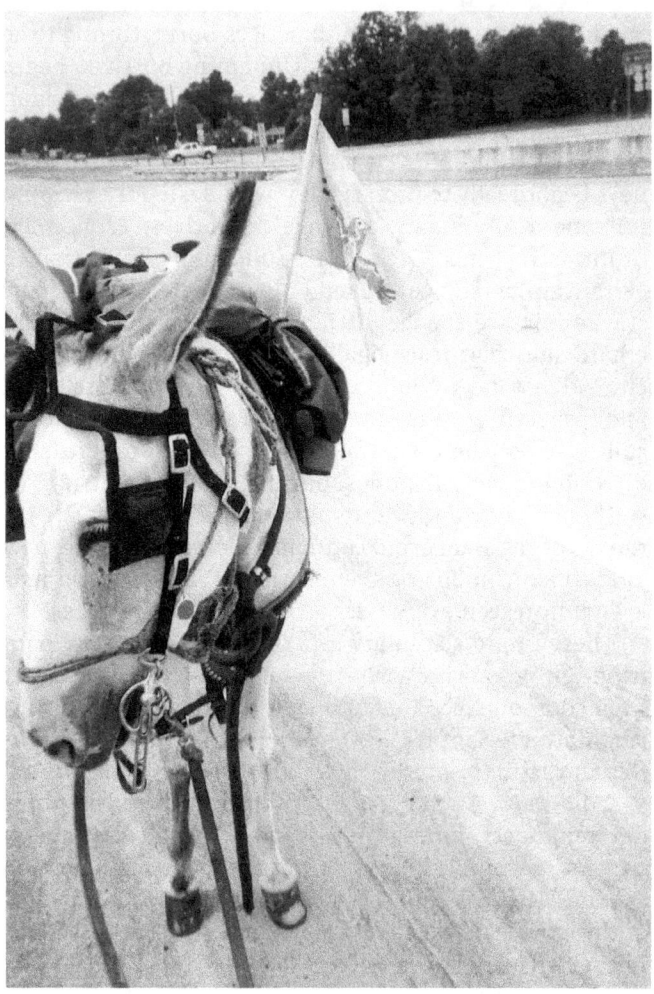

Fig. 1. Aliass on a highway overpass just outside Oxford, Mississippi, June 2002. Photograph by the artist.

Knoxville '99

Dear friend now in the dusty clockless hours of the town when
the streets lie black and steaming in the wake of the watertrucks
and now when the drunk and homeless have washed up in the
lee of walls in alleys or abandoned lots and cats go forth high-
shouldered and lean in the grim perimeters about, now in these
sootblacked brick or cobbled corridors where lightwire shadows
make a gothic harp of cellar doors no soul shall walk save you
— Cormac McCarthy, *Suttree*[1]

... And then in time the ringing hoofbeats on rainy asphalt and the flickering warped window reflections of a
certain unnamed beast of burden, known to some (and
unknown to everyone) as Aliass.

One surreal and humid morning in the early fall of a
former millennium, I made a little literary pilgrimage to
an unfamiliar Southern city in search of a ghostly hero, or
at least faint traces of the fictive protagonist I loved most
in the world, Cormac McCarthy's Suttree. Youthful passion for the viscous, swirling-dark prose of McCarthy's
Tennessee novels beckoned me on this quixotic quest to
Knoxville, as if to another realm. And though I did not
exactly find Suttree that morning, something else of significance transpired. Having never been to Knoxville, or

---

1 Cormac McCarthy, *Suttree* (New York: Vintage, 1979), 3.

much of anywhere in Tennessee, nevertheless I knew the place deeply, in the eerie familiarity of every dank odor and leafy climbing tendril, in the faded colors of warming bricks in the morning sun of the Old City and the slow dirty brown river, and the rust-stained bolted iron spans and cooing pigeons and plastic whiskey bottle relics under the Gay Street Bridge. And strangely, that September morning in 1999, the hazy streets seemed frozen in the '50s setting of the novel. Dust lay thick in the windows of empty department stores, and not a living soul was in sight. As if I had walked onto the abandoned stage set of a movie that could not exist, because how can any vision or memory or dream made solely of word music become visible, tactile, almost habitable like this?

This, I guess, was the main question or quest that brought me to Knoxville that day. More than the reflections of its human protagonist, a thick sense of bodies-in-places is what animates and haunts this particular fiction, and in a way I suppose that's what I was looking for. This visceral thickness is what made me fall so deeply in love with *Suttree*, as a young hungry reader haunted by the flow of hidden, tangled histories and rhythms of ever-changing places – places, both familiar and unknown, that seem to hold us together in nets of memories and experiences lived among others, feeding our lives and longings.

At the end of the street, I came up short on the sidewalk in front of a door with the words "McCarthy and McCarthy, Attorneys at Law" stenciled on the glass upper half in blocky, black-outlined gold letters, like the entrance to an old detective agency. Just then as I stood gawking on the sidewalk, a handsome, gray-haired gentleman with eerily pale blue eyes emerged from the door, peeling a banana. In that awkward moment, the man looked at me quizzically as I stood gape-jawed like an idiot in his immediate path, that 8 o'clock of a weekday morning. I managed to stammer, "Uh, excuse me, sir, could you tell me if this 'McCarthy and McCarthy' is at all related to the author, Cormac McCarthy?" At which the man smiled faintly and said, "Yes, in fact. I am his brother."

I stuttered that I had come because I loved *Suttree*.[2] After a moment's pause, the handsome gentleman invited me to accompany him along the short walk back to his office building a few blocks away, and said along the way he could point out some of the sites from Knoxville's Old City that figure in the novel. We departed on an intense little walking tour of about five blocks, unexpected for both of us and pocked with silences, as we each walked in our own ways with awed wonder and respect that we shared, without saying as much, at the way one writer's singular prose could so richly invoke and haunt a place with distinct ghosts of human (be)longing; how a material place of any kind could be so uniquely and indelibly remade in human imagination in skeins of words and syntax; and the old mystery of how language can or cannot claim to hold certain human places and who we are or might become in them: diverse lives and becomings with others, tracks and traces of loves and losses and slow vanishings.

At the end of the walk across the Old City that morning, the gentleman and I parted on the sidewalk opposite the blocky midcentury office building where he worked. With slight embarrassment, I had admitted along the walk that my dream was to write something like Suttree, even as we both recognized I might as well say I hoped

2 Among the obfuscate, Faulkner-infused Tennessee novels that McCarthy wrote in the 1970s, *Suttree* arguably stands as the masterpiece. After that, McCarthy went West, following the bloody tracks of rapacious and horrifying Westward conquest. Most readers know the singular American author for his Border Trilogy, a series of Westerns written to worldwide acclaim in the '80s and '90s. As Dennis McCarthy told me on our walk that day, the Tennessee novels all got writ in a time of relative anonymity for their author, and Cormac McCarthy mourned that era now that the critics were sitting "like buzzards on his shoulders" as he wrote.

to turn into a unicorn someday. But as we parted, Dennis McCarthy said a thing – most likely out of kindness, tinged with slight bemusement at the unexpected appearance of a literary pilgrim quite literally in the path of his ordinary walk to work that morning. As we shook hands and said goodbye, he asked my name, and to my answer he replied: "Well, maybe I will hear it again in twenty years."

~x~x~x~

More than two decades have passed since that chance encounter with Dennis McCarthy of a Knoxville morning. At the time, in the flame of youthful creative passions, I took those parting words as a challenge – maybe even a kind of benediction, given the unlikely circumstances. But what becomes of literary dreams when an aspiring author gets struck (struck dumb, even) with an urgent sense of responsibility and passion for untold stories that unfold otherwise, in wordless ecologies and timeplace registers?

However moved I was (and still am... sigh) by the incantatory modernist ululations of William Faulkner's *Absalom Absalom!* and McCarthy's Tennessee novels and *Blood Meridian* and *The Crossing* (not to mention Beckett's *Unnamable* and others), I found that newfangled pressures and responsibilities confronted what Stephen Muecke calls the "conditions for writing," fictive or otherwise, in the early twenty-first century. In his fictocritical manifesto, "The Fall," Muecke writes: "Faced with masses of ways of knowing things coming from all points of the compass, the contemporary writer asks what now can legitimate his or her point of view, and then tends not just to add to existing views of the world, but traces a path

[...] showing how we got to this position, and what is at stake."[3]

What seemed to be at stake, in this case, was a sense of authority gutshot by worn-out, broke-ass, outdated American middle school textbook ways of thinking about Biology, History, Geography, Language Arts, Earth Science, and Social Studies – embedded as these subjects were in my early education with primarily unarticulated but no less "taught" ideas and grammars of gender, race, and species.[4] At stake, as well, was the integrity of an imaginative practice that needed urgently to throw off human/animal hierarchies grounded in denials of others' emotional and social complexities – denials that ring false in the experience of anyone who lives with other social mammals (not to mention legions of others who affect our lives and environments directly all the time). What began to seem essential was to trace new paths, as Muecke says, to mobilize ears, hands, and tongues to listen and move past exclusive or downright erroneous texts, maps, and habits of thought that ignore or deny

3 Stephen Muecke, "The Fall," in *Joe in the Andamans* (Sydney: LCP, 2008), 5. Deborah Bird Rose and Libby Robin elaborate the significance of Muecke's fictocritical methodologies for broader environmental humanities work: "[Muecke] provokes us to decentre (not abandon) Cartesian rationality in favour of a more inclusive set of logics. Connections are non-linear (as well as linear), and representation thus requires non-linear forms. It may be that narrative is the method through which the reason of connectivity will find its most powerful voice. This method offers the profound possibility of telling stories that communicate, invoke, and invigorate connections." Deborah Bird Rose and Libby Robin, "Ecological Humanities in Action: An Invitation," *Australian Humanities Review* 31–32 (2004).

4 I like to think things have changed in the US primary education since my days there, but my hopes may be in vain, if fairly recent flaps over Texas textbooks, in which slaves coming across the Middle Passage were referred to as "workers," are anything to go by. Ellen Bresler Rockmore, "How Texas Teaches History," *New York Times,* October 21, 2015, http://nytimes.com/2015/10/22/opinion/how-texas-teaches-history.html.

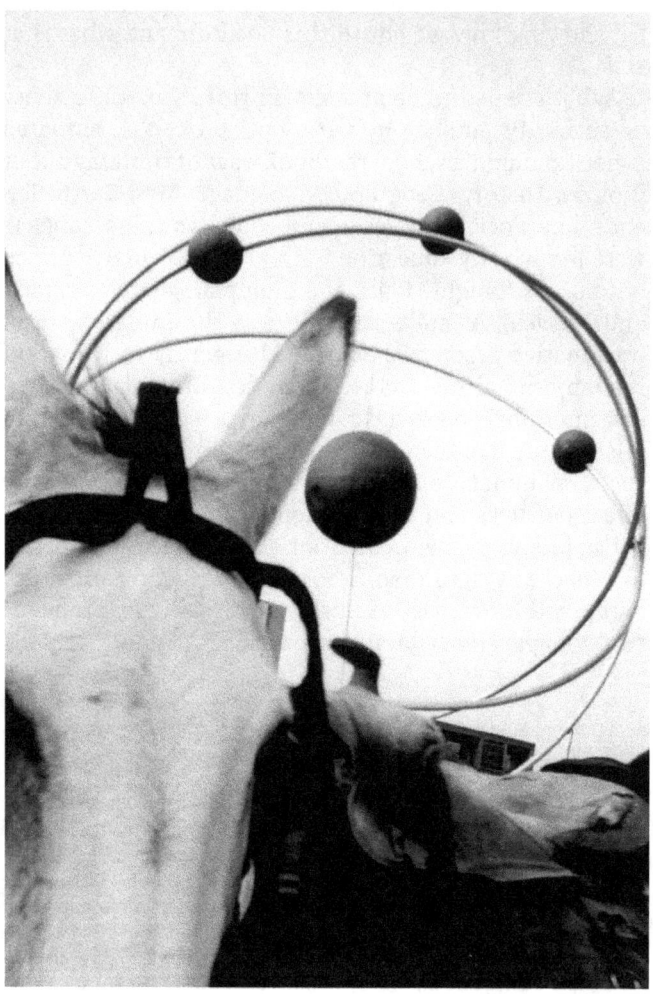

Fig. 1. Aliass outside the Museum of Science and Energy in Oak Ridge, Tennessee in July 2002. Photograph by the artist.

the vital interweaves of beastly bodies and embodied stories that make up all the places we claim to care for and call home. And the light that led the way in this quest was the welter of lively possibilities that bloomed from the beautiful crack of the American Spotted Ass.

Identifications, nominations, trademarks, patrilineal claims, and classifications may all be unavoidable in US Western lives and dealings – those that hope to "make a living," at least. Yet deepest down, somewhere beyond what is even possible to say, the stories of bodies-in-places I set out with Aliass to inhabit, honor, and immerse in can never be claimed by a lone human author's brand. Instead, they must be woven through outward wanderings and cyclical returns that track cracks and fissures discovered in and amplified by the sensitive, fleshly presence of one so-called "ass," along with vast herds of nameless and familiar others who comprise timeplaces we pass through. Meanwhile, as we see plastic trash humans have carelessly tossed years ago tangled in the guts of dead fledgling albatrosses and beached whales oceans away, we begin to grasp that no soul shall walk (or listen, or think) alone – not on Planet Earth, anyway. In light of all this, the name I want to make is not mine but hers.

But then it ain't really hers, either.

5

GOING ASSTRAY
(Carcassonne and Beyond)

A flashback: One night, way back in the Hollow when my own bones seemed caught in a duel between the limits of human poetic imagination and some impenetrable, monumental Nature-Reality, I was moved to memorize William Faulkner's 1957 Nobel Prize Acceptance speech from a recording of the Great Author himself reciting it, from a cassette tape a friend had gifted me. After some hours walking circles in wet grass under the stars, I had the whole thing hardwired into my neural pathways. As it was, those days were full of peculiar passions for mostly male, mostly Southern writers and my own fevered efforts to mimic their distinct rhythms and registers in musical prose. Meanwhile, that same period was also full of awakenings to new ecological awareness of myriad hybrid and multispecies voices – whether cyborg songs or eco-acoustical reports of regional amphibian, bird, and insect dialects. Slowly but surely, revelations of multispecies meaning-making began to render utterly asinine Faulkner's Nobel Prize acceptance assertion that "he alone among creatures has an inexhaustible voice."[1]

1　William Faulkner, "Nobel Prize Acceptance Speech," *Southern Cultures* 12, no. 1 (2006): 71. Weirdly, the speech as memorized that sum-

Meanwhile, I had been intently delving into this one particular Faulkner prose poem story called "Carcassonne" for some time before my first fateful encounter with the American Spotted Ass in 2001. In the same way this surprising ass figure blew open unforeseen paths, something extraordinary happened to the text of "Carcassonne." With the implosive force of "ass," this unusual Faulkner text came to seem like a kind of treasure map, which hid in its tangled syntaxes and images a secret skeleton key to open the gates of conflicted mysteries between names and bodies, romantic figures and real-ass flesh and bones. The rollicking text of "Carcassonne" seemed to rumble anew with vague promises and fraught desires, like a far-off thunderstorm on an oppressively humid afternoon. That is to say, here in the text of Carcassonne, I discovered another crack between porous realms loosely known as "reality" and "imagination."

In the long run, it was this explosive mix of conflicting poetic, political, geographic, and even ontological forces that would make mythically storied Mississippi the inevitable place of departure for our long-ass mission. Mississippi became the point of departure from which to launch into all the untold tales Aliass and I would pass through as we wandered the roads to Nameless and beyond.

Wait, Mississippi? Why *Mississippi*, of all possible places, as the state from which to begin a nascent ass mis-

mer night in the Hollow is still embedded in my synapses to this day (though I can only conjure scraps of it, and only if I imitate Faulkner's Mississippi accent). I would note that there is much in this speech that still resonates (such as the statement that "there are no longer problems of the human spirit; there is only the question 'when will I be blown up?'"; but we also do well to cast a critical eye on some of its inherent assumptions. You can find the speech on YouTube, as it happens, with an eerie visual accompaniment of Faulkner's bust floating and slowly growing closer in dark space, as if video artist Bill Viola turned his eye to ghosts of modernist Mississippi: Artzineonline, "William Faulkner: Nobel Prize Speech," *YouTube*, July 13, 2013, https://www.youtube.com/watch?v=gOg3oJBnik8.

sion? That fall of 2001, I was newly (if shallowly) planted in the Pacific Northwest, having just driven all that way westward to settle in a bustling young (post)industrial city at the westernmost edge of the continental US – a region with its own tortuous, mostly hidden histories.[2] Why turn back to the haggard Deep South so soon, and for that matter to an unfamiliar and fractious state where I had no real ties and knew not a soul? I could not really say, except that somehow these fraught territories demanded imaginative reckoning with questions of home and belonging, the muddles of so-called "realities" and fraught fictions of races and species, specific languages and hidden histories that roil in every storied landscape – but perhaps especially, or at least in special American ways, in the Southern states.[3]

2   Portland seemed especially sad and dark in the gloom of confused post-9/11 American reckonings. Disturbing forces percolated under the shiny surfaces of millennial Stumptown, like a mysterious oil leaking up from the spectral Black Lodge in the woods of Twin Peaks or vague rumblings from the Cascadian subduction zone. This sense of fissures crumbling beneath the bright surfaces of Capitalocene urban green culture, in a postmodern Western city built on tides of displacement and rapacious industrial extraction and racial exclusions, is tapped with visceral brilliance by Vanessa Veselka in her 2011 novel, *Zazen*. From the opening scene, in which punkrocker-geologist narrator Della observes a stranger sobbing hopelessly in a yoga class, the narrative struggles with uncertainty amid regimes of hidden global forces and explosively fragile means of response. Veselka's novel evokes the angst Della feels within shifting terrains of class, race, and activist urban youth culture caught in a desire to respond meaningfully to threats of ecological catastrophe but paralyzed by hidden traps of global capitalism and its various erasures. Says Della: "There should be some kind of price to pay for all this ugliness, especially the pretty kind: especially the kind you don't always see." Vanessa Veselka, *Zazen* (New York: Red Lemonade, 2001), 3.
3   If you listen to Rev Dr. Martin Luther King's "I Have a Dream" speech, listen hard to what rumbles and twists through his voice when he says, "Mississippi." It is a chilling, ominous, yet beautiful and promising thunder that cracks with hope and history in a way you can't hear anywhere else. LogistiKHD, "Martin Luther King | "I

Truth be told, the Mississippi I knew best was not the asphalt and concrete infrastructures of twenty-first-century Lafayette County but rather the fictional "past-that-is-not-past" of rural landscapes, characters, settings, and scenes found within novels and short stories of Faulkner's imaginary realm known as Yoknapawtapha. As it happens, Yoknapawtapha stands uniquely for authorial creation of regional place in modern American literature, Faulkner's famous literary claim to his "own little postage stamp of soil."[4] As a fervent fan of Faulknerian apocrypha, I was long under the spell of this model of godlike literary creation of place, whereby the august human imagination draws from reality to "create out of the materials of the human spirit" works of aesthetic wonder "which did not exist before" (as Faulkner describes the artist's job in his Nobel Prize acceptance speech).[5]

Though I would not have articulated it this way at the time, it was against the old idea of proper, patriarchally authored "reality" of any beastly place, and toward possibilities of more inclusive multispecies storyings, that the "Little Pilgrim of Carcassonne" foray with Aliass sought to simultaneously blast out from and go deeper into Faulknerian Mississippi in a particular way, turning away from patrilineal modes of writing, naming, and knowing within the sway of great modernist Southern literary tradition and its tropes and assumptions (and even its

---

Have a Dream Speech," *YouTube*, August 28, 2013, https://www.youtube.com/watch?v=I47Y6VHc3Ms.

4 As Faulkner famously told Jean Stein in an interview, "Beginning with *Sartoris* I discovered that my own little postage stamp of native soil was worth writing about and that I would never live long enough to exhaust it, and that by sublimating the actual into apocryphal I would have complete liberty to use whatever talent I might have to its absolute top' (LIG 255)." Robert Hamblin, "Carcassonne in Mississippi," in *Faulkner and the Craft of Fiction*, eds. Doreen Fowler and Ann J. Abadie (Jackson: University of Mississippi Press, 1987), 169.

5 Faulkner, "Nobel Prize Acceptance Speech," 71.

lustrous dirty lyricism). So the long-ass journey sought to forge new kinds of stories in imaginal/real Mississippi, with other kinds of authority (or perhaps none at all?) grounded in movement through hot, insect-ridden, unfamiliar Southern territories.

"Little Pilgrim of Carcassonne"

But beyond the lore of Yoknapawtapha that lured my ass to Oxford, Mississippi as a point of departure was a different pseudo-geographic, out-of-the-way junction of Faulknerian cartography, "Carcassonne." More lurid prose poem than short story, "Carcassonne" is shot through with distinctive swirls of unbridled italicized passages that read like conjuration or crazed sermon. At the same time, the text unfolds a rather wry conversation between an aspiring poet's imaginings and the grave wisdom of his skeleton. In the context of this conversation, "Carcassonne" presents a dreamy confabulated site, where a gossamer vortex of lyrical language pits "reality" and "imagination" against each other in a literal duel, like the perennial haggard figure of Don Quixote and his monster windmills. Flat on his back in a garret over a cantina in Rincon, the prone poet dreams of a frenzied horseback gallop that twists and scrolls through histories and landscapes of ancient medieval Crusades: "*I want to perform something bold and tragical and austere* he repeated, shaping the soundless words in the pattering silence *me on a buckskin pony with eyes like blue electricity and a mane like tangled fire, galloping up the hill and right off into the high heaven of the world.*"[6]

The prone poet muses on the timeless, flaming glory of his imaginary courtly ride, even as his own bones dryly remind him that he is a mortal body bound to time: "He

6 William Faulkner, "Carcassonne," in *The Collected Stories* (New York: Vintage, 1995), 895.

lay beneath an unrolled strip of tarred roofing paper. All of him that is, save that part which suffered neither insects nor temperature and which galloped unflagging on the destinationless pony, up a piled silver hill of cumulae where no hoof echoed nor left print, toward the blue precipice never gained."[7]

In an essay called "Carcassonne in Mississippi: Geography of the Imagination," scholar Robert Hamblin writes: "In [Faulkner's] curious geography of the imagination both Oxford and Carcassonne are part of Yoknapawtapha. And the only map on which that fabulous land appears is the one the artist himself drew, the one signed by 'William Faulkner, Sole Owner & Proprietor.'"[8] Meanwhile, it so happens that the real Carcassonne from which Faulkner takes his title is not in Mississippi at all. It is, in geographic fact, a medieval walled castle and surrounding city in the rolling, fertile Languedoc region in the South of France. The marvelous towered ramparts of Carcassonne's castle complex have stood since medieval times, and as a famed tourist destination since the site was reimagined by visionary architect and restorationist Eugène Viollet-le-Duc in the nineteenth century. "Carcassonne" is a site where mythical pasts and modern realities merge, medieval literary traditions and modernist innovations chafe – a situation of which Faulkner was likely aware.[9] Modern tourists love to visit places like this, as they evoke feelings of immersion in a bygone past – as if History was a static and monumental geographic space one can drop into and not just another mode of

---

7   Ibid., 895.
8   Hamblin, "Carcassonne in Mississippi," 169.
9   For instance, Viollet-le-Duc's Victorian architectural renovations/revisions of Carcassonne infuriated influential art critic John Ruskin, who fumed that the so-called restoration was in fact "a destruction accompanied with false description of the thing destroyed." John Ruskin, *The Seven Lamps of Architecture* (New York: Dover Publications, [1880] 1989), 194.

story constructed and maintained by human words and hands. Here in this fraught and fabled realm of "Carcassonne," Faulkner sets up a contest between "reality" and "imagination."

The dueling forces of "imagination" and "reality" seem to echo Wallace Stevens's modernist admonition that all poets (and artists, by association) must somehow reckon with the notorious predicament of Don Quixote. As a believer in outmoded romantic fictions, Quixote is alternately a fool, a dangerous madman, and an enduring hero. Faulkner's precarious poet's circumstances seem to echo this prescription that poets and artists must address quixotic delusions if they hope to contribute meaningfully to their age.[10] At the same time, the prescribed duel between Imagination vs. Reality in "Carcassonne" affirms other hierarchal dualisms that linger in Western art and literature. As Hamblin has it, the duel is between "the power of the creative imagination to reshape and transcend the narrow world it inhabits."[11] And this, Hamblin holds, represents the author's "overall conception of art": The poet/artist "as omnipotent god" creates a fabulous space of representation wherein the glorious force of human creative Imagination wins out against the "shabby, sorry world" of Reality. Whether or not the testy conversation between poet and bones in "Carcassonne" stands for Faulkner's entire "conception of art," the critic Hamblin echoes an enduring tendency of Western thought to view human imagination as a separate and transcendent force of nature, which mysteriously hovers above the muck of the muddy material world where the lower, less imaginative, less technologically adept, and all-around beastlier beings toil and strive and go the way of the flesh

10 Wallace Stevens, "Noble Rider and the Sound of Words," in *The Necessary Angel: Essays on Reality and the Imagination* (New York: Vintage Books, 1951), 27.

11 Hamblin, "Carcassonne in Mississippi," 151.

in mortal time. For what it's worth, Faulkner himself described the poet-protagonist of the story as "a young man in conflict with his environment."[12] Here he is, the isolated (male) artist, separated from the muck of the Real World so as to draw forth immortal beauty *sui generis* from the dross and shit of worldly entanglements, transforming the shabby everyday reality into poetic gold.

"Women are so wise. They have learned how to live unconfused by reality, impervious to it," writes Faulkner in "Carcassonne."[13] Taken out of context, this could seem pejorative. But from another angle, such imperviousness to certain versions of reality may be seen as a heroic trait, a kind of resistance, if for instance the reality in question is the global neoliberal capitalist dominion for which There Is No Alternative, as Iron Lady Thatcher famously put it. Medieval castles, monumental modernisms, and global capitalist schemes are not the only sites where patrilineal versions of what is "real" hold sway, of course. Our ontologies, mother tongues, and creative practices also reify certain ways of worlding along these lines. Despite decades of postmodern, feminist, and environmental artistic interventions, we find traces of separation between what is still considered the exceptional faculty of "human imagination" and the messy material makings of multispecies worlds.

Meanwhile, in a galaxy far from Yoknapatawpha and Carcassonne – and let's say specifically in the realm of twenty-first-century feminist science studies – we observe how the shabby, earthly "reality" that the Modern Poet must transcend has always been a construction,

12 Ibid.
13 Faulkner, "Carcassonne," 898. In an interesting turn, Faulkner scholar Deborah Clarke pitches the idea that some of Faulkner's female characters, like the unflappable Lena Grove, can be read as "outside" voices that push against patriarchal boundaries of their settings. Deborah Clarke, "Gender, Race, and Language in *Light in August*," *American Literature* 61, no. 3 (October 1989): 398–413.

even a reconstruction to suit modern tastes (like Carcassonne reimagined for bourgeois tourists by Viollet-
le-Duc). In *Simians, Cyborgs, and Women,* Donna Haraway
parses how the "real" is constructed, specifically in scientific discourses (and so, in many ways, contemporary
Western secular society): "Reality has an author. The
author always has a proper name, but it has a way of
disappearing into declarative sentences or even graphs
embedded in published papers issuing from well-funded
laboratories."[14]

How do we come to ground in this maze of multiple realities? In recognition of worlds made of complex
meshes, we are duty-bound to balk at the claim of any
universalized version of a Real. Old-fashioned cleavages
of "transcendent" human imaginations from dirt and
flesh and fur betray immersions in specific ecologies, in
kaleidoscopic multi-authored realities. Against this betrayal, relational creative practices work to honor them,
in places where earthly habitations need these interventions. Which is all to say, when I set out with Aliass to
punily pound the Mississippi dirt and asphalt, it was not
so much in hopes of accessing some timeless, universal
Human Real that Faulkner happened to tap and extract
from the landscape like a miner with motherlode. Instead, alongside Aliass I hoped to humbly inhabit new
kinds of largely indeterminate, ecological reals, always
present and evolving through bodies-in-timeplaces, in
every wild, weedy, multi-authored place we pass through.

Going Asstray...

Rumblesome, crackling energies resounded from "Carcassonne" and soon gave way to cracks and crevasses in the
text and new, brackish spaces between names and maps

14 Donna J. Haraway, *Simians, Cyborgs, and Women: The Reinvention of Nature* (New York: Routledge, 1991), 77.

and mortal territories. As if the words emitted a kind of radio static transmitting from some distant island continent believed till now to be uninhabited – maybe even that "last red rock hanging tideless in the red and dying evening," where Faulkner's poet stands alone and laureate on an Olympus of high-blown prose with his "inexhaustible voice." I was compelled to listen to its crazy music with special fascination, with an ever-lengthening ear cocked sideways. And then suddenly one day there it was, hidden in plain sight. From a literary node where transcendent (phal)logos, language, and authority battle the dirty realm of "dumb" bodies, up it flared like a secret signal of rebel life hidden within our overwrought fictions: Carcassonne.

Once again, that powerful little pattern of sounding letters, this little unassuming phoneme, blew open the ramparts between words and bodies, names and things, and made a new opening in the possibility of storying places. "Ass" blasted through the textual surface, shattering assumptions about the unimpeachable grip of logos and language on material (and even poetic, material-semiotic) reality. Lo and behold, this one particular "assinanity" – in the tension between real/imagined Mississippis and other kinds of timeplaces – made "Carcassonne" a vital site for intervention and resistance, and in the long run even an inevitable-ass destination.[15]

Though it could not serve as a real geographic destination for our journey across the US South, this cracked-open textual surface became an attachment site, a jumping-off place for a departure that might interrupt the surfaces of dominant narratives and representations of

---

15 "Assinanity" is a term, adapted from Jacques Derrida, which deals with dominant paradigms of logos, silence, and so on. Isabelle Stengers also offer vital insights on idiocy as a technique of resistance to ecological and global capitalist hegemony. Isabelle Stengers, "A Cosmopolitical Proposal," in *Making Things Public*, eds. Bruno Latour and Peter Weibel (Cambridge: MIT Press, 2005), 995–1003.

places, so as to dive toward untold stories of myriad lives. In choosing to depart (both literally and figuratively) from Faulkner's land-lorded literary landscape, the journey with Aliass became an artistic strategy kin to what Ronald Broglio describes as "minor art" in *Surface Encounters: Thinking with Animals and Art.* [16] Drawing from Gilles Deleuze and Felix Guattari's discussion of "minor literature," with their example of Franz Kafka's "impossible writing" as a Jew in a German-speaking Austrian world, Broglio proposes works of "minor art" whereby certain voices or kinds of meaning that are traditionally excluded from "major," established hermeneutic social circles discover moves that allow them to breach "the impasse that bars access."[17]

As an imaginal site full of flaming manes, thundering hoofbeats, and conflicted poet-skeleton musings, "Carcassonne" presented an odd little outpost on the map of the most majorest Southern literature there is. From the grand patriarchal literary dominion of a "major literature," as mapped across Faulkner's Yoknapawtapha, I set out with Aliass to embark on a thunderously explosive (if puny and humble) literary pilgrimage, seeking to "run astray" – wildly asstray, even – from dominant modern modes of storying in which only human ways of wor(l)ding matter. Meanwhile, a certain irony flickers in the

16 Ronald Broglio's work resonates here all the more so because he is interested in exploring the ways that "minor art" makes new kinds of spaces for thinking "alongside animals" and "against the power of representation, the power of major literature, and, one might add, established aesthetics": "*Man* and *animal* are linguistic subjects only within a properly established language. Once a 'minor literature' [or art] begins dismantling the common-sense ground on which meaning is established, man and animal become fragile signifiers that may run astray or 'deterritorialize.' They become available for 'asignifying intensive utilization of language.'" Ronald Broglio, *Surface Encounters: Thinking with Animals and Art* (Minneapolis: University of Minnesota Press, 2003), 107.

17 Ibid., 105.

notion of working against Faulkner's corpus as a "major literature"; in the realms of broader American literature, Faulkner has been considered by some to be a regional (read: minor) writer. While some readers revel in that special sound and fury that characterizes Faulkner's most gloriously obfuscate prose, other critics claim Faulkner's "thunder and music" are his downfall. As with the low-ass pun, unbridled lyricism allows language's musicality to ride roughshod over meaning, illuminating the limits of human logos to lord over material worlds.[18] So it was that with a coy but hopeful notion of immersing in the thunder and music of untold Mississippis, Aliass and I would bring our own puny ass thunder into the midst of a blown-open "Carcassonne" – where even Faulkner's lonesome "last red rock hanging tideless in the red and dying evening" becomes a more riotously full of life place than we ever thought possible.[19]

Coming into Como (Mississippi Hill County Blues)

The distinct musical thunder of Faulkner's prose certainly played a role in opening paths for the "Little Pilgrim of Carcassonne" mission, but it was a different and unexpected bodily encounter with another kind of Mis-

---

18 In an essay called "Faulkner's Patriotic Failure: Southern Lyricism versus American Hypervision," critic William Meyer holds that Faulkner's "music" is his great failure as an American artist. Faulkner remains a regional (read: Southern) writer, because his overblown lyricism excludes him from the ranks of what Meyer calls the great "hypervisual" American tradition. At the same time, and significantly, Meyer opines that this "failure" is also Faulkner's underdog greatness, tangled as it is in historical, social, and environmental "failures" tied to the South's defeated "past" and enduring racial, class, gender, and environmental frictions. William E.H. Meyer, "Faulkner's Patriotic Failure: Southern Lyricism versus American Hypervision," in Faulkner and the Craft of Fiction, eds. Doreen Fowler and Ann J. Abadie (Jackson: Univ. of Mississippi Press, 1987), 105–26.
19 Faulkner, "Nobel Prize Acceptance Speech," 71.

sissippi thunder that made the act of going back to that land with the spotted ass necessary. It was the same kind of thunder I heard throbbing in Sun Ra's "Nuclear War," which echoes and throbs with hidden violent histories and frayed hopes. And here is a strange but true detail. The first time I heard this special thunder, and came to know it in my bones, was at a place just a few miles from the same Mississippi highway exit for Como/Senatobia where I was struck and transformed by the Arkestra's explosive query – "what you gonna do about yer ass? – on that icy New Year's Day, 2001.

It happens in the previous fall of 2000, in a place called Como not far from the junctions of the state route and Yellow Dog Road. Down from New York on an aesthetic quest for rare "social music" of the American South, Adam Lore and I are hoping to gain an interview with Otha Turner, the 92-year-old king of Hill Country fife-and-drum music, and glean insights into the endemic and endangered fife-and-drum picnic tradition for Adam's zine, *50 Miles of Elbow Room*.[20] We have a set of sketchy directions to Turner's place, where the annual Turner Family Fife-and-Drum picnic is held every Labor Day weekend. The picnic is hardly a secret; at this turn of the millennium it has been happening for generations as a gathering for locals, but recent media interest in Turner and a new record release by his Rising Star Fife-and-Drum band means the yearly gathering has begun to attract a new demographic of middle-class white folks, and even Yankees like us. All are welcome, especially if they bring cash to buy goat-meat BBQ sandwiches and moonshine and hand-made cane fifes.

Coming into Como, the directions bring us along a grid of rural backroads. Single-wide trailers stand on weedy

20 For photographic documentation of this place and its players in the 1960s, see George Mitchell, *Mississippi Hill Country Blues 1967* (Jackson: University Press of Mississippi, 2013).

lots amidst vast swathes of harrowed crop-fields. We find Otha Turner's place, a few acres that sprawl out around a central shack close to the road, surrounded by scattered wooden structures hammered together from plywood scraps and old peeling signs. We pull up on the roadside in front of the shack, across the road from a steep weedy pasture where a billy goat watches from across the barbed wire, and park the Caprice. We then proceed to get out of the car and walk across the yard, blithely at first, still more or less comfortable in our skins, toward where two men sit on a wooden bench in the shade of an open slant-roofed structure in the steamy late August morning. One of the men is middle-aged and grizzled, and he watches us with a quizzical look as we approach. The other man is Otha Turner himself, and he watches us from his weathered wooden bench with an ancient, pale blue and ice-cold stare like nothing I ever saw or dreamed before. His gaze is as opaque and unwelcoming as a darkening sky – a sky that might rip open any second and lash a body with terrible lightning.

In the distance (thirty feet? thirty seconds? a thousand miles?) that we move across the yard in that withering gaze, I learn some things – or rather unlearn them. With every step, each and every tactic I acquired in the makings of a social human – ways I learned to behave over a lifetime among others in a variety of situations – fails utterly, one after another. I scramble inwardly for some kind of composure to click into place, but nothing fits this moment, this encounter. Every means I know to ingratiate myself – to signal goodwill, assume subtle power, or even (last ditch) suggest hair-twirling, girlish innocence – is blankly refused. Never have I felt with such fierce atomic clarity how every identity we perform is a scripted story we tell, and how every gesture and twitch is part of this performance – from the slant of shoulders to the ways we wear our faces. And what makes this so painfully, viscerally clear in this encounter is that Otha

Turner does not give a shit about any story or identity we bring. He plumb rejects any little biography we might offer up, whether in words or the ways we carry our bodies. He gazes at the air around us as if to locate the buzzing of gnats he'd swat away.

Somehow we keep walking across the yard. Adrenalin makes every detail of a passing moment as distinct as if it is frozen in time. In the dirt yard behind the shack, several goats with slit throats hang by their hind hooves and drip blood into plastic buckets. Their carcasses sway slightly in the breeze, and the glint of their eyes is not yet dimmed entirely. A rangy dapple gray colt stands watching from behind a few strands of rusted wire, hind leg cocked and tail flicking slowly back and forth against the flies. A dusty, dark old Buick sedan sits in the middle of the yard with windows rolled down and the radio blaring a thumping blues station. The air is viscous as oil and full of unfamiliar sounds and smells. We make it all the way to the edge of the shade under the slant-roofed structure where Otha and the other man sit. I have the vague, anachronistic sensation – borne of medieval fairy tales or more recent ones, maybe – that we are approaching a king on a throne, cowering for mercy and facing certain doom. My companion Adam summons the courage to speak, to introduce us and explain that we have come down from New York City in hopes of an interview. He says he spoke to someone on the phone a few weeks ago, who said to come on down early and try to catch Otha before the picnic preparations get crazy. Otha looks away toward the tall pines and mumbles, "I don't know nuthin' bout no New York."

High noon in Como, we stand abjectly in the dirt of the yard. Adam presses on, and eventually Otha's friend, Abron Jackson, exchanges some small talk with us in a bemused way. As for me, I am gone reeling. Cannot not look up from the pale dirt... vaguely aware of a low rumble of voices, but words are indistinguishable and very far away.

I have fallen out the bottom of the scene somehow, as if in the failure to present into the human social sphere in any appropriate or recognizable way, I have slipped into another kind of presence, beyond the sphere of social humans where I suddenly find myself so unwelcome. Like a child who is not capable of performing an adult social role, and so falls free to tune into everything else, I dissolve into the environment surrounding us and find, lo and behold, this is where the shit is really going down. In this moment I understand the significance of a scene from *Space Is the Place*, when a drunkard stumbles up to Sun Ra and says, "Hey man, what's happenin'..." And Sun Ra slyly, solemnly intones: "Everything is happening."[21]

The dirt is happening, humming along with strange sounds and smells of Otha's farm vibrating the thick and rich steamy late summer air, meshes of reverberating bodies, all held together in a visceral, immediate, and boundless substrate of living becomings of and in an earthly place. The gray colt stands yonder with his hind leg cocked, tail swishing, familiar and unknown. The shiny eyes of Otha's coonhounds peer through the wooden slats of their kennel, beyond where the goat carcasses sway and drip in the faint breeze under the screaming jay-blue sky, insects buzzing, pokeweed towering and vibrating in the heat, heavy with wine-dark bursting berries that possums and mockingbirds like to get drunk on, vines everywhere twining skyward, the stink-bearded billy goat watching and wandering in the weedy lot across the road, a three-legged dog basking in the middle of the hot asphalt road – a thousand wet and shining eyes, invisible beating hearts and lungs, flowing roots and insect tunnels and flight ways of birds and beetles in the sky above, and the thump-thump-thump and moanful twang of that Blues station coming from the dusty Buick. No el-

21 John Coney, dir., *Space Is the Place* (North American Star System, 1974).

ement separate from any other, no that or this or them or us, if only for a swirling moment. All dissolved in tremendous and tremulous opening, this dissolute immersion in a place both familiar and strange.

Over the years, this encounter in Otha Turner's homestead remained indelible, as a submerged and haunting scene of a world radically unzipped and yet somehow more whole, in a place (un)known as Mississippi. That visit to Como was a bone-shaking wake-up call to real and present, mostly erased histories bound up in historical, political, social, colonial, and ecological conditions both visible and hidden in that (and most any) landscape. Raw shame in the minefields of old and ongoing racial injustices, rooted in distinct ways in the American South, scared me deeply. But it was much more than that, too. Not until all these years later do I come to understand that it was this visceral, fearsome, and ultimately joyful dissolution in a wholly unreckonable Mississippi – more than any love for the "thunder and music" of literary fiction like Faulkner's or even the sublime gut-deep thump and cry of fife-and-drum music endemic to that place – that made me have to come back to Mississippi in the humble, long-eared listening company of a nameless she-ass.

Fearsome as the encounter was as a terminal crack in the edifice of white history and privilege, the experience at Otha Turner's farm that day was also a momentous opening, unfolding multiple Mississippis and eventually all (his)storied landscapes to new reckonings and complicities in their possible futures. That visceral experience – akin to dissolution in the Badlands but more grounded in a specific place's hidden ecologies – demanded immersion as a way of being in and becoming with places, listening into histories and untold stories hidden in flesh, soils, glands, roots, and sounds of environments. Como called for new and deeper reckonings with old stories we get told and believe about places, stories that shape the ones we tell ourselves about who and where we are, what is "real" and what is "imagined." So Como came to demand a different, full-bodied mode of radical listening and responsibility to different ways-of-being-in-places.

In the long run, it was to this blown-open, unmapped "Mississippi" that I was most deeply compelled to go with Aliass, to immerse and walk and listen deep for other histories than the redacted ones I was taught (and with a little prod from Sun Ra along the way). From Como came the hope that shedding dangerous kinds of naming and claiming to know might open more inclusive modes, tuning instead into real-ass presences and unfolding possibilities within them. As if this kind of stripped-down immersion might carry us into dreamy swamps and harrowed histories of Mississippi, Carcassonne, and so many other nameless places we never thought possible – yet always find ourselves passing through.

Snakes of Virginia

Southern thunderstorms are something else. What begins as a far-off throb, what could almost be rumbling guts, the distant rolling thuds at first blur the boundaries of inside and outside. Then the little wind comes to tell it: soon the bruise-colored cumulonimbi roll in and pour over the trees. The dogs slink into hiding, as the atmosphere darkens, darkens, darkens more, and the air grows thick-electric and begins to tremble like flesh. In the barn the horses get restless, stomp and blow, then go tense and still, waiting in their wooden stalls like seafaring cargo for the hammering hiss of hard rain on the metal roof. Thunder cracks close, then a breathless lull, then closer, and closer again, as the big winds roar up in a sudden swirl and the thunder booms and cracks hugely, right here, just as the sky rips opens and the first few splats of rain come, one by one kicking up a tiny cloud of dust before the world disappears in dripping veils. Come the lashes of lightning, and the every-which-way winds twist the heaving branches and pale underleaves as the forest canopy turns wild and inside out.

Thunderboomers like this used to come like gifts to the sweltering, humid dog-day afternoons of summer on the Virginia farm where I grew up. After lunchtime each day in July and August, we'd begin to hope and wait. We listened, mostly with our skins, for the hints of wind and thickening, for rumbles past the hazy blue horizon. The gifts of the storms, when they did come, were not just in the cooling off. All-encompassing atmospheric changes could shift the speed of time and bodies' boundaries, too. Once it happened in the thick moments just before a storm hit. I was racing to get a mare and foal in from the paddock when a black snake hurried across the dirt road in my path, moving fast from one thicket of shrubs to another. The black snake slithered furiously, with its sleek shiny head raised six inches off the ground. It seemed to cast about wild-eyed as it whipped across the open space of the dirt road. How a snake can have an almost comical, Chaplinesque expression of frantic worry is beyond my powers to describe. But I remember how it seemed, along with the strange feelings this chance crossing of paths stirred. In that naked moment with the snake I was struck by an unforeseen sense of kinship, as we each rushed for cover from the coming storm.

Few inhabitants of that old farm in the Appalachian Blue Ridge foothills – full as it was of domestic beasts and wilder ones, each hidden and exposed in our various ways among the rolling hill pastures and cedars groves and thickets of woody shrubs – were more incomprehensible to me than the snakes. I both feared and obsessed over them, and spent hours in the barn office poring over a hardback field guide someone had given us, simply titled *Snakes of Virginia*. That summer, violent and frequent thunderstorms supposedly washed scores of snakes down from the mountains – at least, that was the colloquial explanation for why the little creek pool beneath the culvert pipe became a vibrant and mesmerizing, knotty tangle of reptiles of every size and color for a few weeks: bright milk snakes and corn snakes, thick slit-eyed copperheads, and even the slow and blunt-nosed, seldom-seen hog snakes. Rumors also circulated that summer that the benign, enormous black snakes (who sometimes grew up to eight feet long) were interbreeding with venomous copperheads. This became an excuse for lords of the land to wantonly hack apart resident black snakes, who were mostly left alone otherwise to keep rodents at bay. (One huge black snake thick as a human arm, who lived in tunnels under our barn, grew lumpy-fat one summer on the generations of white and spotted laboratory mice and rats who thrived there after a kindhearted neighbor set them free from their glass cages.)

When they were not spectacularly tangled in the creek pool, the snakes of Virginia were a looming presence just at the edges of perception. I knew they were out there, hidden in the folds and cracks of the land. I used to fantasize that I had a magic power to snap my fingers and suddenly turn everything stark white except for the snakes, thus revealing in an instant exactly where each snake hid coiled or moved through the brush. Aside from the remote threat of viper's bite, danger was not what compelled this special fascination. It was that the snakes commanded a certain respect in their hiddenness. Their vaguely menacing, unseen presence was powerful and challenging. This mystery of invisible, wild presence was something I wanted to learn to *live with*. If asked back in those days, I would have said I'd rather not live with snakes, but the odd feelings stirred by the surprise pre-storm encounter with that black snake, as we crossed paths in a charged and vulnerable moment, said otherwise.

Remembering that encounter now feels like recalling a dear and long lost friend. That crossing-of-paths was a crack, a fleeting sliver of opening across boundaries of species and shared habitat I thought were impassable. The bodies we lived in were as different as vertebrates can get, yet the thunder still meant something to both of us. When the thunder says it's time to move, each and every body heeds it, every one sensing in our own ways that our worlds are about to get changed – whether just wet and muddy or washed away, annihilated.

Mostly summer thunderstorms on the farm were cool relief on sweltering afternoons, but they were laced with dangers, too. Snakes displaced by torrents piled up in the creek. Once my wiry little mother was thrown back ten feet in an arc across the dirt road when a bolt of lightning hit her through the metal pasture gate. And do not forget that phone call from Johnny, from the dark Nelson County hollow hideout where he went to live those years after the farm was lost and the family scattered. The call was unexpected. His voice cracked in a way I'd never heard as he told me how Zak and Tarbaby and the new gray mare whose name I forget were all three lost in a green mountain thunderstorm the day before, when lightning struck their shade oak in the pasture, shot up through the roots and into their bodies through their metal shoes. No human saw it happen. One can only imagine how a few minutes later the storm must have passed, as they do, leaving only cooler air and glistening leaves and grass. Johnny found them later that afternoon, laying where they fell under the big oak tree, their bones all shaken loose and their soft eyes blown out like bulbs.

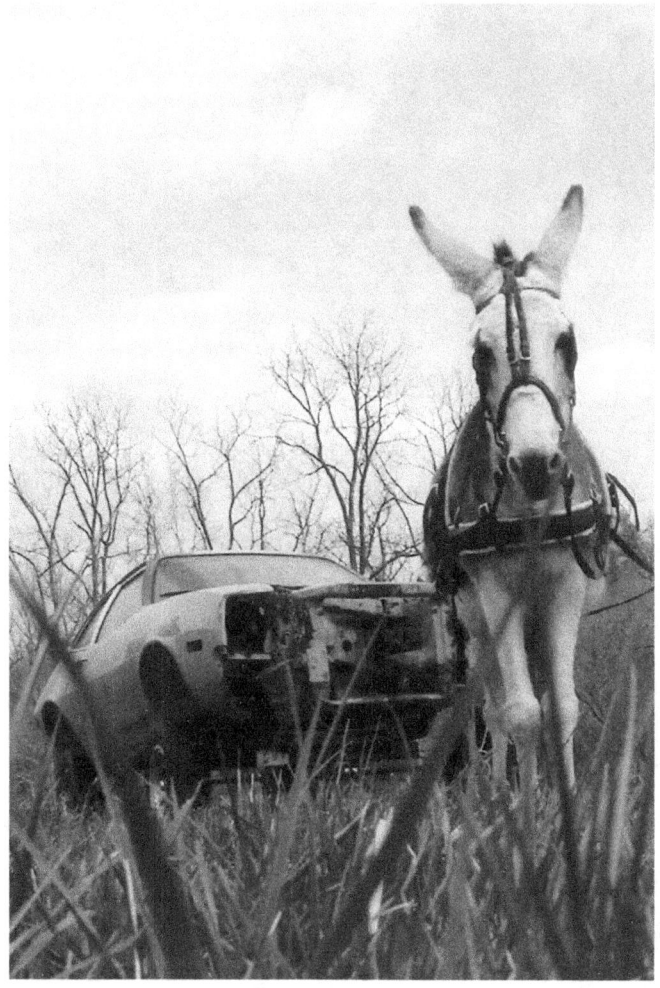

Fig. 1. Aliass with an early incarnation of the Dead-Car Wagon. Photograph by Jack Christian.

6

DEAD-CAR CROSSING

Gee, Death! Haw, Time! Alas, did I truly believe I could keep my hands on the wheel of driving global futures by holing up with my little spotted ass family in a heavenly wild rural Appalachian hideout?

For a while I kind of believed this, yes.

Preserving hard-won idylls of passtoral peace is assuredly a worthy enterprise, as philosophers far back as Lucretius assert. But say we do find the *locus amoenass* we seek. We may glory in it for a time, but eventually we come to see, one way or another, that the shelters we call home are only stable so long as we grasp that no peace (not even a sweet Virginia peace-of-ass) can ever be static. Bulldozing into any idyll of cattle-dotted pastures and wild hard-wooded hills comes the inevitable big *but*. Even the deepest sull (short of death) can only pretend to hold back the Roundup-Ready, Tar Sands-burning geopolitical ravages of our times for so long.[1]

---

1 I like big "buts," I cannot lie, but when it comes to the gravitas of negotiating fraught care of asses in twenty first century global neoliberal capitalist technocracies, they proliferate and grow bigger at times than one might prefer. On the ancient art of idealizing one's pastoral locus amoenass, see Lucretius, *On the Nature of the Universe* (New York: Penguin Books, 1994), 38–39.

Almost Heaven

For two years after we arrived in the Roanoke Valley at the end of our long-ass journey across the South, Aliass and I lived in daily wonder and grassy sustenance on the splendorous 100-acre, mountain-ringed expanse of a magnificent old farm, tucked into the Appalachian range near a little hilltop town of Fincastle. Aliass had a roomy box stall in a corner of the sprawling barn and a little paddock beside, where she slowly ate holes through big round bales of local grass hay. The Mutt of Gold and I settled into a small cabin on a ridge overlooking a sweeping valley pasture, surrounded by woods and blue-black mountains and edged to the northeast by the roiling, magical, many-colored Catawba Creek. The Mutt of Gold had spent that summer with my mother when Aliass and I were on the road. It had been a tough decision, but in the end I realized my concern for her safety and well-being, and hers for me, would make it too difficult to undertake the journey with the kind of openness necessary. As always, reuniting with the Mutt at the end of the journey was like slipping back into my skin. So the Mutt and Aliass and I spent the halcyon late summer and early fall of 2002, waiting for "the Passenger" to arrive. In a fog of blown-out exhaustion after a harrowing summer on the road, coming back to the elusive Lost Virginia – arriving into this phenomenal farmscape of astonishing beauty, grassy swathes of pastures and cedarblown towering sycamore creeksides and ridges – made it feel like we had achieved a kind of happy-ass afterlife. "Almost heaven," as John Denver has it.[2] A veritable passtoral paradise.

2   These are the opening words of John Denver's classic sentimental mountain song, "Take Me Home, Country Roads," and a rather ironic soundtrack, since the present state of many places in West Virginia is about as far from the idea of heaven as one can get. John Denver, "Take Me Home, Country Roads" *Poems, Prayers & Promises* (RCA, 1971), https://www.youtube.com/watch?v=1vrEljMfXYo/. Meanwhile, Beth

The first few nights after we landed on the Fincastle farm, the Mutt and I had slept in the barn beside Aliass's stall, then eventually moved into the cabin. The weeks wore on as we waited. Equines most often give birth at night, but I had none of the fancy stall video monitors or alarm devices that breeders use to keep alert to impending labors and possible complications. In early September, I would lie in the dark of the cabin on the ridge with the windows open all night, listening toward the barn in the valley below through the hoot-owl calls and trilling raccoons. I listened like this all night long, with all my nerves tense, as if the unknown energies of the night woods and tall grass fields might somehow transmit what was unfurling inside Aliass's body. Eventually the Mutt and I moved back to sleeping in the barn, curled up in a tent in the stall next to Aliass, listening in half-sleep. Those nights we dreamed amidst the burping ruminations of sheep in the fold across the barn aisle, the scrabblings of unseen possums in the beams and rafters, and the curious snufflings of a pair of standard poodles named Rubens and Guggenheim, who belonged to another artist-tenant and often stayed in the dog run next to the barn. The poodles peered in at us, on and off all night long, their faces popping up on the other side of the chain-link to sniff and blink from under their curly mops of fur.

When Aliass finally began to labor, it was a bright mid-September afternoon. The foaling went on into the hours of the night. The birthing process was likely fairly normal, but harrowing nonetheless, as Aliass groaned and writhed on the ground for hours with her muzzle contorted in a terrible grimace. Finally a little pale bulb

Stephens and Annie Sprinkle offer a revolutionary ecosexual mode of resistance to the devastations of mountaintop-removal mining in West Virginia. See Beth Stephens, dir., *Goodbye Gauley Mountain: An Ecosexual Love Story* (Fecund Arts, 2015).

began to emerge from her vulva, and then with a few more groaning thrusts from Aliass, the whole shiny wet ghostly-pale sac that held the foal slid out and lay quietly pulsing in the straw. In the dim light of a dusty bulb, Passenger was born at last.

The next morning after the vet's foal-check visit, I followed a deep urge to carry the placenta and amniotic sac out across the Great Pasture and give them to the creek. It was a little ritual, pitched with desire to share the good fortunes and rare treasures we'd gathered on the long-ass journey and harrowing labor's happy outcome, in gratitude for our present habitation in this most beautiful place. I had some vague desire to share the happy event of Passenger's birth within what Gary Snyder calls the "deep world's gift economy."[3] I didn't have much clue who out there might enjoy the placenta (or Hoo, I should say, given an intense encounter with a Great Horned Owl who stared me down with huge yellow eyes one day from a sycamore limb beside the creek, in a way that still makes my hair stand up when I think of it). But I wanted somehow to share the bounty with other inhabitants of the place, recognized and unknown. So I carried the placenta and amniotic sac in a bucket to the creek-side and stood with the Mutt of Gold on the bank, exhausted and grateful. As I released the placenta into the rolling water, the amniotic tissues flowed around shiny black rocks and into a pool, where the deeper creek-water twisted and filled and billowed it up like a ghost. In one sense, I never felt closer to the presence of that other mother tongue I had searched for so long – never felt so deeply part of a matrix of lives and ways unfolding and woven through an environment. Meanwhile, the reception of this ritual

3 Ronald Grimes, "Performance is Currency in the Deep World's Gift Economy: An Incantatory Riff for a Global Medicine Show," *ISLE: Interdisciplinary Studies in Literature and Environment* 9, no. 1 (2002): 149–64.

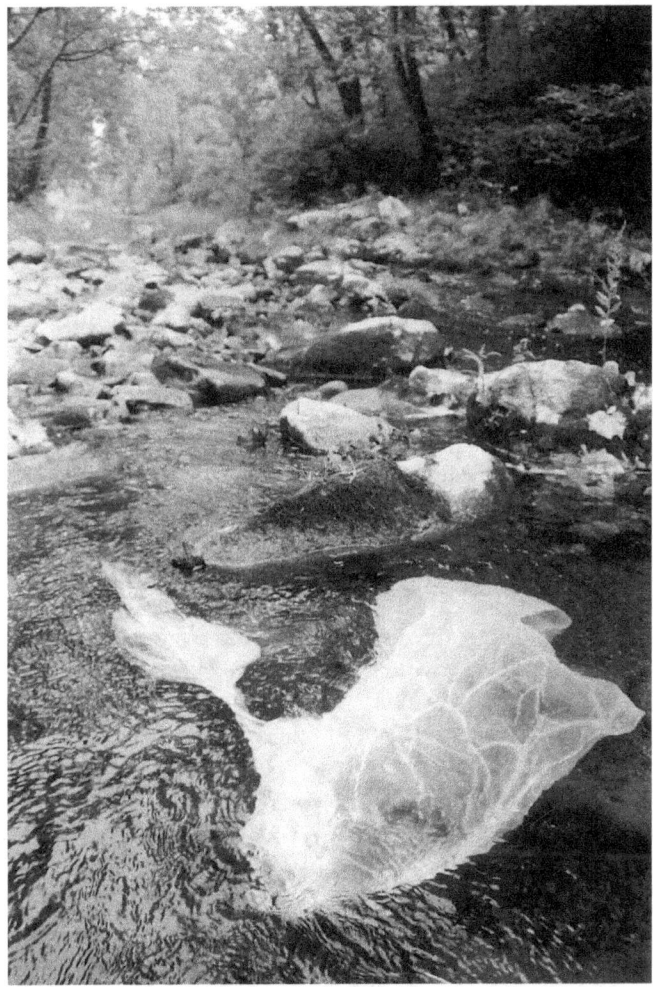

Fig. 2. The amniotic sac that held Passenger within Aliass floats in the Catawba Creek. Photograph by the artist.

in its wider watershed ecology remains entirely uncertain. For all its intentions toward generosity and wishful connection, this same gesture might be for others an act of pollution.

Given all this, I can't fathom if it is easier or harder to reckon with threats posed by ourselves and others to beloved places where creeks and mountains roll, full of wildly unknown lives and energies and torqued histories, where spotted asses graze and frolic among industrialized techno-cattle in historic global pastures. But I do know that writing this, *wanting this*, feels like grasping toward a ragged and fantastic old dream. But no place is safe or unchanging. Porous mortal beasts of every kind must find ever-shifting ways to navigate highways and low ways, ever-changing lands and global cyberspaces. So, like the recognition that holding "timeless wilderness" inside national parks is mostly a quaint tourist's dream or savvy marketing ploy – a mirage maintained by historically fraught and complex territorial and biopolitical negotiations among scientists and other fauna, from reintroduced gray wolves and grizzly bears to mosses and microbes – I slowly grasped that our passtoral way of life in Fincastle was precarious and terminable.[4] At the same time, a certain scrappy resistance, gathered from wanderings with a certain stoic beast, led me to grasp this: if any fragile, contingent peace-of-ass is to survive, its articulated forms must be retrofit for rough roads and turbulent times. In other words, a twenty-first-century nomadic ass family has gotta have some kind of wheels. And when the time comes to move, it better be ready to roll.

So it was that in the summer of 2004, a strange American hybrid vehicle known as the Dead-Car Wagon made a

4   William Cronon, "The Trouble with Wilderness: or Getting Back to the Wrong Nature," in *Uncommon Ground: Rethinking the Human Place in Nature,* ed. William Cronon (New York: W.W. Norton & Co., 1995), 69–90.

slow crossing, departing from the gates of a rural Virginia NASCAR speedway and heading south, to end its journey across the state line in Rockingham County, North Carolina, in a deserted church parking lot in a sad town called Eden. Resurrected from the stripped body of a 1980 Ford Pinto, the Dead-Car Wagon was pulled by a team of American asses, Aliass and Brawnson, and driven by two human "poets" who grappled with a knotty mass of aesthetic and ethical drives and desires, vague hopes, and idyll longings.[5] As a vehicle of human imagination, the Dead-Car Wagon was a strange material-cultural-artistic articulation, hitching vague aspirations of human meaning-making to the fearsome physical and cultural weight of a scary American automobile and then launching it dangerously into a rural Southern transportation infrastructure. Out on the roadways for three harrowing days and nights, the grim and surprising specter of the Dead-Car Wagon rattled southward, creaking ominously amid the groaning frictions of flesh and fur, metal on metal and sweaty leather, and of course rubber on the road. Just exactly where this thing hoped to go, and whether it could ever arrive at any real ass destination, remains an open question.

5   I put the word "poet" in scare quotes on behalf of my own reluctance to claim the designation; fellow Dead-Car teamster Jack Christian is a full-blown, innovative contemporary poet who not only claims the name but gives it new relevance and bad-ass audacity for our age. See Jack Christian, *Family System* (Fort Collins: Center for Literary Publishing, 2012).

Dead-Car Radio (The "Practice of Outside")

The car is still travelling. It runs through the kingdoms of
the dead picking up millions of passengers.
– Jack Spicer, "Ferlinghetti"[6]

Among the beautiful blue-black Appalachian hills and pastures, dwellings, and hardwood forests of rural South-west Virginia – where Aliass and I landed at the end of our long-ass journey, where Passenger was born, and where we found a home that I loved deeply but could not sustain – the Dead-Car Wagon arose like a mangled metal apparition from some oily underworld. It grew up from a site where poetics of fraught American places meet material traces of soils and grasses, mines and metals, trees and shade, and shiny black creeks of Appalachian landscapes with their own secret dreams and half-buried histories.

Taking up residence in the phenomenal environment of Fincastle, Virginia had been a stroke of amazing good fortune for me, second only to finding the wondrous ass herself back in Tennessee. Along with magical conjurations of my mother, who found the Fincastle cabin-for-rent while Aliass and I were out on the road, another factor had also helped to land us in this specific blissful habitation: I had gained a spot in a unique yearlong creative-writing Master's degree program at Hollins University in nearby Roanoke. That fall I began the program, wherein the pressure to generate written works in the form of poems, stories, or literary nonfiction was intense and unrelenting. I was lucky to get in; the program was small and competitive back then, renowned for turning out small batches of writers like a fine whiskey under the loose and ludic guidance of the inimitable literary magi-

6   Jack Spicer, "Ferlinghetti," in *The Collected Books of Jack Spicer* (San Francisco: Black Sparrow Press, 2002), 133.

cian, Richard H.W. Dillard. And really, I should have had it made. As I was told by one of my teachers, it should be a piece of cake to write up my long-ass journey, as a journey is by nature a linear narrative. All I had to do was recollect and render those experiences into colorful prose scene by scene, and I would have a compelling memoir, easy as pie. The golden rule of creative writing: write what you know. Haw!

Indeed, it might have been easy, if not for the insistent, burning desire to find ways to inhabit and frame untold/ untellable tales at the overlapping edges of human–assine adventures – that is, that fervent desire to let wordless interweavings of bodies-in-time *be the text,* which in turn drove a longstanding refusal to take on authorship of experiences with Aliass. Even more so now that we were immersed in the brimming presences of such a phenomenal environment, printed words on a page seemed woefully inadequate as means to reckon with questions of becomings and belongings within in a barely reckoned multispecies world. So that year in Fincastle became a kind of artistic pressure cooker, where pushes to generate good poems and prose rubbed against the drive to make spaces otherwise, for diverse and even imperceptible naturalcultural meshes to express their own stories in places. Even as I immersed in inspiring literary works and churned out page after page of text, the urge to address such questions directly beckoned me to move *beyond* words on printed page, *beyond* writing poems or lyrical short stories in any form previously tapped. How could bodies moving through timeplaces become a different kind of poetic gesture, written (or not) with respect for the hidden layers of places and others we find ourselves among?

This pressing question became the main fuel for the project called the Dead-Car Crossing, which emerged over passing seasons in Fincastle like a scary flowering from roots in performance art, poetics, and most of all from the rural Southwest Virginia landscapes that powered its drives and longings most materially (not with gas but with local grass and hay). Merging poetic urges with the drive to ground human imagination in material bodies and ecologies, the Dead-Car Wagon evolved as a collaborative performance with poet Jack Christian, a native Virginian who also, it so happened, had a newfound passion for possible poetics-of-outside, and an eye for the mangled glories of junkyards and hidden histories sunk in marred and majestic Appalachian hollers.

A.M. Radio (Pontiac)

> The boy perceives the voiceless moment: he hears
> a grim man charging two mules locked in a yoke
> to drag the carcass to the edge of the field.
> – Maurice Manning, "Pontiac"[7]

One fine autumn day I was in the barn mucking out Aliass and Passenger's stall. Lost in thought, I rolled the wheelbarrow down the aisle and out to the manure pile, which was growing day by day in a grassy spot at the back of the barn suggested by the farm's beneficent landlord, Fred Taylor. Oak and poplar leaves fluttered down from the trees. All of a sudden, as if seeing it for the first time, I noticed the hulking frame of an old maroon Pontiac Catalina that was quietly rusting away in tall grass, weeds, and vines in the grassy place next to where I dumped manure. The presence of a dead car was not in itself noteworthy; defunct vehicles are everywhere. Like a new breed of postindustrial ghost or monstrous roadside weed, they sit still in all weathers and slowly rust away in cluttered yards and other abandoned places. That omnipresence made it all the more strange when all of a sudden this

7   Maurice Manning, "Pontiac," in *Lawrence Booth's Book of Visions* (New Haven: Yale University Press, 2001), 28.

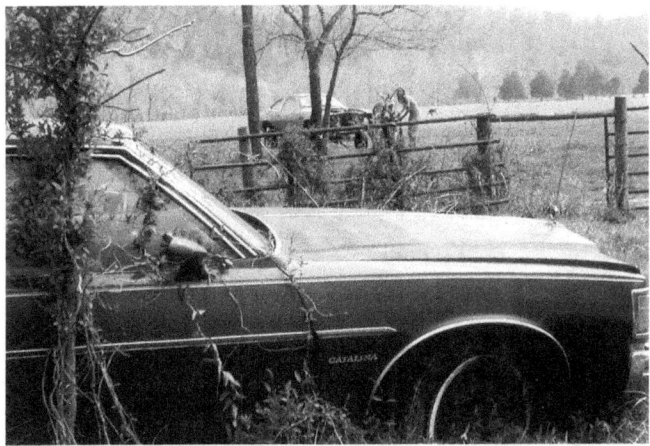

Fig. 3. Dead Pontiac Catalina, aka "American Masturbator," mother of the Dead-Car Wagon. Photograph by Jack Christian.

dead maroon sedan snagged my attention in a different way, almost as if it was emitting a transmission just below conscious hearing. Then an even stranger thing happened. As if the old Pontiac Catalina had spoken directly to me with a desire to reveal its own secret name, a pair of words came blaring into my head: "American Masturbator."

Surprised and delighted by this little irruption from the seeming undermesh of poetic imagination, I seized upon the phrase, and from then on I knew the dead Pontiac – rooted in its grassy site beside a patch of hardwoods behind the barn near the little hidden pond where peeper-frogs make insane springtime choruses – by this peculiar epithet. At the intersection beside the rusty red gate into the Great Pasture, the rusting hulk of metal, plastic, vinyl, oily residues, and mouse-nested wires known as American Masturbator effectively came alive as a vital figure and imaginative transport. This dead car with its stolen Native American name became a kind of opening or intersection in the understoried landscapes of the

Fincastle farm, as the heat-seeking imperatives of poetic imagination slowly fused with hidden histories and wilder environs in which the possible new lives of this dead vehicle were enmeshed. From then on, in daily comings and goings around the barn, I had newfound regard for the Pontiac Catalina and its secret cargos. I began to pay attention, tune in and listen for its transmissions. As if in that unexpected encounter, the dead-car radio was suddenly, invisibly *switched on*.

Looking back on this seminal scene reminds me of an episode in Robin Wall Kimmerer's *Gathering Moss,* in which she describes how one day the familiar forest landscape around her longtime research station seemed to open a lit path and literally lead her to a new place. This encounter gave her both scientific and spiritual insights into her work of studying mosses – insights that seemed to come straight from the assembled ecologies of the rocks and mosses themselves. Kimmerer's scene draws on her native Potawatomi heritage, describing the cultural orientation whereby living lands communicate directly with human inhabitants in webs of mutual respect.[8]

The sense of plants, birds, or mossy boulders "speaking" directly to humans is not an integral part of my own Western cultural heritage or philosophical tradition in the way it is for Kimmerer, but the experience she describes is nevertheless familiar, if from a different cultural inheritance. Artistic and poetic practices of all stripes tend to rely on the sense by which impulses and layered figures seem to arrive from "outside" the sphere of rational thought. And in a way, that day, I was especially primed for such ethereal transmissions. I had just fallen in love with the *Collected Books* of Jack Spicer, a poet whose body

---

8   Robin Wall Kimmerer, *Gathering Moss: A Natural and Cultural History of Mosses* (Corvallis: Oregon State University Press, 2003), 1–6.

of work famously relies on a distinct practice of tapping into an "outside" of language.[9]

This (in)human "outside" is the subject of the influential essay "The Practice of Outside," by Spicer's dear friend and fellow poet, Robin Blaser. In this homage, Blaser describes a distinct mode of drawing on irrational connections as Spicer's means to go beyond "the humanisms which do not measure up."[10] Spicer's poems unfailingly disturb and unsettle logical and linear thought, while at the same time stirring a haunting familiarity and warmth, through a welter of visceral feelings unmoored from rational sources. Reading Spicer feels like having conversations with ghosts – and not necessarily human ones, either. These poems are like dialogues with the humans we have never been.[11]

In "Heads of the Town Up to the Aether," one of the serial poems in Spicer's *Collected Books*, mythical shades like Orpheus and Eurydice flit in and out amid fragments of baseball statistics, commercial jingles, and San Francisco gay-bar jokes. Shadowy presences float through the multilayered poems like scraps of radio heard from a distance, and Spicer makes both ghosts and old-fashioned radios resonate.[12] Mingling in the airwaves of that Fincastle autumn with Spicer's ghostly voices, then, the

9   Jack Spicer's Vancouver Lectures in particular describe this aspect of this practice, which in typical Spicerian fashion he likens to communications of "little green Martians." Major lectures and other important insights are collected in Spicer, *The House that Jack Built: The Collected Lectures of Jack Spicer,* ed. Peter Gizzi (Middletown: Wesleyan University Press, 1998).

10 Robin Blaser, "The Practice of Outside," in *Jack Spicer, The Collected Books of Jack Spicer* (San Francisco: Black Sparrow Press, 2002), 345. o

11 This wording echoes Haraway's specific reinvention of "We have never been human" in *When Species Meet,* which in turn borrows from Bruno Latour's significant assertion that "We have never been modern." See Bruno Latour, *We Have Never Been Modern,* trans. Catherine Porter (Cambridge: Harvard University Press, 1993).

12 In one of his fake "explanatory" footnotes in "Homage to Robert Creeley," Spicer writes, "the recalling of Cegeste's voice was done on a

old dead Pontiac rose up as an ideal poetic vehicle (especially with its odd and monstrous doppelganger known as "American Masturbator"). Maybe because I sensed the impending end of times in our blissful Fincasstle homestead, the desire to stop time and tune into barely audible, beyond-human voices that flowed through the woods and creeksides and deep in the barndark was more intense than ever. After all, in its slow change from gas-guzzling automobile to decaying habitat for birds, mice, and honeysuckle vines, a dead car stands for a kind of stopped time. And as it turned out, I was going to need this special mode of transport sooner than I realized.

Jack Spicer may be onto something when he says that "a poet is a time mechanic and not an embalmer."[13] Either way, in spite of the fact that living with a little happy ass family in the gorgeous hills and coyote howl echoes of southwest Virginia taught me a few tricks by which to slow, distort, and even turn sweet-ass moments inside-out, I could not stop time altogether. Seasons passed in Fincasstle. Little furry Passenger grew bigger, and the grass and vines, thistles and glory-beaming pawpaws came and went. With the end of academic funding, limited prospects in a depressed Southwest Virginia job market threatened the home and barnyard economics of the peace-of-ass rooted in that place.

I did not know where we would go, but I knew this much: If we had to leave Fincasstle, it would be an uprooting unforeseen. If I had to move the ass family from this hard-won dream of Virginia belonging, such a departure would require extraordinary transportation. Indeed, the vision came to me one day that the only way to leave this place would be with a wagon, a kind of catafalque made of the dead Pontiac Catalina, pulled by a team of asses.

horse in one version and a car radio in the other. Both made it seem natural." Spicer, *The Collected Books of Jack Spicer*, 134.

13 Ibid., 25.

Pinto Madness

The articulation began as a notebook scrawl, a stick-fig-ure sketch in which a team of three spectral asses (two abreast and one up front, known as the Unicorn Hitch) pulled the carcass of the dead Pontiac through indeter-minate space.[14] The impulse to make a journey was in-evitably bound to previous experiences on the road with Aliass. Whether writing poems or refusing to do so, simi-lar pressures – to make imagination do concrete and "real ass work in the world" and to attend to beloved places in climates of frayed histories and threatening global fu-tures – fueled the creative energies that went into bring-ing the Dead-Car Wagon from notebook scrawl to mate-rial incarnation.[15]

In any real sense, though, it would require a serious mule team – more asspower than Aliass alone could ever generate – to pull the motherlode of American Mastur-bator from its green hole. Over time, the vision evolved as the impulse did not fade. If the Dead-Car Wagon was really going to take to the road, it would be necessary to find a smaller substitute for the Catalina. That was when the Ford Pinto came onto the scene in a fiery burst of green ass flames. The inevitable companion to the im-plosive cultural figure of American Spotted Asses, this quintessential American car was loaded with its very own explosive hidden cultural weight and woeful scorched capitalist histories. I vaguely remembered the Pinto as the butt of bad-car jokes in the 1980s, but research into the history of the popular Ford model revealed the noto-

14 On "articulation," see Stuart Hall, *Critical Dialogues in Cultural Studies*, eds. David Morley and Kuan-Hsing Chen (London: Routledge, 1996), 113–34.

15 Some of the wording and insights here come from an unpublished talk that Jack Christian and I gave at American Studies Association conference in Washington, DC in 2005, where we spoke on a panel titled "Performance."

rious Pinto's special role as the black burn mark in American automotive history.[16] Most folks are not aware of the actual record of motorists maimed or killed because of a design flaw that the Ford Motor Company engineers knew about but did not fix for max economic gain: the Pinto's bumper was only two inches from the gas tank, and so any rear-end collision over ten miles per hour could, and often did, cause the car to explode. At higher speeds, a bump from behind sometimes caused the doors to jam, trapping passengers inside the burning vehicle. Indeed, on the frozen January afternoon that the Pinto came to Fincastle from rural Maryland, a neighbor came by to look it over and recalled, sometime in the late 1970s, passing the burnt asphalt of an entrance ramp in Indianapolis where a woman and two children were immolated in a Pinto the day before.

But more than all that grim history, it was the Pinto's resonance with American Spotted Asses that made it inevitable, "Spotted Ass" being, of course, a fanciful name for pinto donkeys. As it turns out, even the mottled hides of Aliass and Passenger articulate a darker underside of American history. As a kid growing up around the colonial horse worlds of the Northeast US and later Virginia, I vaguely remembered a time or two when I heard someone say that spotted horses "don't belong in the show ring." When I dug into this a bit – asking friends about their own memories and finding a few relevant texts – I discovered what I suspect is at the heart of this old prejudice, in the US, anyway: a holdover from nineteenth- and early-twentieth-century associations of pinto coloring with the so-called "Indian pony." As Frank Roe put it plainly back in 1955: "The plainsmen regarded

16 Mark Dowie, "Pinto Madness," *Mother Jones,* September/October 1977, https://www.motherjones.com/politics/1977/09/pinto-madness/. This classic article from *Mother Jones* is subtitled: "For seven years, the Ford Motor Company sold cars in which it knew hundreds of people would needlessly burn to death."

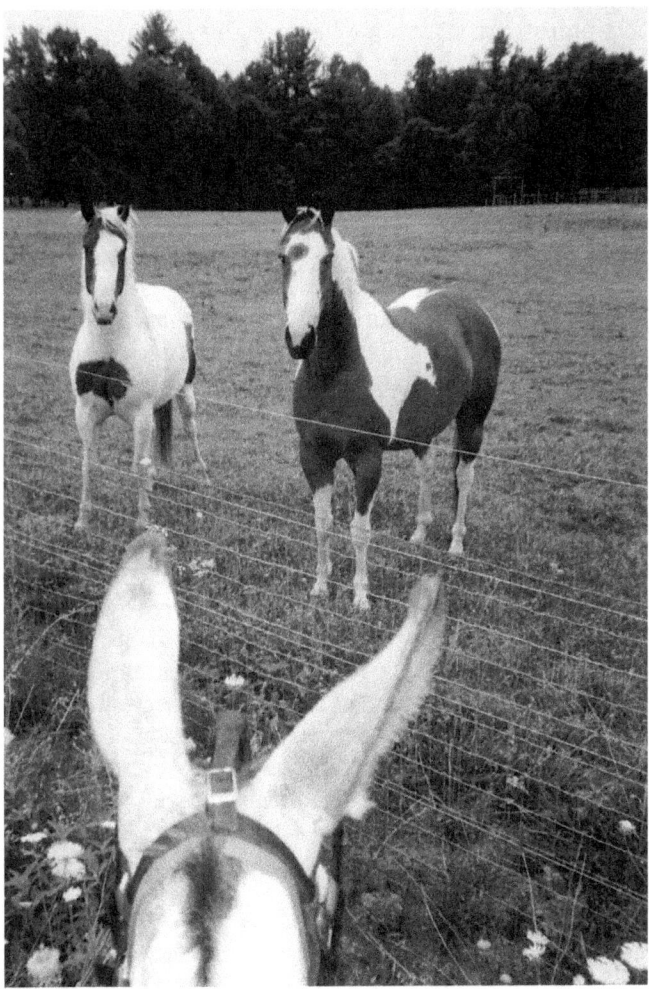

Fig. 4. A pair of Paint Horses that Aliass and I came across one morning as we passed a longhorn cattle ranch in rural Tennessee. The horses were aesthetically matched to the bovines they grazed among. Photograph by the artist.

the pinto with contempt because the Indian liked it."[17] Similar racially charged associations came from England and Europe more broadly, where spotted coats on horses have long been associated with gypsies and considered anathema in thoroughbred breeding (with a few notable exceptions).[18]

In some cultural configurations, pinto coloring is still associated with "bad breeding," while other cultural sites and institutions, like the American Council of Spotted Asses and the American Paint Horse Registry, have embraced the genetic inheritance of spots with fetishistic enthusiasm.[19] In the late-twentieth-century West and beyond, I saw pinto horses come to symbolize certain kinds of "American pride" and even the ubiquitous height of horse color fashion in various arenas. To wit: Countless times I have watched local rodeo queens parade past in a spray of glitter and fake flowers, or gallop into the rodeo arena with a flourish, on black-and-white pintos. They thunder around the arena in spangled red-white-and-blue attire, while the queen waves or brandishes an enormous Old Glory and the loudspeaker blares some stirring modern-country anthem of American patriotism.

By whatever means equine pinto genes came to stand as synonymous with certain breeds of American "freedom," this blurry conflation of piebald spots and stars-

---

17 Frank Roe, *The Indian and the Horse* (Norman: University of Oklahoma Press, 1955), 171.

18 Richard Nash, email communication; Harriet Ritvo, *Noble Cows and Hybrid Zebras* (Charlottesville: University of Virginia Press, 2010).

19 Founded in 1962 against the odds (of racist, misogynist, anti-pinto cultures) by Oklahoma cowgirl Rebecca Tyler Lockhart, the American Paint Stock Horse Association is now the second most successful and popular horse breed association in the world. This promotional video from the American Paint Horse Association on YouTube gives a sense of the history and worldwide scope of present-day Paint popularity. aphavideo, "American Paint Horse Association: A History," *YouTube*, September 10, 2018, https://www.youtube.com/watch?v=U9mLOpt3oik.

and-stripes apparently proved a bold and ready mar-keting tactic for the Ford Motor Company in the 1970s. When I first began to consider the Ford Pinto model for the Dead-Car Wagon, I found a postcard on eBay that provides an interesting articulation, to which I articulate another, different version of the spotty American history hidden in these forms and names. Significantly, this cul-tural shift coincides with the allure of the pinto leading to the organization of the American Council of Spotted Asses in Montana in 1969. If indeed the pairing of the Ford hatchback and young Pinto horse in this postcard was intended to evoke a promising nexus of freedom and speed, as seems to be the case, then the newfangled American Spotted Ass version, where a young Passenger faces off with the dead car, means to present an ironic challenge to the assumptions behind American freedom and need-for-speed, which is anything but free.[20]

I found the broken-down, orange 1980 Ford Pinto on eBay and made arrangements to purchase it and haul it back to the farm in Fincastle from the rural Maryland town where it had sat rusting for years. As it happened, the seller was a young man named Blaze, who ran a vine-yard and, oddly enough, kept a pair of Medicine Hat pin-to horses with his girlfriend. Adding to the somewhat spooky and ominous mood of the Pinto's acquisition is the fact that the town where we picked it up in the dead of winter is the same one where the scary Blair Witch Project legend and film took place. The dead car arrived in Fincastle on a frigid New Year's Day 2004. There it slid ominously off the U-Haul tow dolly and settled on the brittle winter gravel, gloomily awaiting its resurrection in the driveway beside the barn.

In order for the Dead-Car vision to leave the imagined spaces of the hard drive and notebook page, the project

20 Stephanie LeMenager, *Living Oil: Petroleum Culture in the American Century* (Oxford: Oxford University Press, 2014).

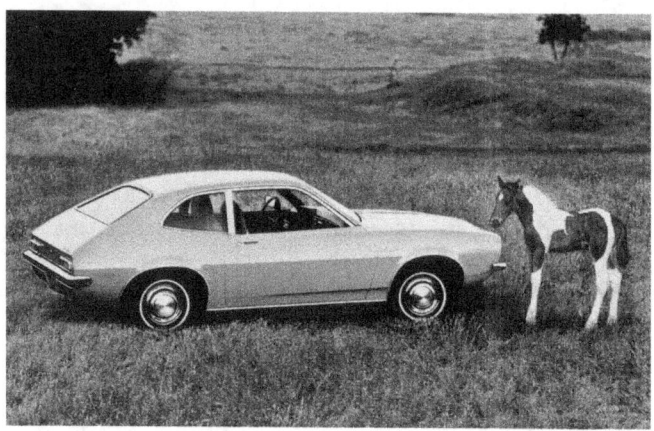

Fig. 5. 1971 Ford Pinto promotional postcard purchased from eBay.

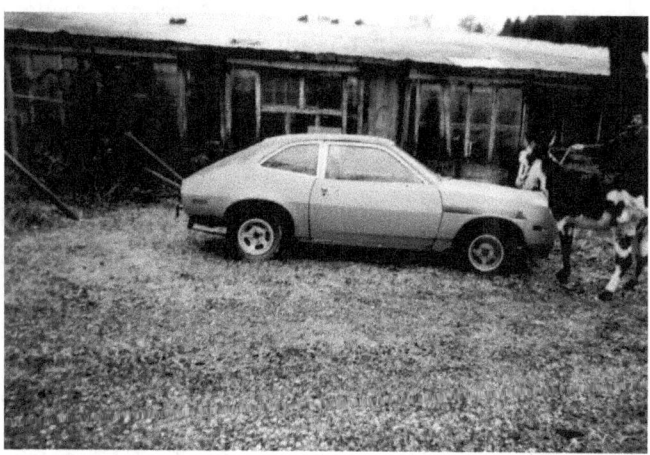

Fig. 6. Passenger poses with Jack Christian and the carcass of the 1980 Ford Pinto in Fincastle, January 2004. Photograph by the artist.

required the real material transformative tools and magic of barn and the body shop. Quite literally, the Dead-Car Wagon was born of a place, when Fred Taylor, renegade engineer and landlord of the Fincastle farm, took the project under his wing – or more specifically, into his fully outfitted mechanical shop and more so his imagination and skill set. Through the deep winter and into the spring, the shop rang with a clatter of hammering, drilling, and welding of mangled metal scraps, while the asses called impatiently from the nearby barn for breakfast or dinner. Deep in the shop night after night, we tore into wire harnesses and rusted bolts and seat-track latches with unbridled frenzy for hours on end, wielding tools undreamed of. What weather and time had already accomplished toward disassembling the Pinto – stripping its capacity for destruction and speed, consuming it in rust and turning its interior into a nest for rodents, its floorboard into a lattice for vines – only fed the hunger to strip it further and, pound for pound, to make it new.[21]

The drive was strong to transform this machine that was responsible for much destruction – stronger than the sting of bloody knuckles and the forces of gravity and rusted bolts. Out came the engine, axles, and other heavy systems; the car was stripped down to its hulking orange unibody, bolted seats and a makeshift brake system Fred devised and built into the engine compartment. Then I welded a hay-wagon's running gear to the front axle so that we could attach a tongue made from a young black walnut tree that Fred and I harvested from the woods. One day in March when the grass was still pale, Jack and I pushed the Pinto out into the pasture, and I tied Aliass to it with a rope. She moved forward, the rope went

21 Echoing, ironically, modern poet Ezra Pound's famous modernist dictum: "Make it new!" Ezra Pound, *Make It New: Essays by Ezra Pound* (New Haven: Yale University Press, 1935). And more so Royal Trux's 2001 album *Pound for Pound,* which I listened to a lot in those car-killing days. Royal Trux, *Pound for Pound* (Drag City, 2000).

taut, and the Dead Car rolled. From then on, the Dead-Car Crossing gathered a frightening, if slow and creaking, momentum. I carved a doubletree from the same black walnut as the tongue, to which Aliass and Brawnson (the long-legged gelding borrowed for the team from my friend Cheryl Haas's herd) were hitched. With one ass on either side of the tongue, the team could just barely pull and steer that awful beast of a dead-car wagon – if only on level ground.[22]

Toward the In-CAR-nated Poem

> We pin our puns on the windshield like
> We crossed each crossing in hell's despite.
> – Jack Spicer, "Car Song"[23]

Poets of all kinds pine, it seems, to diminish the sense of distance between words and the world of things they are supposed to name. From Romanticism and Dada to Spicer's kindred language poets, from Amanda Ackerman's parapoetic collaborations with flora to Adam Dickinson's explorations of his own body's petrochemical burdens, contemporary poetry proffers a diverse range of practices whereby poets radically trouble assumptions about the natures of human language and its material entanglements. Yet most poetic practices remain bound to words on a page in some way, limiting to some degree the possibilities for messy material multispecies co-composings.[24]

---

22 Hills were a different story, and so this problem was handled by un-hitching the team and hooking the Wagon to the Black Caprice on the more treacherous inclines and declines of the journey.

23 Jack Spicer, "Car Song," in *The Collected Books of Jack Spicer*, 119.

24 Even as they remain bound to pages in some formal ways, poets like Ackerman and Dickinson radically expand the limits of collaborative poetic inclusion in wild multispecies directions. See Amanda Ackerman, *The Book of Feral Flora* (Los Angeles: Les Figues Press, 2015) and Adam Dickinson, *The Polymers* (Toronto: Anansi Press, 2013) and *Anatomic* (Toronto: Coach House Books, 2018).

Poets and storytellers have long imagined "Nature" as a source of inspiration or material, sometimes exploiting or undermining the complexities of natural systems in the process. At one brilliant extreme of this is Vladimir Nabokov's Kinbote, the crazed narrator of *Pale Fire*. Megalomaniacal Kinbote believes the natural world, with the poet John Shade as scribe, is busily writing the saga of Kinbote's own biography. As Kinbote exalts when he finally gets his hands on the poem that is supposed to embody his (possibly imaginary) lost homeland of Zembla: "Solemnly I weighed in my hand what I was carrying under my left armpit, and for a minute I found myself enriched with an indescribable amazement, as if informed that fireflies were making decodable signals on behalf of stranded spirits, or that a bat was writing a legible tale of torture on the bruised and branded sky."[25]

Nowadays we recognize by scientific means that fireflies and bats do make decodable signals, if very much on their own behalves. Still, Kinbote's longing resonates and chafes; who among us has never leaned into a cozy feeling of synchronicity where other earthly creatures like birds and insects, trees and grasses, and whole cosmos of living energies seem to be fluttering about to attend to small but significant tasks at the edges of human fates, like Disney birds and woodland creatures who twirl and tie Cinderella's ribbons and bows – or maybe more like invisible migrant laborers who pick fruit and spray weeds to keep North American agricultural economies working, or the diverse species of pollinators who make them possible at all? Kinbote's megalomania seems to warn readers, though: Beware the trick of Western myths that encourage us to see individual (and even collective political) fates as heroic paths of Progress toward futures (whether dystopian or victorious), pitched against Na-

---

25 Vladimir Nabokov, *Pale Fire* (1962; rpt. New York: Vintage International, 1989), 289.

ture. Better to ask: Who rides in the shadows beside our driving human heroic quests, and who makes them possible through movements and lives we don't see? In light of grasses, asses, and untold others whose supposed silence disguises infinite varieties of liveliness, can we learn to tell our own stories in search of belonging without trampling on the tales of everybody in our paths and wakes?

Enter, with creaking uncertainty, the Dead-Car Crossing. Reveling with ironic fervor in the riot of movement-naming, Jack Christian and I called the Dead-Car Wagon "in-car-nated poetics" and imagined it might present a radical new frontier on the map of American poetics – or at least a smirky retort to avant-garde language poet Charles Bernstein's famous call for "the ultimate concretization of poetry."[26] Beyond the jokes and wordplay and renewed passion for Bruce Springsteen, though, the Dead Car vision was driven by sincere desire to enmesh poetic imagination in territorial ecologies. Artistic desire to counteract environmental damage and do ecological good parallels what scholar–poet Jed Rasula calls "ecological imperatives" in American poetry.[27] Such impulses that are not new, by any means, but they do seem especially pressing in times when each of us is more and more aware of harms we perpetrate on places just by driving to and from them.

Even so, while poems and performances may enmesh with specific environmental concerns, most contemporary artists are suspicious of pitching a direct relationship

26 Charles Bernstein, "Introduction," in *With Strings* (Chicago: University of Chicago Press, 2001), 5.

27 In *This Compost,* Jed Rasula connects Walt Whitman's wish for people to read his poems only out-of-doors to Gregory Bateson's *Steps to an Ecology of Mind*: "'The individual mind is immanent but not only in the body,' writes Bateson [...] 'it is immanent also in pathways and messages outside the body; and there is a larger Mind of which the individual mind is only a subsystem." Jed Rasula, *This Compost: Ecological Imperatives in American Poetry* (Athens: University of Georgia Press, 2012), 234.

between art and intended purpose. Even "off the page," the capacities of poetic imagination to affect material matterings remains an open question, which becomes more ethically fraught with uncertainties when other species are directly implicated in the "poem's" realization. We understand that poems, stories, and other forms of human artistic representation have capacities to move thusly attuned human minds in various and particular ways; but we can only wonder what work might poems *do* otherwise (whether directly or invisibly) to intervene in the well-being of worldings? What kinds of unforeseen responsibilities and obligations do we take on when we set out to put poetic visions into material worlds?

Both assthetically and politically, the notion of taking the "poem" out on the road in the form of a Dead-Car Wagon imagined its slow-ass crossing as an intervention, a hope that it might present a rolling, open challenge to rural American infrastructures of place and passage, Fordist-driven car culture, extractive industries, suburban sprawl, hidden histories of colonial migrations and Manifest Destiny, and remembrance of wayside exchanges that are impossible when so many places, along with ecological communities they contain, are rendered into terminal blurs in windshield glass. As it evolved, the Dead-Car Wagon's artistic drive to "blast poems off the page" and into in/visible infrastructures of rural Virginia roadways embodied pressing desires to make art "work" in more direct ways for trees and creeks, green ass pastures, and wild pawpaw trees.[28] In spite of many uncer-

---

28 Steve Baker describes the embrace of irony frequent in postmodern modes. He quotes ecological artist Mark Dion, who claims artists who incorporate environmental concerns into their work do well to "to employ 'the rich set of tools, like irony, allegory and humour,' which are less readily or imaginatively employed by the institutions which seek to promote particular 'truths,' such as science or the entertainment industry." Steve Baker, *The Postmodern Animal* (London: Reaktion Books, 2000), 10.

tainties, the Dead-Car Crossing was driven by urgent questions of "what a poem can do" in times of ecological crises to intervene and act meaningfully in places. So arose the vague hope that putting a "poem" into material form and taking it out on the road might somehow be an act of goodwill toward the wilder worlds of rural Southwest Virginia, if only in some scattered, ethically impossible to grasp way. At the same time, the assemblage as a whole was frayed by ethical and aesthetic tensions where other species are involved, especially when artists pose their works as ecological projects that hope to work for the good of the world in some ambiguous way. What is the possible value of this "incarnated poem" for other species involved in its passing-through places?

Assymmetrical Burdens

Of all the oddly pitched burdens Aliass has borne since that fatesome day we met in Tennessee, the Dead-Car Wagon is surely the most onerous. The act of reanimating a gnarly old Pinto and making Aliass and Brawnson pull it precariously across winding miles of Virginia hills and hollows raises knotty ethical quandaries. As the Dead-Car Wagon's entire conceptual and material weight hung on the delicate body of one little American Spotted she-Ass and her (fortunately brawnier) partner, the asses were knotted and buckled up in representations and material ropes and scraps of harness and tied to the hulking metal weight of the ominous dead car. Always a danger with any traditionally humanist-oriented poetry or artwork is its tendency to stray from its roots in and consequences for assemblages of material bodies. This material-poetic incarnation, which made artistic sensibilities thrill and shiver, made Aliass tremble for other reasons altogether. How was it ever justifiable to hitch gentle Aliass to that ominous mangled-metal, dystopian-ironic road beast

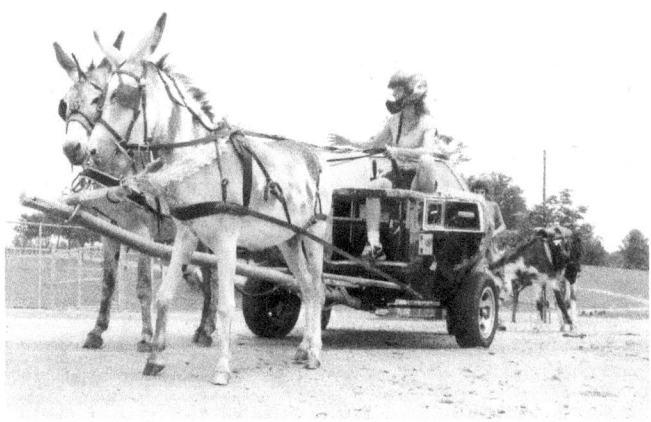

Fig. 7. The Dead-Car Wagon gearing up for the journey to come at the Martinsville Speedway. Photograph by Susanna Hill.

and then make her pull its grueling weight through miles of unfamiliar and dangerous territory?

I have often proceeded with the understanding that Aliass, in her domestic assness, can never fully unhitch from human obligations and desires – specifically, in this case, she is bound to her task as equine ambassador to creative possibilities of human–ass becomings.[29] In return, I am obligated to keep her in good health and company, safely accommodated, and free from suffering, all to the best of my abilities. Yet the human passions and big-ass questions at the core of our adventures together

29 Could I ever "set Aliass free" to live among wild burros somewhere in the US? This is a fraught idea, given the problems facing BLM-managed wild horses and burros in the US West and Southwest. But to consider what this kind of freedom (from obligations, containment, boredom, but also care) would mean for Aliass and her family herd seems vital, even as "wild" donkeys are not free from human intervention in their fates. See, for instance, Abraham Gibson, "Beasts of Burden: Feral Burros and the American West," in *The Historical Animal*, ed. Susan Nance (Syracuse: Syracuse University Press, 2015), 38–53.

are always bigger than our mortal bodies, which I suppose is why I have been willing to risk our lives and limbs out on dangerous American roadsides, time and time again. One of the most perplexing quandaries we've carried along, inside a practice that seeks to disrupt dominant stories and ground more inclusive tales in assemblages of bodies-in-places, is this: How do forms of human poetic imagination either nurture or diminish possibilities for multispecies worldings in places? The sinister tension inherent in the ideas that humans manipulate the "Nature" of others is not a new concept, but increasingly we turn to the ways that species – and not just humans – shape each other in evolutionary co-patterns, both helping and hurting, sometimes with ethical awareness, other times unwittingly. What happens to our ideas about art and poetics, more specifically, as we realize that other species also co-opt each other for practical and possibly even aesthetic purposes, for better or worse?

The Dead-Car Wagon was a fearsome hybrid articulation, a "material-semiotic actor" assembled from an oddly combustible mixture of frayed hopes and ironies, ethical galls and pressures, and unseemly cultural histories.[30] I was also keenly and uncomfortably aware that the very spots on Aliass's body are shaped by human cultural hungers for certain kinds of spectacle – even as the spots

---

30 Contemporary discourses in environmental humanities bring new light to investigations of possible material-poetic narratives. Donna Haraway specifically poses poetics as a tool for rethinking modes of representation/meaning-making and embodied knowledges when she writes: "From the early stirrings of Romanticism in the late eighteenth century, many poets and biologists have believed that poetry and organisms are siblings. [...] I continue to believe in this potent proposition but in a postmodern and not a Romantic manner. I wish to translate the ideological dimensions of 'facticity' and 'the organic' into a cumbersome entity called a 'material-semiotic' actor." Donna J. Haraway, "Situated Knowledges: The Science Question in Feminism and the Privilege of Partial Perspective," *Feminist Studies* 14, no. 3 (1988): 595.

actually elide the histories of bodies beneath. A literal articulation of American Spotted Asses to the fraught history and image of the Pinto hoped to fuse the poetic with the material and thereby present a "concrete" material-semiotic figure to navigate how landscapes change as we roll forward into the twenty-first century.[31] Resonances of its articulation spoked out of concerns about the history and hegemony of US transportation systems and car culture, spiked with resentment and conflicted anxiety born of being trapped inside the flaming car culture infrastructure as it endangers and renders inaccessible so many possible exchanges between places and passage through them – rural or otherwise. Still, whatever sassy articulations of material-poetic imagining the Dead-Car Wagon may have put forth, it was Aliass's and Brawnson's bodies – as representations but also materially – that carried the bulk of the weight of the Dead-Car Wagon from its inception. And in true Aliass style, the she-ass did so with fortitude and grace that make my heart ache for all of us. My dear sweet Aliass, my vocabulary did this to you. I can only hope troubled loves will let us go on.[32]

31 Putting forth the Dead-Car Wagon a "material-semiotic actor" may not justify its most egregious impositions on certain sweet ass bodies any more than calling it a "poem" might do. Yet to disengage from the Romantic ideas of human/Nature relations, as Haraway does here, broadens the possibilities of this relationship: "Like 'poems,' which are sites of literary production where language too is an actor independent of intentions and authors, bodies as objects of knowledge are material-semiotic generative nodes. Their boundaries materialize in social interaction." Ibid., 595.

32 Jack Spicer's last words, spoken to Robin Blaser in a San Francisco hospital bed, offered to readers by Robin Blaser's loving generosity: "My vocabulary did this to me. Your love will let you go on." Blaser, "The Practice of Outside," 325.

The Road to Eden, NC

Come summer, it was time to go. The team of asses grazed in the paddock, trained and ready. Too little to pull, Passenger would walk beside, and the Mutt of Gold would ride. We mapped the distances and hoped the hills wouldn't overcome the Wagon's dubious braking system: Martinsville Speedway to Eden, NC. I screwed a "Farm Use" tag onto the hatchback of the Pinto, and so the Dead-Car Wagon clanked off into the ill-known hills of Henry County, Virginia, toward the Carolina state line. We hitched up on the grounds of the Martinsville Speedway and rolled out, after a slow ceremonial maiden loop around the outside of the Speedway. And went on down, deep into Henry County and toward the border in a three-day trip through a kind of pastoral hell.

There were pleasant moments and exchanges, as well. A local man named Billy Agee saw us pass and later brought us three dozen eggs from his own chickens and enough packages of deer-meat to feed the hordes of nameless ghosts who rode with us. Other folks offered water spigots, weedy pastures, or shade to rest in. In that sense, the Wagon's passage did serve to inspire acts of remembering and connection for some of the local human inhabitants. Ruby Craddock and her yellow dog welcomed the Wagon in her driveway as we passed, and, later, all Ruby's kinfolk up and down the Odell Road came out to meet us. Wesley, a five-year-old boy from the windowless trailer across the road hung around for an hour or so with his mother, where we stopped in a field to rest and water the team. His questions, all beginning with "Hey, y'all..." were as probing and constant as a mockingbird's song. A bearded man named James stopped his pickup in the roadside ditch and told us about all the empty houses up and down the road, many of them abandoned by cancer victims. He said the pistol on his hip was for shooting snakes in the hay pastures.

We liked to imagine that the Dead-Car Crossing as an "in-car-nated" performance reached "outside" traditional poetic spaces and practices, into local environs in ways a poem on the page could never do – especially in regions where many inhabitants (human and otherwise) do not read poetry as a pastime. At the same time, the realization of the journey confronted us with the fact that however we might gesture toward an "outside" of linguistic strictures, we cannot escape certain modes of word-image-bound meaning-makings and representations – any more than the blasted Dead-Car Wagon could escape the infrastructures of global fossil fuel economies or the asses could escape the terrible creaking burden to which they were harnessed.

So we set out sweating and clanking in the Dead-Car Wagon on the rural roads of Henry County to chase ghosts through the "haunted landscapes of the Anthropocene."[33] But if we'd known how real it would get out there, we might have been inclined to "chicken out at the edges of it" (in Spicer's words) and never set foot, hoof, or paw onto that hellish-hot road down to Eden.[34] We did not foresee the first night's plague of huge horseflies that made the donkeys groan and lay down in the dirt like they would die. We forgot to watch out for ticks and poison ivy. We didn't anticipate the bullet-holes in Jack's Toyota, nor the maggots writhing in Brawnson's gall on that endless second day. The road offered no shelter from stress, heat, mechanical grinding, or the wicked thunderstorms from which the herd fled for refuge in a weedy cattle pasture. And most of all came the uncertainty of whether it was worth it – what it was we hoped any of this would do

33 See Elaine Gan, Anna Tsing, Heather Swanson, and Nils Bubandt, "Haunted Landscapes of the Anthropocene," in *Arts of Living on a Damaged Planet*, eds. Anna Tsing, Heather Swanson, Elaine Gan, and Nils Brubandt (Minneapolis: University of Minnesota Press, 2017), G1–G13.

34 Spicer, *The Collected Books of Jack Spicer*, 181.

for the places we passed through or any past present or future lives.

The weight and tensions inherent in the Dead-Car Wagon project were monstrous indeed, in ways that render the hitching of Aliass and others to its unwieldy bulk and conceptual contrivances questionable and ethically dangerous. While these ethical tensions are inextricable from the overall assthetic drive of the Dead-Car Wagon, the question remains open as to whether one can balance the ambiguous "workings" of poetic imagination against the groaning, sweaty labors and hardships, unforeseen perils, and grievous founderings of bodies and souls that unfolded when the "in-car-nated poem" hit the real-ass road. We drove on, nonetheless, saying "Hup, Brawnson! Hup, Aliass!," clucking and cracking the reins to keep the team moving and groaning on into the oppressive heat, all in the belief that if poetic articulations (in whatever form) are to be forces that resist and reckon with violences of toxic parking-lot sprawl, they must press hard into places of conflict to remain vital. Even so, the realization of its harrowing three-day journey demands reckoning with particular questions of responsibility: What do we imagine poetic visions really do for the worlds they inhabit? Whose bodies bear the most onerous burdens of this effort, the galls and scars? At what costs? And who benefits? I guess the real question is: What led us as artists to hope or believe that the Dead-Car Wagon really could do anything for the places and livelihoods into which we imposed its form? As an act of "incarnated poetics," the Dead-Car Wagon set into motion became a monstrous intrusion, even as the social, global-economic, and environmental pressures it moved against made it seem justifiable, even inevitable.

In the wake of it, at intersections of thinking and practice where contemporary art meets academic forays in feminist-materialist science studies and energy humanities, the "material-poetic" articulation of the Dead-Car

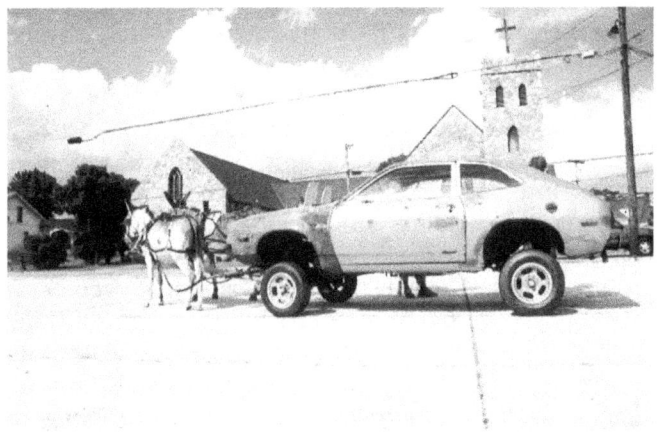

Fig. 8. Dead-Car Wagon arrives at the empty church parking lot in Eden, NC. Photograph by Richard Lucyshyn.

Wagon might bear forth nuanced possibilities for artistic practices to intervene in becomings of American road-ways and barnyards. *Might*, I say. The cultural weight and energy of the project pulled not so much against its seeming opponents in car culture, wracked colonial histories, and fossil-fuel consumerism as toward a vague hope that the crossing might artfully blast black-hole headlights into oncoming traffic, and shoot the green flames ripping from the Dead-Car Wagon's rusty wheel-wells into local woods and waterways. But beyond all this talk of imagining and articulating ideas (if ironically) toward hopeful movements into earthly futures lies a lurking suspicion that it might have been some kind of redemption the Dead-Car Crossing was seeking, deep down – as if to assuage some of the shame of partaking in endless extractive oil-and-asphalt nightmares that harm earthly bodies and beloved places. But if redemption was really what this voyage secretly sought, in the end, in Eden and onward, it was nowhere to be found.

At the end of that strange road trip, we were glad (and a little surprised) to have survived. Yet a nagging sense of failure and uncertainty haunted the afterlife of the Dead-Car Wagon. In human social circles, Jack Christian and I spoke of the Wagon's aims as a radical and risky artistic intervention driven by genuine concerns for rural Southern ecologies and sociopolitical struggles. But in recollecting the swell of uncertain feelings that settled in like clouds of exhaust as the Dead-Car Wagon came creakingly to rest that final hour, in that empty church parking lot just up the road from an abandoned mill in postindustrial Eden, we were maybe not so sure. Ambivalence about what (if anything) the Dead-Car Crossing actually gave to the world (whether politically, assthetically, or ecologically) throbs through the final lines of a poem Jack Christian wrote called "After the Project." In the exhausted wake of a journey fueled by fretful concern for past and future earthly places, what we have done and/or might yet do, the passage feels more like an epitaph, writ in the cracked rearview mirror of one more haggard-ass American road trip:

> We arrived in Eden hungry, and camped open on a thin sheen
> of leaves beneath a giant tree growing from the center of a
> vast parking lot. Its roots ran like rivers through nearly all the
> vacant spaces. Weeping, the tree asked us what we needed.
> Then, without a word, it dropped its fruit, which in a frenzy
> we horded.[35]

---

35 Jack Christian, email communication.

7

Passing-Through
(Nomads in the Valley of Dooms)

Belonging becomes a tricky proposition in any place one might call home these days. The lands where we make our lives and livings are always inhabited by hidden (often explicitly erased) histories and unheard voices. Sometimes these phantoms guide us to good places, and sometimes they lead us astray. Either way, it was certain ghosts of old Virginia and their makeshift promises of newfound belonging that brought my little ass family reeling back, again and again, to reckon with hopes and hauntings scattered in roadside ditches, hot parking lots, and waysides left behind in the hills and hollows of the so-called Old Dominion. At the same time, it was always real bodies – lives and loves caught up in unforgiving systems and structures – that we remained bound to as we were passing through.

A decade earlier, the abrupt collapse of a family horse farm had kicked off for me (if obliquely) a spinning spate of wanderings and tenuous dwellings in the company of an unnamed American Spotted Ass. Sure enough, the old Appalachian range that runs like a spine along the mid-Atlantic US state known as Virginia played a significant role in that first summer Aliass and I spent on the byways of three Southern states and beyond. The Dead-Car

Crossing, in turn, could be said to reflect an aching reluctance to leave that state. In different ways, each journey performed aspects of a much larger quest to tune
into particular places in more inclusive ways. This special brand of twenty-first-century passing-through has
sought to arrive at some kind of resolution of fraught,
conflicted belongings within the unseen, untold, and
unknowable stories of places. Meanwhile, acts of unnaming and passing through places with Aliass are also
driven and shaped by more basic and mundane material
and economic necessities – long-term negotiations with
pushes and pulls of many different and often conflicting
forces. Through years of wayward-ass wandering, the ever-present need to secure amenable living spaces for the
herd was complicated by the situation of being a land-
less, rural–urban-divided female artist, whose access to
"pastures of plenty" was limited by different hot-wired
political, economic, and biographical factors.

Certain pastoral necessities are inescapable when it
comes to living, traveling, and making temporary homes
with/in a herd of grazers. Certain hard to satisfy, nomadic hungers for a nourishing and safe place to stay is one
of the main forces that brought us back to Virginia in the
spring of 2005, less than nine months after crossing the
southern border into Carolina in the Dead-Car Wagon. A
hazy promise of belonging brought us reeling back once
more to assemble, in both creative and commonplace
ways, amidst the psycho-geographic patchwork of pastures, asphalt, landfills, interstates, hardwood mountain
forests, and hidden underground spaces known (for the
most part affectionately) as the Valley of Dooms, Virginia.

The move back to Virginia in 2005 – back, that is, from
a yearlong graduate school stint in Athens, Georgia – was
first sparked by the happenstance discovery of a ramshackle rural speedway in a town called Dooms. This find
was reported to me by L-Haw (aka Lydia Peelle), who had

recently moved to Charlottesville, Virginia from Whites Creek, Tennessee. As L-Haw happened upon the place on an exploratory bike ride one day, Dooms revealed itself to be a small rural hamlet, tucked like evidence of a bad habit into a shadowy Appalachian fold just northwest of the Afton Mt. Pass, whereby Interstate 64 crosses the Blue Ridge. So L-Haw's discovery of this backwoods motor speedway in Dooms, Virginia resonated with certain unresolved questions still leaking from the creaky morass of the Dead-Car Crossing. And so it was that this Dooms speedway was the catalyst that brought our little herd reeling back to Virginia – not six months after the Dead-Car Wagon had rolled away from the glorious Fincastle farm in the grievous grind of reluctant departure. Suddenly I had to get us back to Virginia, no matter what it took.

This was hardly the first round in an ongoing cycle of departure and return to a state of troubled barn-dark belonging. I had come and gone from Virginia many times, by a dizzying assortment of means and speeds, in the nearly ten years since my family's farm had blown apart like a seedy dandelion on the other side of the Blue Ridge. Yet the Shenandoah Valley to the west of the mountains was new territory, if close enough to the dark heart of Albemarle County to maintain a certain psycho-geographic charge. It was still Virginia, after all, the impossible home, the onerous state of perpetual (if not exactly Sisyphean) departures and returns. But this time would be different. This return to the Blue Ridge foothills and valleys below was not so much out of homesickness for the mythical Lost Paradise of the Past or wishes for an everlasting peace-of-ass. This time, it presented a shift toward something more present and pressingly possible, if speculative. Promises of grounding a new kind of nomadic-ass pastoral belonging resonated in the prospect of starting a brand new life in Dooms.

Oh yes, darkly hopeful promises attached (with only faintest irony) to this oddly named hamlet, just on the outskirts of gritty old Waynesboro, home to a few collapsing dairy farms, clusters of modest houses and trailer homes, a dusty and sprawling antique shop, and a downtown hot-dog stand. And so we did – go (back) to Dooms, that is. And so begins (again) the quest to secure an amenable home for a little nomadic ass herd – at the very least, a fenced pasture and some kind of barn for shelter – in the ravaged and glorious forests and fields of a rolling rural-industrial Appalachian valley. This effort to find and colonize a little homestead in the storied old Shenandoah landscapes was doomed from the get-go, of course. Nevertheless, the year spent wandering in the Valley of Dooms – on various county routes, wayward paths, and interstate exit ramps, searching in vain for a place to call home – would in its ultimate failure reveal unforeseen states of creative nomadic possibility. Though a bust in that way, that year in the Valley of Dooms boomed for a time, through hidden underground connections and wholly new creative modes for listening, composing with, and passing through beautiful, lively, endangered and untold places.

Pleasant Valley

Heaven knows I looked high and low for a place to call home with Passenger and Aliass and the Mutt of Gold. Lo and behold, it is not easy to find those longed-for pastures of plenty. It takes a long time, as I found out over the seasons of false starts and broken dreams in the Valley of Dooms, Virginia. What we did find – when we found it at last in an industry-encrusted, landfill-perfumed place on the southern edge of Harrisonburg, in the dubiously named Pleasant Valley – never did turn out to be the hoped-for peaceful-ass homestead it seemed at first to promise.

While humanly psycho-geographic longings haunt the push-and-pull necessities of making homes, other pressing material, economic, and logistical questions matter, too. Shuttling back and forth from place to place, we are driven by bodily needs and capital lacks, pulled by faint hopes and half-seen desires. More specifically, in our case, we were driven by distinct material requirements of caring for (not to mention transporting) a little ass family. With some premonition of complexities to come, before departing Athens, Georgia I had spray-painted a stencil of the full first stanza from a poem called "The Dog of Graffiti," by poet Mark Bilbrey, onto the still-mangled passenger-side door of the Black Caprice:

Wholivesheresundaysorever
yotherweekendorforthatmat
terwhenicomebyinthenylon
thinkingcapcauseafteralltha
tswhenhomemovesandwew
homakerightherewestayput[1]

Like pastoral landscapes with their seemingly timeless, mostly inscrutable histories of conquest, displacement and constant change, Bilbrey's poem challenges a reader to make meaning of a mass of possible patterns and configurations. The poem's coy and haunting opacity resonated with my own special set of complex questions borne of twenty-first-century nomadic-ass homemaking in fragmented rural US places: Who lives here? What are you looking for? Where do you go now? Is it a place, or a way of life? And what is on the other side?[2]

1 Mark Bilbrey, "The Dog Poems and the Poetics of Prayer," PhD diss., University of Georgia, 2009, 28.
2 I call these the R.A.W. Questions, though they predate the actual establishment of the Rural Alchemy Workshop by a year or two. I have animated and inhabited these questions in various performances of

I can't recall how I came upon the property in Pleasant Valley, especially since it was more or less uninhabitable and not yet officially for rent. It was a derelict farmstead of two thickly thistle-blown acres, haphazardly fenced and scattered with peeling and crooked outbuildings and piles of toxic trash. The old two-bedroom farmhouse was "under renovation," which is to say it had been gutted by the landlord's crew – bathroom and kitchen stripped, doors off the hinges, holes in the floor, piles of raccoon shit littering the skeletal upstairs rooms – and the work had pretty much stopped there, indefinitely. The house was by no means ready for habitation, and I probably should have walked away right then and there. But then I saw the barn. As soon as I glimpsed that oddly perfect little white barn – with its old warped boards layered with peeling white paint and peculiar graffiti, perfectly sized for a pretty pair of spotted she-asses – I fell perilously in love. I looked past the fearsome dilapidation of the house and fences and the surrounding stretches of industrial gravel lots, steaming green chemical ponds, and fuming factories, blinded by a visionary future in which the asses grazed in peaceful perpetuity in grassy pastures, eating hay and dozing happily on cold nights or hot afternoons inside that humbly beautiful little white barn.

The landlord was dubious: Did I really want to wait around for him to finish renovations on the house? The answer was a desperate yes. For months I had sought hard for an affordable place with basic shelter and space requirements for Aliass and Passenger. I was willing to hunker down and wait for the house if it would mean realizing the fragile dream of a little homestead in the Valley of Dooms in the long run. So Mr. Landlord took pity on my plight, invested in an old camper with Cadillac hubcaps, and parked it next to the broken house, run-

rural-urban ass husbandry and home-making over a decade of practice.

ning power out by extension cord. And there we dwelled, me and the Mutt of Gold, for several months through the late summer and fall of 2005, while I worked to make the place ready for Aliass and Passenger to come "home."

From August into the fall, I worked on mending the brokedown fences, trying to make a safe enclosure for Aliass and Pass, so I could bring them up from their temporary accommodations near Roanoke.[3] Neither house nor camper had running water, so I had to drive up Route 11 a few miles toward town to the Sheetz gas-station convenience store to enjoy the luxury of indoor plumbing. By early October, I had strung a makeshift electric fence around a part of the pasture, and the barn was ready. Aliass and Pass arrived at last one day, and a week of blissful browsing on thistles and weeds ensued. A passtoral dream materialized – not without irony – as the she-asses dozed behind the graffiti-marked barn door where someone had scrawled the word "PEACE" along with what appeared to be an upside-down, incomplete peace sign and some other indecipherable hieroglyphs.

Along with the inevitable need for a suitable place to dwell with the donkeys, this move to the Valley of Dooms was also a nascent performance – a deliberate, experimental, and exploratory in-habitation of one specific form of "relational assthetics," seeking to investigate and frame relations within these places and our possible roles within them. For this reason, and for lack of other options, I was ready to inhabit not just the (un)Pleasant Valley farmstead but also to fully and performatively inhabit the situation of being a single-woman-with-herbivorous-herd in the throes of trying to find and make a good-ass

3   Aliass and Passenger were living it up in grassy fields with a rowdy multigenerational herd of rescued donkeys on the ever-welcoming Cheryl Haas's farm near Fincastle. They were happy, but I missed them terribly. Home is, after all, where one's ass is.

home in a ragged Appalachian rural–agricultural–industrial zone.[4]

Had it worked out, this might have been a little victory. This manifestation of Virginia homemaking, where the home we made was no longer bound to a static, Lost Place in the Past but hitched instead to a dynamic inhabitation of lively possibilities in fraught, fragile, and transitory twenty-first-century passtoral places. Stretching feminist philosopher Dehlia Hannah's frame, I might go so far as to describe the effort to establish an amenable locus for the family herd in the Valley of Dooms as a kind of psycho-geographic-sociocultural-economic-aesthetic-multispecies "performative experiment."[5] In any case, this performative-experimental approach to homesteading, undergirded as it was by darkly hopeful visions of a radical little dairy-ass enterprise in Dooms – and of course a

4   It helped that I was newly engaged in the vibrant socially engaged artistic community of Goddard College's low-residency MFA-Interdisciplinary Arts program, and so generating biweekly projects and reflections of this process as a durational performance-art practice. Had it not been for the intellectual–artistic support of the Goddard network and friends closer at hand, I might not have been able to take such a rosy view of, say, having to drive several miles to the Sheetz up the Route 11 commercial strip to use the bathroom, or having to reckon with nightmares about what was hidden in the naked walls in the torn-open house, or whatever phantoms or residues made the Mutt of Gold tremble whenever we went inside the supposed soon-to-be home.

5   Dehlia Hannah describes performative experiments as "aesthetic interventions […] calculated to illuminate features of experimental design, materials and methods, and conventions of interpretation that tend to escape attention in the practice of everyday science." Eben Kirksey, Dehlia Hannah, Charlie Lotterman, and Lisa Jean Moore, "The Xenopus Pregnancy Test: A Performative Experiment," *Environmental Humanities* 8, no. 1 (2016): 37. Emphasizing the performative–aesthetic aspect over specifically scientific engagements, I look to interdisciplinary fields of ethological, social-scientific, and philosophical–artistic bodies of knowledge to experimentally illuminate practices of nomadic home-makings with multispecies herds in the twenty-first-century Valley of Dooms, Virginia.

need for somewhere to hang our hats and halters – gave a certain outlaw courage to my efforts. We hunkered down, in spite of prevailing discomforts, uncertainties, and the all-night clanking, buzzing, and big-rig braking from the windowless factory right across the road.

But lo, the Valley of Dooms lived up to its name. That late summer and fall of 2005, disasters darkened the already prickly dream of Pleasant Valley homesteading. For one thing, Hurricane Katrina. I had no TV and scant internet access while living in the Cadillac-hubcap camper, but the news came through the radio as I drove around the valley in the Black Caprice. I will never forget sitting at a red light near an exit ramp off Interstate 81 and hearing New Orleans Mayor Ray Nagin's tearful pleading for help from slow-moving federal forces, as the city's inhabitants drowned and struggled to survive, huddled against the storm's ferocity and lack of aide in the aftermath. Meanwhile, the nights turned cold in the camper, which had only a small borrowed space heater. I would wake up in my sleeping bag to find the Mutt of Gold shivering in spite of the Joan Jett t-shirt she wore and the heater blowing directly onto her bed on the floor. And it was getting too cold to pee outside (the only option). So in a flurry one day, I gave up. I made some calls and found a place to board the donkeys down Route 11, in a small hilly pasture with a cozy shed they shared with a fuzzy, fat miniature horse named Andy. And that was when the Mutt and I moved into a rented room with Libby, a divorced mother of two grown kids who worked at the local community college where I was adjunct-teaching English composition, mostly at night.

Other misfortunes visited us through the fall and into that winter in the Valley of Dooms. In late November some thieves broke into my storage unit in Waynesboro, rifled through all my belongings and stole everything electronic or seemingly valuable. Most heartbreaking was the theft of my solar-powered electric-fence charger, which had made it possible in most places for me to single-handedly construct and wire up a little ass paddock, anywhere I could sink a ground-rod. I was devastated by this loss, and maybe more so by the inability to make clear – to the policeman to whom I reported the theft, or to the pawn-shop owners I questioned in search of my fenced fencing goods – just how vital that particular (pricey) piece of agricultural equipment was to a fragile, nomadic-ass livelihood. The charger never turned up. Winter was coming. For the time being Aliass and Pass, the Mutt and I were safe in temporary refuges (if separated by a ten-mile stretch of Route 11). We settled into the rented room in Weyers Cave, defeated but grateful for homely comforts like baseboard heat and indoor plumbing, and more so for the woods and grassy meadow by the little river where the Mutt and I wandered daily. Pleasant Valley was behind us, and we had no truck with it anymore. And yet, certain shadowy structures lingered hidden in that ever-shifting, shadowy Shenandoah landscape, and soon they came a-knocking in unexpected ways.

Black Stallions in the Mud

One site in particular rose up in a fierce and daunting way. Back in early October, when I was still struggling to make the derelict Pleasant Valley property habitable, I had needed to go away for a weekend. I could not leave Aliass and Passenger in the makeshift paddock without supervision, though, so I was in a fix. One day a neighbor named Darrell, a widower who would come by sometimes to chat when I was out working on the fence, told me, "There's an old feller up the road who keeps horses. Maybe he could help. He's Black feller, but he's alright."

A few days later I drove up the road over the hill in hopes of checking out the place Darrell mentioned. About a mile along, I saw a rundown stable, set down a steep hill off on the side of the road. In a maze of muddy, hap-

hazardly fenced paddocks and manure piles sat a sprawling, patchwork-tin-roofed barn that looked like a sinking
ship, surrounded by a sea of broken-down cars and trucks
and refuse piles. I turned the Black Caprice slowly down
the steep gravel driveway, rolled through a metal gate,
and parked in front of a single-wide trailer with a pallet
porch and tarp awnings. I got out and walked toward the
barn, looking for someone to talk to. Wandering into the
labyrinthine barn, I found that it was full of horses, submerged in dark stalls and moving eerily in the dimness
like underwater creatures.

A metallic hammering sound came from around a
corner. I followed the hammering to find a burly man,
roughly in his thirties, in a ripped t-shirt and banging
on a tractor part. I introduced myself and told him I was
looking for a place to board my donkeys for a day or two,
though even as the words came out I already knew I could
not leave Aliass and Passenger at this stable, even for a
weekend. Something about the establishment felt precarious, endangered. (Looking back, I am amazed how
even in transient pastoral-nomad mode, a sense of safety
is a privilege to which I felt entitled, for myself and Mutt
and asses.) The man told me that the farm belonged to
Charlie, who wasn't home, but to come back another time
and maybe he could work something out. I got back in
the Black Caprice and drove off, with no intention of re-
turning. A couple weeks later, I abandoned Pleasant Valley for good, leaving only traces of our brief habitation
– scattered piles of manure and hay and some more mysterious graffiti to add to the odd palimpsest in the little
white barn's hayloft.

But something about Charlie's precarious rundown
stable settled like a stormy cloud-shadow over my comings and goings in the Valley of Dooms. One night in
February, curled up safe and warm under blankets in
the rented room, I had a furious nightmare in which a
flood came and – precisely as a bull's-eye shot – washed

Charlie's farm off the face of the earth. In the dream, and then again in a brief surge on waking, this felt like the saddest thing I could imagine. The sadness was so huge, and especially strange, too, because I had not been back to Pleasant Valley or thought consciously about Charlie's farm in months. The intensity of the nightmare was such that it required immediate attention, and even action. In the performative mode of Valley of Dooms habitation, I realized that I had to go back to Charlie's and find out what was happening there.

What I discovered when I worked up the guts to go back was this: Sunk off to the side of the rural byway and slowly going under, Charlie's stable was a barn-dark motherlode of uneasy histories and forces where humans and horses and landholdings in racially divided, colonial Virginia chafe against wheelbarrow-loads of broken dreams, frayed connections, and impossible cares stretched to the breaking point. Feeling weird about driving, I borrowed a friend's bicycle and rode out from a municipal-building parking lot, past the spuming factories and landfill and cattle pastures through Pleasant Valley, and then uphill for a mile or two along the shoulderless highway, until I came to Charlie's place. No one was around, it seemed, so I left a note on a barrelhead in the barnyard, with my phone number and a message saying that I was a horse-lover and to call me if he had need for help with chores or working with any of his horses. Weeks went by, and then one snowy day in February came a muffled voice-mail message. Charlie's thick Virginia accent and mumbled words in the message were hard to make out, but I got enough to understand that he welcomed me, if tentatively. He said he probably had some horses I could ride, if that's what I was after.

In early March of that year, I began to drive out to Charlie's barn once a week or so, when the weather allowed. I came to know Charlie a little, and his one-eyed beagle named Trouble even stopped barking at me after a while. Charlie was ambiguously aged and mostly crippled. He walked with a crutch when he did walk, and otherwise he drove a little muddy golf-cart around the place, though mostly it was broke-down and he often just sat on it and watched over the farm's goings-on. Charlie had some help with the burden of relentless chores that come with caring for thirty-some horses, or the horses would not have survived long. But from what I could tell and the little he chose to share, he was mostly on his own, living in the single-wide trailer with only one-eyed Trouble and the tremendous burden of caring for a large and needy equine herd.

For reasons I will never grasp, Charlie's barn was full of stallions. I believe it had been years since he did any horse-breeding, but there they were, wasting away in dark wooden confinement. For all the familiar and pleasant smells and sounds of stable life – all of which kicked my family-farm-exiled, 4-H-raised horseperson-body into high gear – this barn was also a nightmare. I often found horses standing in stalls up to their fetlocks in excrement, with no water in their buckets. Enormous rats raced back and forth across the aisles and stopped to stare a person down. When I showed up I would ask Charlie what he needed, feed and fill buckets and clean stalls as I could. But I could not come every day, and I didn't know who otherwise was doing the at-least twice-daily feeding chores. Charlie had helpers, but I hardly ever saw anyone when I was there. He was doing the best he could, as he had been doing for decades. In a rare moment of conversation one day, Charlie told me how in the 1960s he had worked as a stablehand until he raised enough cash to buy the thirty-two acres of brushy cedar hills we stood on. He cleared it by hand, built the barn and fences. One winter he had lost his entire herd in a barn-fire, and then slowly rebuilt, board by warped board. He had been young then.

Going out to Charlie's gave a difficult pleasure. There was satisfaction in moving around barn-spaces and smells and sounds, tools, and implements in forgotten ways, yet the situation was deeply troubling. I admired Charlie for maintaining the old dream of his horse farm, somehow holding it together with bent nails, leaky hoses, duct tape, and baling twine. But every time I showed up, I witnessed devastating neglect: horses imprisoned in the dark stalls, their cracked and overgrown hooves rotting in urine and excrement, their moods depressed (or sometimes crazed) by lack of fresh air and sunlight. The friction was especially fierce after I made friends with one little black pony stallion, whose name I never knew, and who never got out of his cramped stall (in which he could barely turn around), unless I came to take him out to the paddock or to graze on a leadrope. The first time I tried to groom the little black stallion, he pinned his ears, bit and struck at me with a front hoof when I tried to brush his head. Later I realized I had been hurting him because the halter he wore was never taken off, and the nylon strap had galled the flesh beneath it.

Charlie never seemed to care one way or the other if I showed up or not. But the black pony stallion did come to care, after a while, because my appearance meant he could get out of his stall into the fresh air for a time – and even get a taste of new spring grass that grew in a lush patch by the broken-down horse van. After a while, he would brighten when he saw me appear over his stall door. Over time I came to feel the pull of the little black pony stallion waiting in his dark stall as a constant, no matter where I was in my daily comings and goings around the Valley of Dooms. In every moment I was somewhere else, I was failing to show up for him, and he was waiting, maybe suffering.

This right here, what swarms in the mysterious energies and affects that built Charlie's barn and all the fences, stall latches, gates, bits and bridles, and other ap-

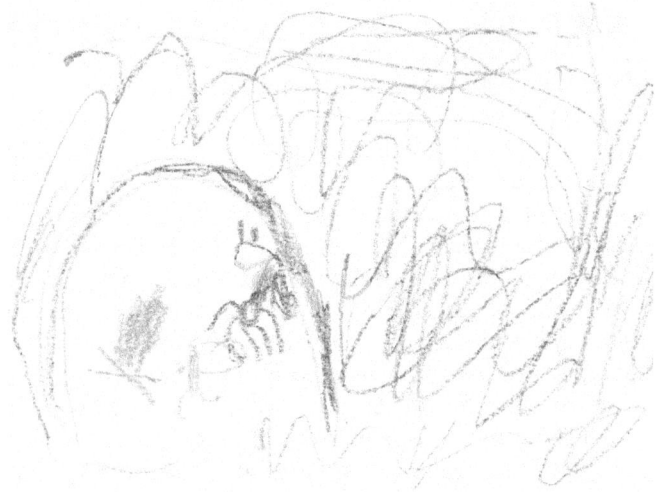

Fig. 1. I drew this at the age of six, after this and other scenes from the 1980 film *The Black Stallion* took root deep in caverns of a childhood imagination. Courtesy of Christie Bolender.

paratuses that have held domestic equines and humans bound and harnessed and knotted together for thousands of years, in (mostly untold) histories that are perhaps as full of joyful intimacies and mutual benefits as they are of galls and exploitations.... Right here is the primal push and pull of a nameless bond that forms through different bodies across domestic species. And if this passion for connection is not the fundament of all human image-making – as some scholars and poets suggest from the flickering depths of Paleolithic cave paintings – it is certainly at the root of desires to draw entangled empathies across representations and unnamed bodies in new ways.[6] This bond is the deepest drive of living with Aliass

---

6   Contemporary poet and Paleolithic art scholar Clayton Eshleman makes this case throughout his hybrid book, *Juniper Fuse: Upper Paleolithic Imagination and the Creation of the Underworld* (Middletown: Wesleyan University Press, 2003).

and herd, too. Let me testify to this cave-deep rootedness at the heart of artistic representation, with a document of my own earliest image making, which is a picture I drew as a child of six after the 1980 film *The Black Stallion* carved a wild dark horse-shaped hole in my guts that that has never closed up.

Some might call this horse hole a "soul," of the kind Gary Snyder evokes when he says, "Our 'soul' is our dream of the other."[7] Others describe it otherwise, through scientific-philosophical-biocultural registers like Donna Haraway's "sympoeisis" or Vinciane Despret's "anthropo-zoo-genesis."[8] What matters more here is not so much the names we give (or don't) to this tremulous opening, but rather the anomalously powerful black-hole gravitational pull of it. And even more important is the fact that this possible bond, this affective push and pull and chafe and gall of beastly bodies, is never pure and free, but always compromised in thousands of complex ways by the situations in which we find ourselves trying to live and make livings in each other's midst. Bonds become especially barbed and twisted in sites where kinships are undermined by classified hierarchies like breed and bloodline. These forces often determine the chances each beast will have for well-being and access to basic necessities like fresh air and grass, or whatever a given body happens to desire and need. In these places, capitalist commodifications play a role in valuing some lives as more or less worthy of having what they want and need than others. Under conditions like these, fragile ties fray and chafe against every living body they touch, like the nylon strap

---

7   Gary Snyder, *The Practice of the Wild* (New York: North Point Press, 1990), 180.

8   Donna J. Haraway, *Staying with the Trouble: Making Kin in the Chthulucene* (Durham: Duke University Press, 2016), 97–98 and Vinciane Despret, "The Body We Care For: Figures of Anthropo-zoo-genesis," *Body and Society* 10, nos. 2–3 (2004): 111–34.

of a halter left on so long that the fur wears away and the tender flesh begins to absorb it.

More than any other site in the Valley of Dooms, Charlie's farm presents haunting challenges and troubling specters inherent in certain nomadic ass tendencies, where escape is not only the privilege of freedom to move on to better and brighter places, but also to abandon the places where our nerves or ethical capacities fail. Charlie's farm sheltered and sustained valued ways of life that have historically bound horses and humans together in this and other configurations, but at the time I came across it, the farm was also a disaster of suffering and impending doom for those who lived there. Sunk off the side of the rural highway in a shifting zone where Harrisonburg suburban sprawl pushes against older farms, county landfill sites, and factories, Charlie's place was full of knotted histories of horses and humans and others, whose lives and unwritten biographies persist even as political and economic forces mobilize to bulldoze them under rapid human housing sprawl. Or more slowly, by the waysides of naturalcultural obsolescence in which certain lives might find ways to persist or else fail, and bail, falter and fade.

In Charlie's barnyard I found a muddy morass I could not see a way through, where practical ethics and imagination both failed to provide a clear path.[9] I did not know

9   I might present my engagement with Charlie's farm as an artist–researcher engaged in creative intervention, through the lens of contemporary relational aesthetics and site-specific, socially-engaged performance practices. I might, but I won't. It feels more appropriate here to echo Kathryn Gillespie and Rosemary-Claire Collard, who bring to light certain ethical conflicts that come with witnessing sufferings of other domestic species from a certain (academic) remove, calling attention to "a larger problem with the act of witnessing and field research in general – namely that this work is done in service of long-term future change, but frequently does nothing for the individual whose suffering is being witnessed." Kathryn Gillespie and Rosemary-Claire Collard, eds., *Critical Animal Geographies: Politics, In-*

what to do. For the horses, I probably should have called someone, some animal welfare organization. I was fairly sure that if Charlie's motley herd of mostly aged, crippled grade horses were seized by a rescue group or the county, many would likely end up going to slaughter. Some of them might have been saved. But I could not bring myself to betray Charlie in this way.

Did I betray the horses, then? How do we navigate through lives filled with loved ones otherwise known as livestock, who we may be compelled to sell, put down, or otherwise abandon to another's care when money runs low or time comes to move on? I did not have access to the necessary capital, either economic or political, that might have settled matters in other ways. One thing seemed certain: the ship was going down, and one way or another it would all be over before long. I could not save Charlie's farm, whatever that might have looked like, and after all nobody asked me to. I had not been able to save my mother's farm, either. And anyway, I was only passing through.

tersections, and Hierarchies in a Multispecies World (London: Routledge, 2015), 204.

Nomads in the Valley of Dooms

It is a lucky few who can easily uproot and leave behind places that fail to meet needs or standards, who can up and go at will by lines of flight that track or flee flows of capital, changing climates, and other forces that benefit some while wreaking havoc on others. Some privileges allow or obligate us to migrate after "pastures of plenty," but freedom to move nomadically is not equally available to everybody, human or otherwise. We are tied together in and across specific spaces and the shadow places connected to them, in various ways – be it Charlie and his black stallions bound to the fate of those precarious thirty-two acres in Pleasant Valley, or omnipresent invisible ties across global pathways that link diverse lives to faraway places never seen or imagined.[10] We are always connected to places we pass through and those we leave behind, along with the scattered ways we choose to inherit or resist prevailing systems within specific places' vanished histories and faulty infrastructures of race, gender, and species.

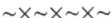

~×~×~×~

In the early spring of 2006, everything changed. Love came rolling up to Weyers Cave in an old red Ford F-150 with a silver stripe, driven by a seethingly brilliant philosopher-farmboy. Soon formidable new passions and promises of hopeful ass husbandry beckoned our herd to another place, another Southern state. And so it was time to go again.

Leaving Virginia was never easy. From this looming departure, and all the other failures to dwell deep and enduringly in the Valley of Dooms, came a series of journey

10 Val Plumwood, "Shadow Places and the Politics of Dwelling," *Australian Humanities Review* 44 (2008).

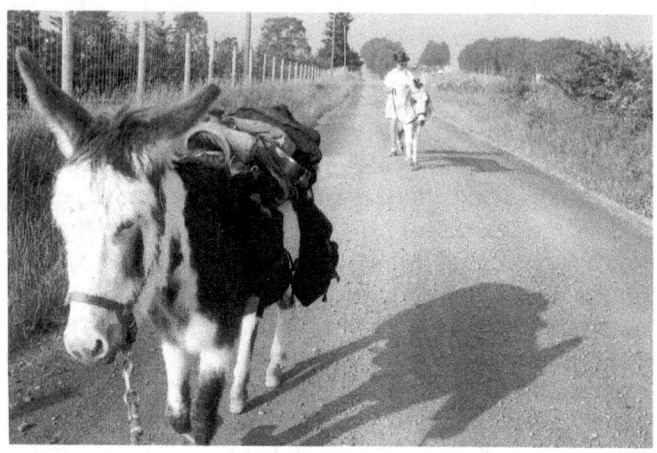

Fig. 6. She-Haw Transhumance passing through the Valley of Dooms in June 2006. Photograph by the artist.

projects that sought to creatively address, if not assuage, the shames and the creative forces borne in practices of passing-through. Adapting our proceedings from traditional movements of domestic herds of humans and herbivorous mammals who make their livings by *transhumance* – migrating seasonally from one grazeable land to another – two different but linked projects called the She-Haw Transhumance and the "Can We Sleep in Your Barn Tonight?" Mystery Tour assembled to move, play, listen, and improvise in slow deliberation through this particular pastoral, agricultural-postindustrial landscape.

In different configurations and assemblages, each of these projects plays on speculative past and future resonances of transhumance, limned by contemporary artistic, poetic, and (cosmo)political nomadic theory (à la Isabelle Stengers and Rosi Braidotti), to pitch into places and explore unique possibilities for "assthetic" acts of passing through.[11] Together, She-Haw Transhumance and the "Can We Sleep in Your Barn Tonight?" Mystery Tour became a bizarre ass farewell tour, as nomadic assemblages of mammalian companions and insects and birds and grasses came together in a peculiar sort of wake for the untold pasts and futures of old barns, valley fields and watersheds, and ways of life woven through them. In search of nourishment for the hordes of ghosts and future friends who may walk these hills, we set forth into the roadside ditches, overgrown meadows, dusty barn-darks, and interstate winds of the Valley of Dooms, to acknowledge, embrace, and even celebrate the necessary failure of any safe, stable, or static place to call home in an age of frayed belongings for so many earthly inhabitants.

She-Haw Transhumance

– I speak as one silenced. Transhumance, as understood and utilized in late 12th C., early 13th C. France, was an agricultural motion or migration, a seasonal moving of livestock and the people who tend them [...] but transhumance also was a possible personal~social act of symmetry, reciprocity and redistribution. Co-mercy, the art of harmlessness [...] to let, to kneel, along the places of the abyss,

11 A number of contemporary artists incorporate modes of performative walking into aesthetic and political explorations of places. The practices of Hamish Fulton in the later twentieth century and the work of contemporary artist Angela Ellsworth delve into the aesthetic and political possibilities and consequences of creative walking. Theoretically speaking, She-Haw's artistic listening-walking performance of becomings-with-asses-and-grasses addresses pressing questions of multispecies belonging that are kin to Rosi Braidotti's nomadic theory, seeking "a regrounding of the subject in a materially embedded sense of responsibility and ethical accountability for the environment s/he inhabits." Rosi Braidotti, *Nomadic Theory: The Portable Rosi Braidotti* (New York: Columbia University Press, 2011), 122.

> to linger as long as possible [...] where the same relation
> may be observed throughout the whole universe, where
> significance "bleeds into an unconstrainable chain."
> – Lissa Wolsak, "an_heuristic_prolusion"[12]

Just past the crack of dawn on a hot May morning in 2006, She-Haw – an assemblage of two spotted she-asses, Aliass and Passenger, led by two bipedal human artists, L-Haw (Lydia Peelle) and K-Haw (yours truly) – set off from the weedy verge of the interstate exit ramp just outside Mt. Sidney, Virginia. We tacked up on the roadside and packed the saddlebags with water bottles, bug spray, and sunblock, and then ambled off into the morning heat, four femammals making our ways slowly along country roads that wound through farm fields and industrial accretions, in the valley below darkly folded foothills of the Appalachian Blue Ridge mountain range. The wind from eighteen-wheelers buffeted us as we made our ways along an access road between the roaring interstate on one side and sprawling nursery for residential landscape shrubs on the other. As we walked, we did not talk. The impulse to put our bodies in place of our speech (in choreographer Emily Stone's words) drove us to make the journey in silence that day. Well, not silence, exactly. We humans agreed in advance that during this She-Haw Transhumance we would refrain from speaking, from sharing verbal observations or otherwise imposing our voices into the landscape (unless for safety alerts, like "Car!" or "Snake!"). We would still our tongues for the duration of the trek, and instead listen for untold stories in the places we passed through, in deeply embodied ways.

Artistically speaking (or rather not-speaking), She-Haw Transhumances perform and explore complex quandaries of multispecies belonging and human artistic

12 Lissa Wolsak, "an_heuristic_prolusion," *Raddle Moon* 18, no. 2 (2002): 81.

representation – most specifically the galls and thralls
found in such seamy rural–industrial places where the
ontological, ethical, and "assthetic" desires of a pair of
nomadic storying women meet the mysterious surfaces
and depths of long-eared embodied equine wisdoms and
different practices of living with them. She-Haw is a collaborative venture that brings together different artistic
practices and strategies to track untold stories through
places where we find all kinds of beastly bodies meeting the burdens of domestic human desires. L-Haw (aka
Lydia Peelle) writes fiction, including a celebrated 2009
story collection, *Reasons for and Advantages of Breathing*,
and the 2017 novel, *The Midnight Cool*.¹³ Meanwhile, She-
Haw Transhumance also draws on different contemporary artistic strategies to actualize twenty-first-century,
rural–postindustrial beastly situatedness, and so open up
what Rosi Braidotti describes as "virtual possibilities that
had been frozen in the image of the past."¹⁴ In this regard,
as much as we are (dis)inheritors of our grandfathers'
barnyards, She-Haw is heir to Sun Ra's slick earthbound
inversions of Space-Age Afro-futurisms and also bastard
cousin to artist-provocateur Praba Pilar's cyborg–shaman–Coyote interventions in transhumanist techno-
transcendence.¹⁵ With an ear to these modes, She-Haw

13 In the guise of a historical novel, *The Midnight Cool* makes delicate
lacunae for the untold stories of others, especially the thousands
of Tennessee mules shipped to the bloody mire of wwi battlefields
in Europe. Lydia Peelle, *The Midnight Cool* (New York: HarperCollins,
2017).

14 Rosi Braidotti also evokes the key roles of creative imagination
and memory in this process of "becoming-woman-animal-insect-
indecipherable": she writes that "imagination plays a crucial role in
[...] conceptual creativity and ethical empowerment. It is connected
to memory [...]. When you remember in the intensive or minority-
mode, you open up spaces of movement and of deterritorialization
that actualize virtual possibilities that had been frozen in the image
of the past." Braidotti, *Nomadic Theory*, 53.

15 Distinct from "transhumanism," which expects humans to "transcend" biological limitations through ever-advancing futuristic

Transhumance navigates fraught realms of imaginative representation and conflicted wonderings of who we are and how we might entwine our cares and tongues with the fleshly webs of other lives, ghosts, and swarming motes in pastoral ecologies.

So She-Haw made the walk that day without talking, in exclusively non-verbal human ways at least. At the same time, what we hoped to honor and attend in the course of this "silent" passage through the valley is really as far from silence as you can get. In openings where strange voices and unknown presences proliferate, She-Haw Transhumances amplify the force of James Clifford's insight that, "Silence is stories that do not translate."[16] L-Haw evokes the resonance of meaningful silences like these in her award-winning short story "Mule Killers." As the narrator recollects the time when tractors arrived on farms in the early twentieth century to take the place of mule labor, he recalls how "all across the state that year, big trucks loaded with mules rumbled steadily to the slaughterhouses. They drove over the roads that mules

technologies and exceptional rationality, these modes of creative Transhumance take an opposite tack. As Cary Wolfe describes "transhumanism" as a direct descendent of "ideals of human perfectibility, rationality and agency inherited from Renaissance humanism and the Enlightenment," he distinguishes that mode of thinking from a "posthumanism" that names the "embodiment and embeddedness of the human being in not just its biological but also its technological world" and also recognizes "a historical moment in which the decentering of the human by its imbrication in technical, medical, informatics, and economic networks is increasingly impossible to ignore." Cary Wolfe, *What Is Posthumanism?* (Minneapolis: University of Minnesota Press, 2010), xv. Like Sun Ra's Astro Black Mythology, artist-scholar Praba Pilar's Church of Nano-Cogno-Info-Bio intervenes brilliantly in notions of transhumanism whereby humanity is expected to "transcend" its mortal animal nature. See Praba Pilar's website, http://www.prabapilar.com/pages/projects/churchnbic2.html/.

16 James Clifford, *Returns* (Cambridge: Harvard University Press, 2013), 23.

themselves had cut, the gravel and macadam the mules themselves had laid. Once or twice a day, you would hear a high-pitched bray come from one of the trucks, a rattling as it went by, and then silence."[17]

For our human parts, at least, the experience of moving slowly on foot and hoof through earthly places with the wary, watchful, grass-hungry, and attentive she-asses is a creative effort to listen differently and to open environments in ways exclusive human-centered storyings can't do – to honor and make new spaces for the different ways that others might story themselves in places. Vinciane Despret and Michel Meuret describe a similar collaborative, "cosmoecological" approach among contemporary European humans and domestic sheep, who have taken up transhumant herding practices in spite of these traditions' local cultural and economic obsolescence. These newfangled herding practices are "arts for living on a damaged planet," as they pitch transhumance into blasted landscapes in ways that change everybody involved; their mixed herds of mammal, plant, insect, and microbial communities "inhabit and compose with" the landscapes they pass through in newfound ways: "We say compose with because to inhabit is at once to be transformed by the environment and to transform it. [...] [T]ranshumance is one of these ways of inhabiting and so composing with a place, a space in time."[18]

So She-Haw set out through the Valley of Dooms that morning to compose-with the she-asses, grasses, and untold others. She-Haw Transhumances are acts of listening-in-places (as best we can) within the limits of our human attunements and umwelts alongside those of our long-eared, dusty-furred, otherworldly friends.

17 Lydia Peelle, "Mule Killers," in *Reasons for and Advantages of Breathing* (New York: Harper Perennial, 2009), 1.
18 Vinciane Despret and Michel Meuret, "Cosmoecological Sheep and the Arts of Living on a Damaged Planet," *Environmental Humanities* 8, no. 1 (2016): 32.

Geographically, the distance we walked on foot and hoof in the stifling humidity of early-summer Virginia was roughly seven miles – a fairly straight shot along back roads, with a little stretch of county highway and the tiny town of Weyers Cave in between. We ambled slowly along at the preferred speed of the she-asses (roughly <2 mph), in a steady rhythm of bare hoofbeats on asphalt and occasional whiffs of blooming honeysuckle on the breeze. Aliass and Passenger were eager as always to snatch bites of the tall roadside grasses, and their long hollow ears swiveled constantly, catching little sounds from near and far. As the heat of the day came on, we walked in slow immersion within a wild swell of sounds, from the click of the she-asses' hooves on the macadam to crickets in the grassroot shadows to the lows of dairy cows inside an old tin-sided barn, where we stopped to bask in that swollen sounding resonance for a time. The pale asphalt road rolled and wound up and down hills, past pastures and hayfields and neatly tended flowerbeds that wrap around single-story brick ranch houses with long paved driveways and two-car garages. The grassy, gravelly, asphalt patchwork of agricultural, industrial, and residential zones we plodded through were thickly crisscrossed with strands of barbed, cedary longings and raw-ass hopes and fears – all of which wove us more deeply than we could ever know into (in)visible traces of myriad lifeways that abide in that shifting landscape.

Alongside our lovely long-eared companions, She-Haw Transhumance holds spaces for untold stories in places where human perspectives and ways of knowing and navigating are never the only ones we need to attend to, whether in the Valley of Dooms or anywhere else. Over the years various forays have led She-Haw to transhumance through different kinds of seamy sites: From the spectacular Mule Day Parade in Tennessee, to dim cobwebby corners of county-fair barns where we find ourselves following mysterious handwritten signs that feature inkjet pictures of indigo buntings and promise "this way for *REAL* beauty...," to the damp and gravelly paths into Paleolithic caves in the Perigord Noir and Hotel Cro-Magnon, where we meet cloven-hooved and spotted-fur ghosts of ancient earthly herds. We wander into and through supposed silences of marginal others, from disregarded beasts to unseen kinships that unfold in hidden processes and paths: in other words, we chase new forms of flocks and folds in meshes of untold stories of beastly becomings with(in) places.

The "Can We Sleep in Your Barn Tonight?" Mystery Tour

While She-Haw Transhumance evokes and composes with others' stories by not-speaking as we pass through places, the "Can We Sleep in Your Barn Tonight?" Mystery Tour took a different approach for tuning in to inscrutable compositions in the places we passed through. The Mystery Tour was a three-day trek of a motley band, including (but not limited to) a fluctuating crew of human musician/artists, Aliass and Passenger, two borrowed miniature goats (Pink and Green), and a number of canine companions, among others. The Mystery Tour departed on a bright Tuesday morning in June (a few days after the She-Haw Transhumance) in a fanfare of handheld drums and hoofbeats and bells and goat bleats. For the next three days, this nomadic band of wayfaring strangers rolled along on foot and hoof through roadsides, fields, barnyards, and even a hidden cave, in a rollicking wake for what's hidden and endangered in present Appalachian landscapes. Most especially we honored what lives in the old wooden barns that are quite literally subsiding, along with their unwritten languages and ways of knowing, by the wayside of interstates, suburban development, and industrial agribusiness.

While the trek along rural roadsides toward the town of Dooms itself was a vital part of the performance, the

"Can We Sleep in Your Barn Tonight?" Mystery Tour had another distinct method for tuning into indeterminate plays between all the living presences (known and unknown) in the old barns and underground. As we moved through the valley, The Mystery Tour band assembled in specific spaces to perform musical improvisation – specifically within two remarkable old barns (known to us as The Churchbarn and the Octagonal Barn) and one spectacular show cave.[19] The "Can We Sleep in Your Barn Tonight?" Mystery Tour comprised a postmodern melding of sources and inspirations, from the Beatles' Magical Mystery Tour to the gritty echoes of North Carolina old-time banjo player Charlie Poole (who recorded an especially haunting version of the old-time tune, "May I Sleep in Your Barn Tonight, Mister?"), along with a certain homage to James Joyce's notion of language asleep in *Finnegans Wake*. The human crew who gathered to walk and play in the Valley of Dooms came in from cities and towns all over the US. With a common grounding in experimental improvisation, the Mystery Tour band mixed diverse musicological passions and improvisational skills. Main players Pamela Albanese, Rennie Elliot, Layne Garrett, Jacob Mitas, Melanie Moser, George Murer, Alex Ney, and Eli Queen all improvised and listened together, merging influences from punk and neofolk and eerie old-time fiddle tunes, fringed and flayed with George's shredding electric guitar and Middle-Eastern drums in the Octagonal Barn, Alex's wicked clawhammer banjo, strange vocal rounds summoned by Melanie from hand-painted religious signs in the Churchbarn loft, Rennie's rollicking Dolly-Parton-inscribed banjo, and Jacob Mitas's hints of Arvo Pärt in the cave, among many other resonanc-

---

19 Grand Caverns, as it is known, has been in use as a commercial show cave beneath the valley since the time of the US Civil War in the nineteenth century. We gained access to this cave for the final night of the Mystery Tour thanks to a winter I spent employed there as a part-time cave tour guide.

es woven through. So the band played on, improvising with all kinds of analog and digital electronics, strangely resonant religious placards, dusty radio waves, hayblown night-barn vocal harmonies, and the quivering vibrations of Pamela Albanese's musical saw.[20]

In each of the two special barns we passed through, and especially on that last night deep in the cave, the band practiced improvisation in response to the distinct spaces where we found ourselves. This creative mode of deep listening (with roots in the works of John Cage and Pauline Oliveros, especially) in places set out to fathom and celebrate – through acoustical presence and musical, lyrical improvisation with stringed instruments, woodwinds, drums, and whatever else was along – what and who is hidden, yet present and resonant, in the motes, seeds, stalagmites, and oak-beams of these spaces' own wilder creaks and hums, and how they harmonize with entangled roots and hides and bones.[21] At the same time, we also try to recognize the limits of our listening in territories with complex histories, full of untold stories in which we are always more deeply implicated than we ever reckon.[22]

20 Sean Hart held it all together and kept things running on the roads and campsites. We were also joined at stages by poets, artists, and wanderers Jessica Bozek, Kate Herron, Douglas Smith, and photographers Shane Carpenter and Susanna Slocum.

21 In other registers, Rosi Braidotti has some fascinating insights that resonate with the Mystery Tour's modus operandi in her essay, "The Cosmic Buzz of Insects"; here she discusses the ways in which "nomadic or rhizomatic musicology attempts to make us hear the inaudible. [...] The becoming-minoritarian of music produces a practice of expression without a monolithic or unitary subject that supervises the operations and capitalizes upon them. It literally brings the cosmos home." Braidotti, *Nomadic Theory*, 109–10.

22 Again, for all the creative intentions of these practices, the privileges we take for granted in accessing places are never innocent. Take, for example, the role of show caves in the proliferation of the vicious white-nose disease that has been extinguishing bat species around the world. See Tessa Laird, *Bat* (London: Reaktion Books, 2018).

In these different, nomadic radical-listening assemblages, She-Haw Transhumance and the "Can We Sleep in Your Barn Tonight?" Mystery Tour wound through the Valley of Dooms in their distinct modes, buffeted doubly by invisible histories and the roar of interstate truck-traffic along the rural roadsides, then deeper into the landscape, past dairy-farm barnyards dotted with veal-calf igloos. From Weyers Cave and the banks of the foamy green North Fork of the Shenandoah River, we moved through shadowy hopes and brighter visions hidden in the folded hills and barn-dark infrastructures of this colonial, agricultural-postindustrial Southern US state of Virginia – which is to say, trying to locate ourselves within different kinds of belonging and to make ourselves more "response-able" to the wholeness of places, even as we know we are only passing through. From within different orientations (both biographically chartable and utterly unknown), we made our ways – walking, listening, wondering, improvising – on grassy edges in diesel-laden winds with many different hungers and hopes for where we might be headed on the supposed road to Dooms, and what we might find when we get there.

Must Be Moving On…

Transhumances became one creative way of reckoning with all the barn-dark chafes and galls, sources and sites of painful conflicts and betrayals found in the Valley of Dooms, and everywhere else that is haunted by extractive global capitalism and other hungry forces. Each body carries (through the Valley and its shadow places) a distinct burden of embodied memories, hungers, and fears, gathered from past places, from places' buried pasts, and from the worrisome ways things always seem to be headed. Even so, nomadic-ass forays and home-makings are pitched to resist the bulldozing of multispecies futures and blaze trails toward more just assemblages –

whatever those may be amidst thickets of bodies in the mangled, wondrous, and often toxic places where we find ourselves. And so, through failed and fleeting experimental habitations in the Valley of Dooms, I learned that the letting-go of static notions of belonging can open vital paths toward future possible-ass pastures. In *Emergent Ecologies*, Eben Kirksey calls out the dominant mode of doom-saying in contemporary environmental discourses, and the book as whole beckons readers to "reject apocalyptic thinking" and grasp "the possibility of grounding hopes in shared futures": "Tactfully guiding interspecies collaborations, new generations are learning how to care for emergent assemblages by seeding them, nurturing them, protecting them, and ultimately letting go."[23]

So this is how we say goodbye to obsolete dreams and fractured belongings scattered through the Valley of Dooms: Seeking hope for new, more inclusive kinds of belonging, we keep passing through blasted places, in the aura of unnamed associates. Moving on together in the common search for nourishment, in recognition of the shifting sources of what each body needs, while seeking shelter from whatever one must try to evade, too: from hot sun and unprecedented storms to shady landlords, rampant global corporations, and other dangerous or predatory forces less easily named. As we seek to find ourselves-with-others more wholly in places, it matters who is here, who and how "we" are, and how we compose ourselves with/in twisted-together stories of other species, where a lack of history as such is too often deployed to write off and erase others' lives as meaningless silence.

It matters whether, and how, different lives and their distinct voices are bulldozed and buried, or instead brought to light and soundings in collective revelries. Vibrantly untold stories might be otherwise heard and sung

23 Eben Kirksey, *Emergent Ecologies* (Durham: Duke University Press, 2015), 214.

in intimate meshes of bodies' pulsing unknowns, in the shadowy folds of foothills, fields, and undergrounds we might call home and must always, in the long run, let go of.

8

R.A.W. ASSMILK SOAP

Black Milk

Years before I met Aliass, or ever dreamed of American Spotted Asses, I had a secret name for an otherwise unnamable substance I desired to tap in flows of words and submerged memories. I called it "the black milk." Every time I sat down to wrangle with poetic imagination, I would begin by asking: "Where is the black milk now?" By this means I would begin a descent into dark crevasses of longing and memory and work my way toward shadowy figures and desires buried in remembering tissues. Even as it stood for something inchoate, fearsome, and hard to grasp, I sensed that this black milk also possessed some kind of homeopathic, transformative power to cleanse and redeem. Years later I found something akin to this ghostly poetic material, but more real and powerful, in Aliass's singular mammalian brew – as I imagined into the milk she made for Passenger during our first long-ass journey from Mississippi to Virginia in the summer of 2002.

Eventually, I rediscovered a black-milk inoculant in Paul Celan's 1945 poem, "Deathfugue": "Black milk of daybreak we drink it at evening."[1] The milk in this poem is black with ashes from Auschwitz, which rained from the sky overnight and darkened the morning milk of a nearby dairy, thus staining the quintessential substance of maternal nourishment and bodily intimacy with irrevocable traces of atrocity. As I looked deeper at this metaphorical articulation, Celan's poem brought to the surface a vital, if latent, association between black milk and "the mother tongue" – that is, the primary language we are born into as humans and live within, inescapably, the language we begin to learn inside our mothers' wombs before we are even born. When Celan lost his mother and father to the Nazi death camps, his German mother-tongue became, as translator and biographer John Felstiner puts it, "his mother's murderers' tongue."[2] The language itself became stained with atrocity and motherloss. In light of this, and from the depths of unfathomable trauma, Celan wrested a new language, hybrid word forms forged from mangled remnants of his mother tongue, in his attempts to recover meaning and memory from so profound a void.

Black milk as a trope figures as a kind of absence inscribed into material substance. The blackness of milk becomes a shadowy residue of lost connection to somebody, some-where, however formless or unnamable. While the losses that haunted me are nowhere near as horrific or devastating as those to which Celan's poems bear witness, I've come to understand that my own struggles with language-as-mother-tongue are also driven by a sense of loss and betrayal. Guided deeper into the black-milk/mother-tongue nexus by Austrian poet Ingeborg Bachmann, and later by the psychoanalytic insights of Julia Kristeva, I looked back at my own black-milk hungers to try to find out what shadowy figures abide

---

1   Paul Celan, *Selected Poems and Prose of Paul Celan*, trans. John Felstiner (New York: W.W. Norton, 2001), 19.
2   John Felstiner, "Preface," in ibid., xxii.

in them. In an essay on Bachmann's fiction called "Living and Lost in Language," Gisela Brinker-Gabler writes: "Rejecting contact with the mother tongue cuts off the past and might be a life-saving strategy, if there is some profoundly detested experience."[3] As a contemporary of Celan's, Bachmann shared his struggle to cleanse language of the terrifying ways it was twisted and stained by the Third Reich. That idea resonated for me, though I didn't know then what "detestable experience" might be the source of my troubles. Later, I came upon Kristeva's description of the mother tongue in *Strangers to Ourselves*, in which she describes: "Not speaking one's mother tongue. Living with resonances and reasoning that are cut off from the body's nocturnal memory, from the bittersweet slumber of childhood. To cut off one's mother tongue cuts off one's childhood and whatever past there was in that language."[4] But what if that mother-tongue language is not, and never was, a strictly linguistic or exclusively human one?

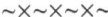

Technically speaking, I was born on an Air Force base, and not in a barn. But the barn is nevertheless where a native tongue came upon me, in time. From my earliest reckonings, an ancestral family farm in Ohio was a visceral source of the most profound wonder, encountered whenever we came from our suburban Vacaville cul-de-sac to visit my grandparents there. An ordinary patch of grass or motes spiraling in a lofty beam of barnlight brimmed

3   Gisela Brinker-Gabler, "Living and Lost in Language: Translation and Interpretation in Ingeborg Bachmann's 'Simultan,'" in *If We Had the Word: Ingeborg Bachmann, Views and Reviews*, eds. Gisela Brinker-Gabler and Markus Zisselsberger (Riverside: Ariadne Press, 2004), 86.

4   Julia Kristeva, *Strangers to Ourselves*, trans. Kelly Oliver (New York: Columbia University Press, 1991), 83.

with infinite richness, all particles of the greater mystery that lived there in the dusty aura of common beastly being. This mystery was most fiercely embodied in the other big domestic mammals who lived there, along with the bright-eyed ghosts of their own ancestors, going back generations. On that old farm my mother had frolicked in her childhood with spotted horses named Marblecake and Cupcake, and this same barnyard is where I first encountered the magic of my Aunt Angelique's mesmerizing friendship with the big chestnut gelding, Irvy.

When I was little, my aunt's long-legged thoroughbred horse Irvy was the lone inhabitant of the old barnyard, and some of my first memories are of his boundless and thrilling presence. Irvy was more than a big equine; he was an entire environment. Being near Irvy was an utter immersion in a presence of rich earthy odors, sounds, and sensations. His head seemed as long as my whole body. The rubbery lips and whiskers of his big kind muzzle coming down from way above, looming close and sniffing, then blowing out a cloud of sweet hay-smelling breath.... Irvy could not have seemed more magical if he was actually a friendly fire-breathing dragon. He was just "horse," of course, and soon enough I learned to call all the beasts by their proper names and put them in their places.

Thinking back on those primal experiences on the Ohio farm, I later came to believe that my own black milk sought to somehow recover forms of kinship with the mysteries of otherworldly lives I'd first tasted in my mother's barnyard, so to speak. No doubt these experiences taught me wonder and respect toward friendly muzzles found on the other sides of stable doors and barbed-wire fences. But why this looming sense of loss and shame lurking in the cobwebby corners and lively dust of barns I find myself in to this day?

As I grew up into the late twentieth century, I began to glimpse the darker elements of agricultural systems and histories, even as the culture I lived in was beginning a profound shift of awareness toward what came to be called "animal rights," broadly speaking. I noticed the many different ways that human exceptionalisms, hierarchies, and materialist commodifications of lives shape relationships bound to stables and barnyards. I became aware of enduring colonial and racist legacies, indigenous genocides, and the effects wrought on ecologies by neoliberal industrial-capitalist techno-cultures – and, more and more, how all these elements are interconnected. Slowly over time my education and linguistic proficiency gave me a framework of words and concepts to name these forces, yet still none of them could encompass what I long for most, nor assuage the growing sense of betrayal: that what I have been taught to believe is all wrong; that there are multiple, possibly infinite mother tongues woven through all kinds of lives in places, not just the syntactical languages of human speech and thought. But the betrayal comes in ignoring all the others, as the blustery arrogance of human logos always seems to bulldoze over quieter, less visible wisdoms of untold stories and becomings in timeplaces.

Here we come again to the conundrum of mysterious black-milk hungers, and to that specific site where, for me early on, the conflicted desire seems to have taken root in my own troubled mother tongue, that is to say, the bygone Ohio barnyard animated by the specters of big domestic friends like Irvy, and later a bay gelding named Moon, who belonged to a transitory vet-student tenant, and whose sweet sweaty fur I can still conjure the smell of, from the one time the vet student and Moon took me for a ride at Christmastime some forty years ago. Even more poignantly, perhaps, those encounters with Irvy and Moon took place in the landscape where my mother spent that singular summer of her own childhood in the mid-1950s, away from the strict rules of her military family and living for a spell with her wild young Aunt Jean,

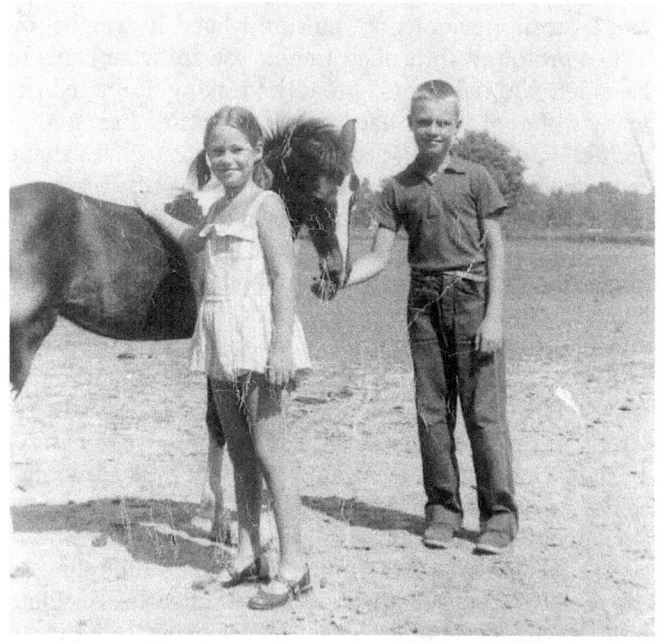

Fig. 1. Cupcake as a filly with my future mother Christie and her big brother, Alan, in Ohio, circa 1955. Photo courtesy of Christie Bolender.

who was seemingly half-horse herself (and who was, incidentally, the first woman to earn a degree in animal husbandry from Ohio State University). My mother would recall running wild in the pastures all summer with her older brother and a friend named Bonnie, riding bareback and braiding flowers into Marblecake's mane. An old photo of my eight-year-old mother shows her in a short dress with her hand on the sleek spotted shoulder of Cupcake, Marblecake's foal. And other old photos plucked from the family scrapbook: Cupcake grown up and in her winter fur, hitched to a sleigh in deep snow; Cupcake in a sea of green grass, carrying one of my mother's cherubic younger cousins bareback, surrounded by a flock of family Dalmatians.

I suspect that, in some magic and fateful way, Aliass began with Cupcake.[5] I only ever glimpsed Cupcake in the flesh once, a far-off patch of bony brown and white seen fleetingly from a car window as we passed an impossibly green Virginia hollow where she'd been turned out to pasture with cattle in her old age. From all I'd heard about her, it was like seeing a mythical beast across the veils of time. My mother's recollections of that halcyon summer with Marblecake (Cupcake's mother) became part of my own story before I even had ears, and more so thereafter, as the generations, horse and human, twisted down through the later decades of the twentieth century. Through my childhood, my mother's stories, and the longings and kinships borne in them, took earthly forms in encounters with real dogs and horses. I can still recall the sweet-edged, dusty smell and wiry mane of Cupcake's own foal, Crumb, a black gelding who was a beloved and notorious trickster. He was a member of the extended family, whom I befriended during the springtime trips we took over the years to visit Great Aunt Jean on her own family's horse farm in Virginia.

The ancestral farm in Ohio mostly succumbed to the sprawls of Columbus. Needless to say, it was not the only one. As more and more family farms disappeared under housing developments and parking lots, the sprawl of asphalt and mown lawns gradually cut off access to certain reliable sources of raw mysteries and dusty interspecies

5   I can't resist evoking Nabokov's narrator Humbert Humbert here: "I am convinced, however, that in a certain magic and fateful way Lolita began with Annabel." Vladimir Nabokov, *Lolita* (New York: Vintage International, 1997), 14. Since technically there is no law on the books forbidding it, my platonic love for Aliass may not demand quite the same degree of frightful eloquence that Humbert calls upon to try to justify his immoral dealings with the underage human girl, Dolores Haze. Nevertheless, I think Nabokov might recognize the gesture of homage, given the ways questionable adult passions are sometimes kindled by vital encounters submerged in the murky depths of childhood.

kinships found in such places.[6] Primary among these de-sertions was the loss of my own family's horse-boarding enterprise in Virginia, though I was not present to wit-ness its demise, exactly. And eventually I realized this: it was not just the abstractly troubled mother tongue that haunted my negotiations with language in the purgatory chasm we humans inhabit between words and living bod-ies; it was also the loss of my mother's *place of belonging*, both real and imagined, the place she loved and nurtured and fought for and lost – her own family horse farm, and the dreams and desires that manifest for a time in sixty acres of rolling creeks and pastures, slatted barn-light, cedar groves, and hardwood forests all around.

My special brand of black milk may have welled up from that lost Virginia farmscape and the familial mesh-es rooted and left buried there. But, importantly, the sense of haunting loss is bigger than any one biography: all landscapes bears witness to cascades of displacement, vanishings of all kinds from any given place in the tidal waves of colonial and extractive enterprises over centu-ries past, along with looming losses ahead. Most of all, the black milk figured a sense of having lost connection to a matrix – a beyond-mammalian mother tongue as a way of belonging in places – much larger than that of any single bodily being or species.

So my black milk figured a specific breach – the body of language as a substance darkened with the loss of some embodied m<other tongue, held (but not wholly)

---

6 Encounters with barn dust are not immaterial to the shaping of microbial mother tongues, it seems. One widely reported study in *The New England Journal of Medicine* found that incidences of autoim-mune diseases decreased significantly in Amish children regularly exposed to the mix of special microbes in familial barn dust, versus other groups of children who had no such exposure. Gina Kolata, "Barnyard Dust Offers a Clue to Stopping Asthma in Children," *New York Times*, August 3, 2016. https://www.nytimes.com/2016/08/04/health/dust-asthma-children.html/.

in the "body's nocturnal memory," as Kristeva calls it in *Strangers to Ourselves*.[7] At the same time, I glimpsed a vague promise of redemption, the shadow of what was lost reabsorbed into substance, made present again – as assmilk. The black-milk-as-assmilk trope promised a new way in, somehow – one that could flow through the barriers made of words and names that are supposed to distinguish "us" from "them," where I was cultured to assume that taxonomies and syntaxes are exceptional faculties that hold us humans high and clean above the mud that killable beasts (beloved or otherwise) are mired in.[8]

Soap

> As soon as our soap has been put into
> orbit, none of this will be necessary.
> – Francis Ponge, *Soap*[9]

When I received an unexpected gift package from France in 2005, the *savon au lait d'ânesse* (assmilk soap) I found inside presented an ideal form in which to hold all the poetic musings and material possibilities of assmilk as a metaphorical cleansing agent. In the mid-twentieth century, French poet Francis Ponge wrote an experimental text titled Soap, wherein he explores the idea that his "processual poetry" on the essence of soap might act to cleanse habitual and crusty ways of reading, writing,

7 Kristeva, *Strangers to Ourselves*, 193.
8 Following Giorgio Agamben, Eben Kirksey and Stefan Helmreich illuminate a vital emergence that animates a mesh of practices they call multispecies ethnography: "Animals, plants, fungi, and microbes once confined in anthropological accounts to the realm of zoe or 'bare life' – that which is killable – have started to appear alongside humans in the realm of bios, with legibly biographical and political lives." Kirksey and Helmreich, "The Emergence of Multispecies Ethnography," *Cultural Anthropology* 25, no. 4 (2010): 545.
9 Francis Ponge, *Soap*, trans. Lane Dunlop (Stanford: Stanford University Press, 1998), 8.

and using language to interface with the material world: "So we slip from words to meanings [...] by a glistening inebriety, or rather an effervescence, a cold ebullience which, besides, we come out of, and here is the great lesson – with cleaner, purer hands than before this exercise began."[10] While I find much to love in the wild bubbling wordplay of Ponge's *Soap,* for my own purposes the poem alone could not go far enough. While inevitably rooted in semiotic processes, I wanted to find a way to propose wordless intra-actions of bodies in timeplaces as the *stories that matter most,* in this case. And then suddenly, *savon au lait d'ânesse* offered a way to hold tangled bodies' unwritten storyings, through milk made of immunological interactions in timeplaces.[11]

Drawing on its own distinctly embodied sources of black (ass)milk and poetic hope, R.A.W. Assmilk Soap proposes that cleansing certain "lyes" of the land, mixing them with the beneficent properties of locally brewed assmilk, might work with imagination to neutralize some of a place's buried ailments. Along with the not-to-be-taken-for-granted cooperation of she-asses, the milksoap-making act also depends on a transformative chemical process known as saponification, which significantly changes both assmilk and another essential soap

10 Ibid., 19.
11 The ways that milk-making bodies and systems respond in specific immunological ways to local encounters – and also hold and transfer less beneficial substances that accumulate in mammalian bodies through biomagnification – are detailed in the introduction. See again Mirium Simun, "Human Cheese," in *The Multispecies Salon,* ed. Eben Kirksey (Durham: Duke University Press, 2014), 135–44 and Winona LaDuke, "Akwesasne: Mohawk Mother's Milk and PCBs," in *Sing, Whisper, Shout, Pray! Feminist Visions for a Just World,* eds. M. Jacqui Alexander, Lisa Albrecht, Sharon Day, and Mab Segrest (Fort Bragg: Edgework, 2003), 159–71. On bodily porosities and their biopolitical implications and possibilities, see Stacy Alaimo, *Bodily Natures: Science, Environment and the Material Self* (Bloomington: Indiana University Press, 2010) and Astrida Neimanis, *Bodies of Water: Posthuman Feminist Phenomenology* (London: Bloomsbury, 2017).

ingredient, lye (sodium hydroxide). Lye alone will burn the skin fiercely, but when mixed with milk and base oils and stirred until it "traces," lye neutralizes to become the solvent agent in soap, and so the ultimate cleansing substance.[12] The chemical transformations embodied in saponification echo back to the black milk as it functions in Paul Celan's poetics. In his "black milk," Celan (whose name I often mistype by accident as "Clean") seeks to "find words for 'that which happened,' as the poet called the Holocaust or *Shoah* [...] how to speak of and through the 'thousand darknesses of deathbringing speech.'"[13] Transformative power abides in the poetic act, as John Felstiner observes: "The cadence and imagery of ["Deathfugue"] engage atrocity with art, as Celan would go on doing during the next quarter century."[14]

Later in the twentieth century, artists began to reckon directly with toxic legacies, not only within languages polluted by "deathbringing darknesses" but also within living bodies and earthly ecologies. The environmental stains, shames, and fears that ecological artists address and seek to cleanse have chemical names that read like twisted inverses of Celan's distinct and breathless neologisms, from phthalates to dibenzofurans – many of which can be found, biomagnified, in the milk of any mammal living today. Artists hoping to reckon with toxic legacies must seek conduits for hopeful gestures in landscapes blasted by past horrors and present complex global economic and political forces. Through different media and political and historical trajectories, ecological

12 As one stirs the mixture of milk, lye, and oils for anywhere between twenty minutes to two hours, it gradually thickens. When it has thickened such that a line of it dripped onto the surface remains there without sinking, this is called "tracing," and it means saponification has begun and the mixture is ready to be poured into molds to fully saponify and harden.

13 Felstiner, "Preface," xxii.

14 Ibid.

artists and poets perform acts of remediation via biological processes, as in the cleansing work of mosses and hyperaccumulators in significant works by Jackie Brookner, Mel Chin, Deanna Pindell, and others.[15]

I return to again and again to Brookner's *Prima Lingua*, as it performs both bioremediative and metaphorical action on polluted agricultural runoff flowing over mosses and other plants that clean the waters as they roll over a big rock shaped like a human tongue. Brookner's early biosculpture suggests that the healing powers of invisible, biological processes are an essential part of an original mother tongue that all earthly bodies speak. At the same time, the work of contemporary multispecies storytellers and poets – like Adam Dickinson in his feisty metabolic explorations of embodied chemical legacies – remind us that words, however toxic or tonic they may be, are also irremediably part of naturalcultural inheritances that permeate earthly lives and generations to come.[16] With careful attention, we might come to recognize how the mother-of-all-tongues is a porous matrix of bodies-in-process that always enfolds us, whether we are aware of it or not.

---

15 Sue Spaid, *Ecovention: Current Art to Transform Ecologies* (Cincinnati: Contemporary Arts Center, 2002).

16 Adam Dickinson's practice of metabolic poetics explores the question of whether poems too can act on bodily systems, rather than just reacting to the myriad toxins imposed upon them. Adam Dickinson, *Anatomic* (Toronto: Coach House Books, 2018).

Rural Alchemy Workshop (R.A.W.)

Our *paradise*, in short, will it not have been the others?
— Francis Ponge, *Soap*[17]

Like any dairy product laced with violent histories and persistent global toxicities, assmilk must always be a product of its time and place. Indeed, the means to transform assmilk's potential meaning-making properties from conceptual blueprint to material manufacture of R.A.W. Assmilk Soap required much more than just amenable she-asses. This speculative ass dairy also needed a home base, a hideout from which to reckon with our implicit immersions in both global webs and local ecologies. In 2008, it happened that our familial herd settled precariously on a neglected farm of nearly ten acres on the edge of a town called Carnesville in rural northeast Georgia. It was on the anxious outpost of the Carnesville farm that the Rural Alchemy Workshop was founded, thanks to the keen determination of Sean, my indefatigable partner in R.A.W. husbandry, who applied his formidable gifts to navigating the tribulations of small-town law and shady backroad rural real-estate dealings. In time our place in Carnesville became a little secret scrappy-ass rebel base. We nurtured lives and dreams in a backwoods barnyard of wire-fenced paddocks, surrounding a lofty old slatted barn that sheltered the long- and short-eared equines, a weird assortment of chickens, and the wild rats, deer, squirrels, ants, and snakes (to name a few), alongside a squat cinderblock dwelling for the humans, dogs, cat, and mice by the millions. Here the makings of R.A.W. Assmilk Soap became materially possible – and achingly necessary.

Even as we assiduously nourished a certain familial peace-of-ass within the fence lines and wooded edges of

17 Ponge, *Soap*, 14.

our Carnesville homestead, the R.A.W. was threatened on every side by economic, political, environmental, and cultural forces that chafed and galled, beyond the meager means of rural alchemy to assuage. As trash left behind by the farm's past inhabitants continuously surfaced in the barnyard mud, I was haunted by these and other looming ghosts and monsters of all kinds of historical and environmental pollution.[18] As in many places across the American South, traces of racial and environmental exploitation are barely buried in the sandy soil. White-columned front porches of antebellum mansions and crooked slave shacks renovated as backyard garden sheds evoke memories of plantation economies founded on slave labor, reliant on the suffering of humans, mules and others and the plundering of forests and soils and whatever other entities could be made to serve its rapacious hungers. Alongside this fraught history, the postindustrial South these days is scarred by other more visible and voracious global consumer economies, evidenced by acres and acres of asphalt, endless Walmart and Dollar Store parking lots and Pay-Day check-cashing places in half-abandoned strip malls edged by gas-station convenience stores and fast-food drive-thrus.

I remember with a shudder one day in 2002 when Aliass and I got lost driving on the Alcoa Highway on the outskirts of Knoxville, Tennessee. I was hauling Aliass in the ramshackle trailer behind the Black Caprice, looking for a place to leave the rig and set out on foot and hoof again. What I encountered on the Alcoa Highway made me lose my nerve entirely. The horizon was nothing but acres of blinding car dealerships and heavy-machinery lots for as far as the eye could see in any direction – an

18 Elaine Gan, Anna Tsing, Heather Swanson, and Nils Bubandt, "Haunted Landscapes of the Anthropocene," in *Arts of Living on a Damaged Planet*, eds. Anna Tsing, Heather Swanson, Elaine Gan, and Nils Bubandt (Minneapolis: University of Minnesota Press, 2017), G1–G13.

impermeable desert far more forbidding than Death Valley could ever be. If the vision of an endless Alcoa Highway is not enough to unsettle lingering pastoral idylls, one can always turn to gut-wrenching images of ravaged Appalachian mountain ranges, clear-cut old-growth forests, Gulf Coast beaches strewn with tarballs and dead seabirds, or drowned neighborhoods in the paths of unprecedented storms.

But as Merle Haggard has it, "If you don't love it, leave it."[19] From our perspective within the R.A.W. homestead, Haggard's "it" might have been Carnesville, the country, or even Planet Earth. But in any case, love it we did – that little plot of compromised land and every mortal body living on it – with every means at our disposal. One steamy summer night in 2010, the R.A.W. ass herd grew by one more when Passenger gave birth to a foal sired by Henry. Aliass stood by quietly on guard in the dark while Passenger labored, pacing back and forth until the time came when she lay down in the paddock dirt and with a tremendous groan birthed the little wet wisp, who was born solid black as a shadow under the full moon.

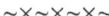

Six months after Nicholass Moon (aka Little Nick) was born, the R.A.W. Ass Dairy was in full swing. Passenger made milk for Nick, and I collected some of it for Assmilk Soap, with essential guidance from our gracious veterinarian, Dr. Alice Beretta, and advice gleaned from Jean-François Wambeke of L'Asinerie D'Embazac, an utterly magical ass dairy near Toulouse in the South of France.[20] Beside the twinkling waters of the foamy brown creek, I

19 Merle Haggard, "The Fightin' Side of Me," *Merle Haggard: 40 Greatest Hits* (Intersound, 2004).
20 You can glimpse the magic of L'Asinerie d'Embazac on its beautiful and informative website: http://www.embazac.com/.

stirred a mixture of lye and oils and Pass-milk, and dark as it was with local, historical, and global-industrial-capitalist-petrochemical traces, it was just as densely sweet with abiding desires, kinships, and intimate rememberings. Even as Passenger's body biomagnified the many invisible pollutants in our midst, her udders also nourished numerous beneficent processes, from the growth of Little Nick's bones and whiskers and thick ass fur (so thick, in fact, that on winter mornings I often found him covered in a layer of frost, like icing on a warm little cake) to the nurturing of distinctly human poetic hope, however strained, that this inextricable mixture of toxins and intimate exchanges might homeopathically heal some of our times' most catastrophic disconnections.[21]

At the same time, other shadows lurk within the assumptions that allow me to hold a herd of asses conscripted to my poetic purposes – some of those same forces that shape and distort the lives and bodies of millions of bovine mothers around the globe. Embedded in Assmilk Soap is the hard-to-ask question of how the she-asses feel about contributing to it. Passenger would let me express her milk without objection. But then again, she was born into my hands and tends to trust (and even scheme to manipulate) them. But Passenger's role as a dairy ass has a darker precursor. The first she-ass to contribute milk for the project had a different story to tell. Rose, as we called her, was a wary and beautiful black jennet with a striking white muzzle and underbelly, whom we bought from a shady Southern ass dealer with her fluffy black three-month-old nursing foal. Rose had not been handled much, and she didn't take kindly to being milked, being mistrustful of humans in general and me especially, and with good reason, I guess. Nor did she like it much when our farrier, Hoyt Silvey, had to knot her up

---

21 Isabelle Stengers, *In Catastrophic Times: Resisting the Coming Barbarism* (London: Open Humanities Press, 2015), 129–37.

in a cat's cradle of ropes so he could trim her hooves. Rose would tense up to flee or fight whenever I approached her, and needless to say she was unwilling to let down her milk in response to my pullings and proddings. After a while she would trade about a teaspoonful of milk for a few carrots, but it was a tense and unpleasant negotiation for both of us every time.

Wranglings with Rose present a dark episode in the history of R.A.W. Assmilk Soap. After recognizing Rose's misery in her role as a dairy ass, we delivered her to a neighbor who needed a companion for his lonesome Arabian horse. But she left a fertile legacy in her troubled wake. Her foal, who we call Henry, stayed with us and grew up to be a handsome jack. When Henry was about two years old, he sired Little Nick (at Passenger's persistent urging), passing on his rather rare, all-black coat color to the herd's newest member. As Nick grew up, he and Henry became a striking pair, both solid black from muzzle to tail and nearly indistinguishable.

Over the years, the R.A.W. continued to explore new forms of artful ass husbandry within the knowns and unknowns of the makeshift home we all made together on the edge of Carnesville, insulated to some degree from the nearby interstate commerce by the burbling coolness of the shady, glittering creek, the buzzing cicadas, and haunting calls of invisible whip-poor-wills from the evening woods. Yet it was not easy to feel at home, for a variety of reasons. Along with a general sense of ominous presences in the local landscapes, there was the woe that welled up in me every week when our nextdoor neighbor Mr. Crump burned his plastic household trash, and the noxious black smoke wafted through the scraggly pine trees and into the lungs of the herd – donkeys, dogs, horses, humans, cat, birds, and every other breathing being, even coating the leaves of the trees and garden greens. Traces of it likely ended up in Passenger's milk. And let's never forget the chickenshit. Carnesville was

the seat of a Georgia county that boasted the most industrial chicken houses of any in the United States, and every winter the farmer who leased the hayfields next door
would spread the reeking manure of millions of bald and
miserable birds onto the fields as fertilizer, so that the
next rain would roll it downhill and into our soils, creek,
and well water. Carnesville is stained in other ways, so
many ways, and it is our fault; all of us are implicated.
As we well know, Carnesville is hardly the only place so
stained in this so-called Anthropocene age.

  With all these R.A.W. reckonings in mind, I went out
one January morning with a special bar of Assmilk Soap,
made especially for our Carnesville barnyard with bits of
plastic trash and broken mirror, fur and creek-mud and
leaves and acorns from the massive old water oak by the
barn. I scrubbed for hours with everything I had. I washed
the mud, the fouled creek, the sad depleted soil. I soaped
up the dead pine trees in the asses' paddock where the
powerline crew sprayed herbicide one day when we humans were not at home to stop them. I spent that whole
winter afternoon with my bare feet sunk in the cold mud
and manure of the barnyard, washing Carnesville with
the faint hope that it's possible to maintain a plot anywhere on this wracked earth that remains unpolluted
enough for porous bodies to thrive.

  R.A.W. Assmilk Soap must be a powerful solvent to
equal the fearsome pollutions of hopes and homelands
it goes up against. But I can testify to this much: every
time I poured the measured ounces of powdered lye into
foamy assmilk in the process of making soap, the mixture
sizzled and steamed and glowed bright and hot as a barn
fire. The first time I poured lye into Passenger's milk, the
reaction was so strong it cracked the jar. That last batch
I made in Carnesville, the mixture of assmilk and lye got
so hot it actually turned black.

~×~×~×~

Of course R.A.W. Assmilk Soap's cleaning powers are more metaphorical than material. It cannot wash away the visible scars of industrial wastelands, but it does try to reckon with hidden stains in embodied muzzles and tongues – poisonous ideas and classifications that enforce asymmetrical burdens borne by exploited bodies and ecosystems, and the ways distinct toxins linger in our bodies, thoughts, and utterances. R.A.W. Assmilk Soap really finds its potency by calling upon human imagination to bring buried stains to the surface of attention. These ordinary-looking bars of soap foam up in the usual way when they mix with water, but the real power resides in collective meaning-making gestures.

Tapping this, R.A.W. Assmilk Soap has engaged a collaborative approach, inviting human individuals to encounter the beneficent properties of assmilk in cleansing suds, and to lather through layers of whatever forms of pollution (chemical, psychological, linguistic, and so on) threaten the places and bodies we love. Along with assmilk, each bar of soap also contains other unique "ingredients" gathered by a collaborator. These ingredients evoke a place, way of life, memory, conundrum, or relationship that the soap's imaginer wants to wash in some way. A few significant batches of R.A.W. Assmilk Soap have included mixed milks from both she-ass and human sources.[22] In keeping with the aims of a collaborative project called *Domestic/Wild,* artist-choreographer Emily Stone's R.A.W. soap bar included her own breastmilk. The label of this soap tells a story of imaginative exploration

---

22 One early batch of R.A.W. Assmilk Soap was part of a collaboration with artist Emily Stone called *Domestic/Wild,* which culminated in an experimental performance that Stone produced in Portland, Oregon in January 2010. *Domestic/Wild* explored explored tensions between the bounds of domesticity – especially as they are experienced by homebound mothers of small children – and the body's inherent mammalian wildness and wisdoms.

into feral places we find even inside our own bodies and homes:

> Ingredients: 100% RAW milk (ass and human), organic base oils; question; dust from under couch (terra incognita); grass, leaves, and sticks picked up by Athena at night; a green note from my Dad; small portions of a nest that had two dead baby birds in it; a burnt match and a small bit of firewood. (Emily Stone, 2010)

Ingredients of R.A.W. Assmilk Soaps have ranged from bits of botanical species of a specific bioregion to personally or culturally loaded objects or substances, like artist Bill Kelly's mix of rain, motor oil, and blood, or poet Claire Hero's teeth of a road-killed coyote. Each soap label reads like a dark little love poem to the complexities of our multispecies habitations. Each bar of soap is an experiment, an ongoing interrogation.

Meanwhile, we know too well that almost anything can be traded on the global market these days, from preteen girls to cloned embryos. Much as I invest conceptually in the power of Assmilk Soap, though, it is not a product for sale. It isn't pretty or packaged, and it isn't scented with alluring perfumes. Aside from the fact that R.A.W. Assmilk Soap is intimately bound to the fortunes of one little ass herd, the scale of any ethically sound ass dairy is limited by economic and sociocultural realities that affect the lives of domestic donkeys around the world.[23] Meanwhile, as a cleansing product R.A.W. Assmilk Soap is only as solvent as the imagination that a washer is will-

---

23 Way too many abused and neglected domestic donkeys live in the United States and Canada, with way too few humans with the will and means to properly care for them. Meanwhile, the ferocious market for donkey hides to boil down for medicinal and cosmetic products in the global market would gladly swallow up any additional donkey lives, were I to keep breeding asses in order to make milk for soap.

ing to wet it with, and it is not for the squeamish. Each soap is embedded with objects of significance (gnarly tufts of assfur, or shards of found veal-calf bones), along with other special ingredients and whatever affective layers of meaning, longing, memories, and taboos a washer imbues it with.

In the end, I would say that I make Assmilk Soap because I am a member of a strange and uniquely language-laden species, trying to find a place in the world with respect to others while navigating minefields of shame, divisive definitions, and earthly desecrations. Everybody alive must come to recognize the sources of what sustains us in order to survive, and by those recognitions and connections we each come to grasp what and who we become, where and how we belong. In its own distinct ways, R.A.W. Assmilk Soap holds foamy hopes for more inclusive storyings through loving and careful attentions to recognizable knots that bind lives together within specific timeplaces. Where earthly belonging in changing worlds is not a static claim to specific real estate or exclusive way of being, we might begin to imagine new forms and practices of belonging: make new paths, plodding with hoofworn and hope-ridden persistence, toward more just and inclusive stories for possible ass futures.[24]

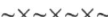

And this brings me back one last time to the black milk, and to the particular forms of reckoning with both exclusions and newfangled (be)longings embedded in Assmilk Soap. In spite of all the buried trash and broken mirrors in our Carnesville barnyard, years of careful R.A.W. husbandry in the woods and paddock mud finally revealed another source for my shadowy assmilk hungers. Not

24 See again Emily O'Gorman, "Belonging," *Environmental Humanities* 5, no. 1 (2014): 286.

surprisingly, this source was discovered once more in the cracks between names and bodies, and more so in the flowing and fertile spaces-between.

For a brief spell in the early days of his life, we called Passenger and Henry's little black foal by the name MoonPie, after the trademarked chocolate-coated cookie-and-marshmallow snack product manufactured by a secret industrial recipe at a factory in Chattanooga, Tennessee. I bestowed this name on the newborn ass with a dash of irony, in the unspoken desire to simultaneously claim and refute legacies of Cupcake, the long-gone spotted ghost-horse of my mother's childhood memories. In other words, I wanted to acknowledge the inheritance of my mother's storied barnyard loves – so fundamental to my growing up and sustaining a mixed-species family of my own – while at the same time marking the more unwholesome elements of industrial-consumer exploitations of bodies, lives, and labors that infiltrate global systems and earthly places. These mostly hidden elements permeate and reshape tissues and landscapes, from the gnarly knots of enduring beastly affinities to the sharp and shiny techno-industries that engineer bovine bodies to be milked dry by relentless robots.[25]

But then things did not go smoothly in the first few days of the foal's life. In the heavy summer heat, Passenger was ornery with postpartum discomfort and difficult lactation, and I ended up having to encourage the newborn to suck canned goat's milk from a bowl in order to stay hydrated and nourished. In that precarity of the foal's first days, I found myself regretting the name MoonPie. Every name has its hidden histories and associations, of course. But along with the load of chemical preservatives and lesser-known iniquities of colonial sugar production that taint every sweet treat, the MoonPie brand is his-

---

25 Scout Calvert, "Ready for the Robot: Bovines in the Integrated Circuit," *Humanimalia* 10, no. 1 (Spring 2019).

torically entwined with industries reliant on the hungry, laboring bodies of coal miners and field hands to whom the MoonPie was primarily marketed through the first part of the twentieth century.[26] Traces of linguistic toxins remain, too. Paul Beatty reports that "chocolate moonpie" was one of a robust lexicon of racial slurs familiar to Black Southern ears.[27]

I didn't know all this then, but as the frail foal seemed to swing in a liminal space between life and death, I sensed a danger in associating his fate too closely with that cellophane-wrapped, petrochemical-preservative-laced industrial snack product, as this life he inherits already teeters unsteadily between (auto)biographical being and killable commodity. So it happened that in keeping with a new ass family tradition, I came to un-name the newest member of Aliass's herd, from MoonPie to Nicholass Moon (aka Little Nick). Invested in this gesture was a hope that his unnaming might repel certain associations, carry on a different legacy and maybe even nourish possibilities for more wholesome ass futures.

We all made it through the postpartum rough patch, and after a few days Pass and Nick established a good nursing equilibrium. The darkest days of that summer (if not the hottest) were behind us as we rolled into a steamy August. One morning when Little Nick was a few weeks old, I was hanging out in the paddock with him and Pass and I saw him do something interesting. He was bent down awkwardly between his still-wobbly, widespread front legs, trying to nurse from a small clump of grass.

---

26 For a seemingly wholesome history of the perennial favorite Southern snack, see Abbey White, "The Out-of-This-World, One-Hundred-Year-Long History of the Moonpie," *Food and Wine*, September 20, 2017, https://www.foodandwine.com/articles/moonpies-history-one-hundredth-anniversary/.

27 Paul Beatty, "Black Humor," *New York Times*, January 20, 2006. https://www.nytimes.com/2006/01/22/books/review/black-humor.html/.

His little black muzzle worked at the green wisps with the full force of his nursling hunger, puckering around the stems in an earnest, if experimental, effort to suck sustenance from it. He gave up after a minute, as his efforts failed to yield sweet assmilk from the grassroots and dirt. But he was onto something, nonetheless. His moment of conflation foreshadowed a big leap he would take soon enough from milk to roughage. He was already beginning to learn to pluck and chew, and so laying claim to the herbivorous life he was born into.

At the time, I was amused by his mix-up of mother-body and other lively presences in the surrounding environment. For the young ass, this was just a transitional moment. But as I reflected on this episode later on, I came to realize that my own confusion on this matter – of where and how we find sustenance and ways of belonging in earthly places – has been lifelong. Like Little Nick, I've been seeking nourishment among the roadside weeds and dirt and asphalts of landscapes, places where I found myself entwined with others in time: I've tried in vain to suck a black-milk brew of flowing places and otherly ways of knowing from the landscapes I have passed through with Aliass and others, from lichen-crusted rocks and barks and tall seedy grasses, from birdcalls and cattails and thorny brambles and mud-puddles, and from blazing asphalt, endless mown lawns, and moony hayfields. In the circuits of all these long-ass journeys and habitations, I never could find one sweet spot that would yield it. But I always felt some rich dark earthly substance was present, flowing just under the surfaces of seemingly discrete bodies, coursing invisible and potent through infinite webs of nameless tissues and minerals and leaves and watersheds.

In this experience, the search for nourishment in compromised ecologies is as much a psychological or spiritual hunger as a biological one. Each in our own special ways, Little Nick and I felt around our shared environments, looking for what we needed most to help us stay alive and find sustaining ties. And in different ways, through that sweltering Carnesville summer and beyond, we each found what we needed in the bright eyes, lickings and fly-kickings, and familiar dusty fur of an ornery ass family (humans, dogs, pine trees, and other wild unknown lives included). For the nursling foal, Passenger's milk gave essential antibodies, microbes, and proteins he needed to develop and grow. For a human with other hungers, R.A.W. Assmilk Soap continues to hold the inscrutable stories that interwoven lives are always making together, full of shadowy hopes, sticky knots of care and desire, and foamy residues of deeply-lived immersion in places we pass through.

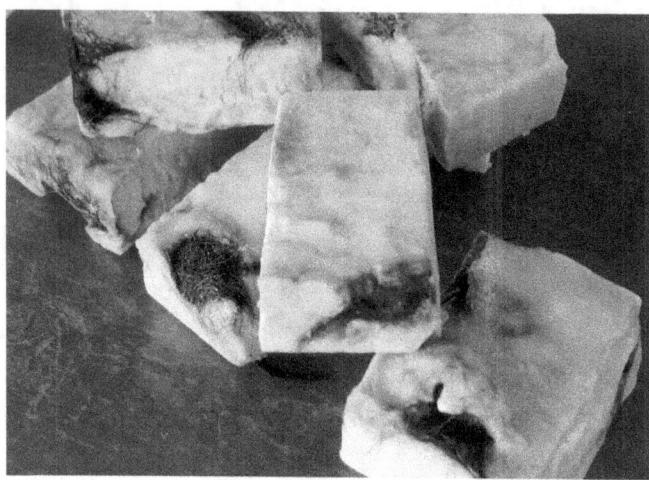

Fig. 2. The last batch of R.A.W. Assmilk Soap may be its fullest expression, and maybe also the most potent postscript. Made in our new ass homestead in Oregon in 2013, this R.A.W. Assmilk Soap contains the remains of frozen milk I saved from Passenger's lactation after Nick was weaned, prior to our move from Carnesville to the West Coast in 2011 (aka the Big Ass Family Road Trip). This soap batch also contains fresh milk my own mammalian body made, mixed with the requisite lye and oils and three generations of ass family furs. But this last batch is NOT more potent because of the fact that it contains my own human milk – supposed to be endowed with exclusive potential for meaningful expression, then provocatively mixed with the bodily fluids of a beastly Other, whose exotic stories are thus privileged but nevertheless held apart. No, that's not it: this last batch of Assmilk Soap is the most potent because it holds and binds so many tangled knots and traces of a familial herd of mammals and many others in timeplaces, not-archiving in its inscrutable ways the tales composed among meshes of vertebrates, microbes, plants, and myriad unnamed others. Our most intimately unknown stories, passed on in m<other tongues and otherwise. Photograph by the artist.

Bibliography

Agee, James, and Walker Evans. *Let Us Now Praise Famous Men*. 1941; rpt. New York: Houghton Mifflin, 1980.

Alaimo, Stacy. *Bodily Natures: Science, Environment and the Material Self*. Bloomington: Indiana University Press, 2010.

———."Trans-Corporeal Feminisms and the Ethical Space of Nature." In *Material Feminisms*, edited by Stacy Alaimo and Susan Hekman, 237–64. Bloomington: Indiana University Press, 2008.

Ackerman, Amanda. *The Book of Feral Flora*. Los Angeles: Les Figues Press, 2015.

Anderson, Virginia. *Creatures of Empire: How Domestic Animals Transformed Early America*. Oxford: Oxford University Press, 2004.

aphavideo. "American Paint Horse Association: A History." *YouTube*, September 10, 2018. https://www.youtube.com/watch?v=U9mLOpt3oik.

Artzineonline. "William Faulkner: Nobel Prize Speech." *YouTube*, July 13, 2013. https://www.youtube.com/watch?v=gOg3oJBnik8.

Baker, Steve. *Artist/Animal*. Minneapolis: University of Minnesota Press, 2013.

———. *The Postmodern Animal*. London: Reaktion Books, 2000.

Barad, Karen. *Meeting the Universe Halfway*. Durham: Duke University Press, 2007.

———. "On Touching – The Inhuman That Therefore I Am." *differences* 23, no. 5 (2012): 206–23. DOI: 10.1215/10407391-1892943.

———. "Posthumanist Performativity: Toward an Understanding of How Matter Comes to Matter." *Signs* 28, no. 3 (2003): 801–31. DOI: 10.1086/345321.

Basso, Keith. *Wisdom Sits in Places*. Albuquerque: University of New Mexico Press, 1996.

Bateson, Gregory. *Mind and Nature: A Necessary Unity*. Cresskill: Hampton Press, Inc., 2002.

———. *Steps to an Ecology of Mind. With a New Foreword by Mary Catherine Bateson*. Chicago and London: University of Chicago Press, 2000.

Beatty, Paul. "Black Humor." *New York Times,* January 22, 2006. https://www.nytimes.com/2006/01/22/books/review/black-humor.html/.

Beckett, Samuel. *Molloy*. In *Three Novels*. 1955; rpt. New York: Grove Press, 1991.

———. *Murphy*. New York: Grove Press, 1955.

Berlin, Jeremy. "So That's Why the Long Face." *National Geographic,* October 2017. https://www.nationalgeographic.com/magazine/2017/10/explore-animals-horse-facial-expressions/.

Bernstein, Charles. "Introduction." In *With Strings,* 1–2. Chicago: University of Chicago Press, 2001.

Bey, Hakim. *T.A.Z.: The Temporary Autonomous Zone, Ontological Anarchy, Poetic Terrorism*. Brooklyn: Autonomedia, 1991.

Bilbrey, Mark. "The Dog Poems and the Poetics of Prayer." PhD diss., University of Georgia, 2009.

Blaser, Robin. "The Practice of Outside." In *Jack Spicer, The Collected Books of Jack Spicer,* 271–326. San Francisco: Black Sparrow Press, 2002.

Bolender, Karin. "If Not for Her Spots: On the Art of (Un)naming a New Ass Breed." *Humanimalia* 10, no.

1 (2018). https://www.depauw.edu/humanimalia/issue%2019/bolender.html/.

———. "Silly Beasts in Sacred Places." *Arthur Magazine* 8, January 2004. https://arthurmag.com/tag/karin-bolender/.

———. "The Unnaming of 'Aliass.'" *Performance Research* 22, no. 5 (December 2017): 80–84. DOI: 10.1080/13528165.2017.1383779.

Boson Amos, Soul Sistah Serrata E. "Mule Day: A Lasting Community Tradition." *Daily Herald* (Columbia, Tennessee), March 31, 2013. https://www.columbiadaily-herald.com/article/20130331/LIFESTYLE/303319921/.

Bough, Jill. *Donkey*. London: Reaktion Books, 2011.

Bourriaud, Nicholas. "Relational Aesthetics." In *Participation,* edited by Claire Bishop, 160–71. London: Whitechapel, 2006.

Bowker, Geoffrey, and Susan Leigh Star. *Sorting Things Out*. Boston: MIT Press, 1999.

Boyd, Brian. *On the Origin of Stories: Evolution, Cognition, and Fiction*. Cambridge: Harvard University Press, 2009.

Braidotti, Rosi. *Nomadic Theory: The Portable Rosi Braidotti*. New York: Columbia University Press, 2011.

Branigan, Tania. "China Bans Wordplay in an Attempt at Pun Control." *The Guardian*, November 28, 2014. https://www.theguardian.com/world/2014/nov/28/china-media-watchdog-bans-wordplay-puns/.

Brant, Linda. "Pet Cemetery Project." *Linda Brant*. http://www.lindabrant.net/#!pet-cemetery-project/cstx/.

Bresler Rockmore, Ellen. "How Texas Teaches History." *New York Times*, October 21, 2015. http://nytimes.com/2015/10/22/opinion/how-texas-teaches-history.html/.

Brinker-Gabler, Gisela. "Living and Lost in Language: Translation and Interpretation in Ingeborg Bachmann's 'Simultan.'" In *If We Had the Word: Ingeborg Bachmann, Views and Reviews,* edited by Gisela Brinker-

Gabler and Markus Zisselsberger, 123–52. Riverside: Ariadne Press, 2004.

Broglio, Ron. *Surface Encounters: Thinking with Animals and Art*. Minneapolis: University of Minnesota Press, 2008.

Bulliet, Richard. *Hunters, Herders, and Hamburgers*. New York: Columbia University Press, 2007.

Calvert, Scout. "Ready for the Robot: Bovines in the Integrated Circuit." *Humanimalia* 10, no. 1 (Spring 2019). https://www.depauw.edu/humanimalia/issue%2019/pdfs/calvert-pdf.pdf/.

Cassidy, Rebecca. *The Sport of Kings: Kinship, Class and Thoroughbred Breeding in Newmarket*. London: Cambridge University Press, 2002.

Cassidy, Rebecca, and Molly Mullin, eds. *Where the Wild Things Are Now: Domestication Reconsidered*. Oxford: Berg, 2007.

Celan, Paul. *Selected Poems and Prose of Paul Celan*. Translated by John Felstiner. New York: W.W. Norton, 2001.

Chao, Sophie. "In the Shadow of the Palm: Dispersed Ontologies among Marind, West Papua." *Cultural Anthropology* 33, no. 4 (November 2018): 621–49. DOI: 10.14506/ca33.4.08.

Chen, Mel. *Animacies: Biopolitics, Racial Mattering, and Queer Affect*. Durham: Duke University Press, 2012.

Christian, Jack. *Family System*. Fort Collins: Center for Literary Publishing, 2012.

Cixous, Hélène. "Writing Blind: Conversation with the Donkey." In *Stigmata*, 115–26. New York: Routledge, 2005.

Clarke, Deborah. "Gender, Race, and Language in Light in August." *American Literature* 61, no. 3 (October 1989): 398–413. http://www.jstor.org/stable/2926827/.

———. "Humorously Masculine – or Humor as Masculinity – in *Light in August*." *The Faulkner Journal* 17 (Fall 2001): 1–19. https://www.jstor.org/stable/24908298/.

Clifford, James. *Returns*. Cambridge: Harvard University Press, 2013.

———. *The Predicament of Culture*. Cambridge: Harvard University Press, 1988.

Cronon, William. "The Trouble with Wilderness: or Getting Back to the Wrong Nature." In *Uncommon Ground: Rethinking the Human Place in Nature*, edited by William Cronon, 69–90. New York: W.W. Norton & Co., 1995.

Crosby, Alfred. *The Columbian Exchange*. Westport: Greenwood Press, 1972.

Culler, Jonathan. "The Call of the Phoneme: Introduction." In *On Puns: The Foundation of Letters*, edited by Jonathan Culler, 1–16. Oxford: Basil Blackwell, 1988.

Da Costa, Beatriz, and Kavita Philip, eds. *Tactical Biopolitics: Art, Activism, and Technoscience*. Boston: MIT Press, 2010.

Debord, Guy. "Towards a Situationist International." In *Participation*, edited by Claire Bishop, 96–101. London: Whitechapel, 2006.

Deleuze, Gilles, and Felix Guattari. *A Thousand Plateaus: Capitalism and Schizophrenia*. Translated by Brian Massumi. Minneapolis: University of Minnesota Press, 2009.

Deloria, Philip. *Playing Indian*. New Haven: Yale University Press, 1999.

Derrida, Jacques. *Memoires: For Paul de Man*. New York: Columbia University Press, 1986.

———. *The Animal That Therefore I Am*. Edited by Marie-Louis Mallet. Translated by David Wills. New York: Fordham University Press, 2008.

Despret, Vinciane. "Responding Bodies and Partial Affinities in Human-Animal Worlds." *Theory Culture & Society* 30, nos. 7–8 (2013): 51–76. DOI: 10.1177/0263276413496852.

———. "The Body We Care For: Figures of Anthropo-zoogenesis." *Body and Society* 10, nos. 2–3 (2004): 111–34. DOI: 10.1177/1357034X04042938.

————. *What Would Animals Say If We Asked the Right Questions?* Translated by Brett Buchanan. Minneapolis: University of Minnesota Press, 2016.

Despret, Vinciane, and Michel Meuret. "Cosmoecological Sheep and the Arts of Living on a Damaged Planet." *Environmental Humanities* 8, no. 1 (2016): 22–36. DOI: 10.1215/22011919-3527704.

De Waal, Frans. *Are We Smart Enough to Know How Smart Animals Are?* New York: W.W. Norton and Co., 2016.

Dickinson, Adam. *Anatomic.* Toronto: Coach House Books, 2018.

————. *The Polymers.* Toronto: Anansi Press, 2013.

Dowie, Mark. "Pinto Madness." *Mother Jones,* September/October 1977. https://www.motherjones.com/politics/1977/09/pinto-madness/.

Dumit, Joseph. "Writing the Implosion: Teaching the World One Thing at a Time." *Cultural Anthropology* 29, no. 2 (2014): 344–67. DOI: 10.14506/ca29.2.09.

————."Foreword: Biological Feedback." In *Tactical Biopolitics,* edited by Beatriz da Costa and Kavita Philip, xi–xiv. Cambridge: MIT Press, 2010.

Emmons, Scott W. "The Mood of a Worm." *Science* 338, no. 6106 (2012): 475–76. DOI: 10.1126/science.1230251.

Eshleman, Clayton. *Juniper Fuse: Upper Paleolithic Imagination and the Construction of the Underworld.* Middletown: Wesleyan University Press, 2003.

Faulkner, William. "Carcassonne." In *The Collected Stories,* 895–900. New York: Vintage, 1995.

————. "Nobel Prize Acceptance Speech." *Southern Cultures* 12, no. 1 (2006): 71. DOI: 10.1353/scu.2006.0005.

Felstiner, John. "Preface." In *Selected Poems and Prose of Paul Celan,* translated by John Felstiner. New York: W.W. Norton, 2001.

Ferris, William. *Mule Trader.* Oxford: University of Mississippi Press, 1988.

Gan, Elaine, Anna Tsing, Heather Swanson, and Nils Bubandt. "Haunted Landscapes of the Anthropocene." In *Arts of Living on a Damaged Planet,* edited by Anna Tsing, Heather Swanson, Elaine Gan, and Nils Bubandt, G1–G13. Minneapolis: University of Minnesota Press, 2017.

Gibson, Abraham. "Beasts of Burden: Feral Burros and the American West." In *The Historical Animal,* edited by Susan Nance, 38–53. Syracuse: Syracuse University Press, 2015.

Gigliotti, Carol. "Leonardo's Choice: The Ethics of Artists Working with Genetic Technologies." In *Leonardo's Choice: Genetic Technologies and Animals,* edited by Carol Gigliotti, 61–74. Dordrecht: Springer, 2009.

Gillespie, Kathryn, and Rosemary-Claire Collard, eds. *Critical Animal Geographies: Politics, Intersections, and Hierarchies in a Multispecies World.* London: Routledge, 2015.

Grimes, Ronald, L. "Performance is Currency in the Deep World's Gift Economy: an Incantatory Riff for a Global Medicine Show." *ISLE: Interdisciplinary Studies in Literature and Environment* 9, no. 1 (2002): 149–64. DOI: 10.1093/isle/9.1.149.

Gruen, Lori. *Entangled Empathy: An Alternative Ethic for Our Relationships with Animals.* New York: Lantern Books, 2014.

Hall, Matthew. *Plants as Persons.* New York: SUNY Press, 2011.

Hall, Stuart. *Critical Dialogues in Cultural Studies.* Edited by David Morley and Kuan-Hsing Chen. London: Routledge, 1996.

Hamblin, Robert. "Carcassonne in Mississippi." In *Faulkner and the Craft of Fiction,* edited by Doreen Fowler and Ann J. Abadie, 148–71. Jackson: University of Mississippi Press, 1987.

Haraway, Donna J. "Anthropocene, Capitalocene, Plantationocene, Chthulucene: Making Kin." *Environmental Humanities* 6 (2015): 159–65. DOI: 10.1215/22011919-3615934.

————. *Simians, Cyborgs, and Women: The Reinvention of Nature*. New York: Routledge, 1991.

————. "Situated Knowledges: The Science Question in Feminism and the Privilege of Partial Perspective." *Feminist Studies* 14, no. 3 (1988): 575–99. http://www.jstor.org/stable/3178066/.

————. *Staying with the Trouble: Making Kin in the Chthulucene*. Durham: Duke University Press, 2016.

————. *The Companion Species Manifesto: Dogs, People, and Significant Otherness*. Chicago: Prickly Paradigm Press, 2003.

————. *When Species Meet*. Minneapolis: University of Minnesota Press, 2008.

Harding, Susan. *The Book of Jerry Falwell: Fundamentalist Language and Politics*. Princeton: Princeton University Press, 2001.

————. "Get Religion." In *The Insecure American: How We Got Here and What We Should Do About It*, edited by Hugh Gusterson and Catherine Besteman, 368–82. Berkeley: University of California Press, 2009.

Hearne, Vicki. *Adam's Task: Calling Animals by Name*. New York: Harper Perennial, 1989.

High, Kathy. "Playing with Rats." In *Tactical Biopolitics: Art, Activism, Technoscience*, edited by Beatriz da Costa and Kavita Philip, 465–78. Cambridge: MIT Press, 2010.

Hodgetts, Timothy, and Jamie Lorimer. "Methodologies for Animals' Geographies: Cultures, Communication and Genomics." *Cultural Geographies* 22, no. 2 (2014): 285–95. DOI: 10.1177/1474474014525114.

Hoffmeyer, Jesper. "Some Semiotic Aspects of the Psycho-Physical Relation: The Endo-Exosemiotic Boundary." In *Biosemiotics: The Semiotic Web*, edited by Thomas Sebeok, 132–53. Berlin: Mouton de Gruyter, 1992.

Howe, Fanny. "Bewilderment, or, the Incarnation of the Author." *Raddle Moon* 18, no. 2 (2002): 41–64.

The Humane Society of the United States. "Tennesse Walking Horse Investigation Exposes Cruelty." *YouTube,* May 16, 2012. https://www.youtube.com/watch?v=gxVlxT_x-f0/.

Hustak, Carla, and Natasha Myers. "Involutionary Momentum: Affective Ecologies and the Sciences of Plant/Insect Encounters." *differences* 23, no. 3 (2012): 74–118. DOI: 10.1215/10407391-1892907.

Hyde, Lewis. *Trickster Makes This World: Mischief, Myth, and Art.* New York: Farrar, Straus, and Giroux, 2010.

Jewett, Robert, and J.S. Lawrence. *The American Monomyth.* Second edition. Lanham: University Press of America, 1988.

Kac, Eduardo. *Telepresence and Bio Art: Networking Humans, Rabbits, and Robots.* Ann Arbor: University of Michigan Press, 2005.

Kalenian, Ruth. "The American Council of Spotted Asses and John Conter." Personal website.

Kim, Claire Jean. *Dangerous Crossings: Race, Species and Nature in a Multicultural Age.* Cambridge: Cambridge University Press, 2015.

Kim, Meeri. "Can Plants Hear? In a Study, Vibrations Prompt Some to Boost Their Defenses." *Washington Post,* July 6, 2014. https://www.washingtonpost.com/national/health-science/can-plants-hear-study-finds-that-vibrations-prompt-some-to-boost-their-defenses/2014/07/06/8b2455ca-02e8-11e4-8fd0-3a663dfa68ac_story.html.

Kimmerer, Robin Wall. *Gathering Moss: A Natural and Cultural History of Mosses.* Corvallis: Oregon State University Press, 2003.

Kirksey, Eben. *Emergent Ecologies.* Durham: Duke University Press, 2015.

———, ed. *The Multispecies Salon.* Durham: Duke University Press, 2014.

Kirksey, Eben, and Dehlia Hannah, Charlie Lotterman, and Lisa Jean Moore. "The Xenopus Pregnancy Test: A

Performative Experiment." *Environmental Humanities* 8, no. 1 (2016): 37-56. DOI: 10.1215/22011919-3527713.

Kirksey, Eben, and Stefan Helmreich. "The Emergence of Multispecies Ethnography." *Cultural Anthropology* 25, no. 4 (2010): 545–76. DOI: 10.1111/j.1548-1360.2010.01069.x.

Kohn, Eduardo. *How Forests Think: Toward an Anthropology Beyond the Human.* Berkeley: University of California Press, 2013.

Kolata, Gina. "Barnyard Dust Offers a Clue to Stopping Asthma in Children." *New York Times*, August 3, 2016. https://www.nytimes.com/2016/08/04/health/dust-asthma-children.html/.

Kristeva, Julia. *Strangers to Ourselves.* Translated by Kelly Oliver. New York: Columbia University Press, 1991.

Kwon, Miwon. *One Place after Another: Site-Specific Art and Locational Identity.* Cambridge: MIT Press, 2004.

LaDuke, Winona. "Akwesasne: Mohawk Mother's Milk and PCBs." In *Sing, Whisper, Shout, Pray! Feminist Visions for a Just World,* edited by M. Jacqui Alexander, Lisa Albrecht, Sharon Day, and Mab Segrest, 159–71. Fort Bragg: Edgework, 2003.

Laird, Tessa. *Bat.* London: Reaktion Books, 2018.

Latour, Bruno. *We Have Never Been Modern.* Translated by Catherine Porter. Cambridge: Harvard University Press, 1993.

Leithead, Alastair. "Why Are Donkeys Facing Their 'Biggest Ever Crisis'?" *BBC News*, October 7, 2017. https://www.bbc.com/news/world-africa-41524710/.

LeMenager, Stephanie. *Living Oil: Petroleum Culture in the American Century.* Oxford: Oxford University Press, 2014.

Lestel, Dominique. "Friends of My Friends." Translated by Jeffrey Bussolini. *Angelaki: Journal of Theoretical Humanities* 19, no. 3 (2014): 133–47. DOI: 10.1080/0969725X.2014.976062.

Lipton, Eric. "Come One, Come All, Join the Terror Target List." *New York Times,* July 12, 2006. https://www.nytimes.com/2006/07/12/washington/12assets.html/.

Liss, Andrea. *Feminist Art and the Maternal.* Minneapolis: University of Minnesota Press, 2009.

LogistiKHD. "Martin Luther King | "I Have a Dream Speech." *YouTube,* August 28, 2013. https://www.youtube.com/watch?v=I47Y6VHc3Ms.

Long, William G. *Asses vs. Jackasses.* Portland: The Touchstone Press, 1969.

Loveless, Natalie. "Maternal Ecologies: A Story in Three Parts." In *Performing Motherhood: Artistic, Activist, and Everyday Enactments,* edited by Amber E. Kinser, Terri Hawkes, and Kryn Freehling-Burton, 149–69. Bradford: Demeter Press, 2014.

Lucretius. *On the Nature of the Universe.* Translated by R.E. Latham and Revised with a New Introduction and Notes by John Godwin. New York and London: Penguin Books, 1994.

Manning, Erin, and Brian Massumi. *Thought in the Act: Passages in the Ecology of Experience.* Minneapolis: University of Minnesota Press, 2014.

Manning, Maurice. *Lawrence Booth's Book of Visions.* New Haven: Yale University Press, 2001.

Marcus, Greil. "The Old Weird America." Liner notes, *Anthology of American Folk Music.* Smithsonian Folkways, 1997.

Marzluff, John. *Welcome to Subirdia.* New Haven: Yale University Press, 2014.

Massumi, Brian. "Becoming-Animal in the Literary Field." In *Animals, Animality, and Literature,* edited by Bruce Boehrer, Molly Hand, and Brian Massumi, 265–83. Cambridge: Cambridge University Press, 2018.

Matthews, Jacqueline. "Ivermectin Resistance in Equine Nematodes." *International Journal for Parasitology: Drugs and Drug Resistance* 4, no. 3 (2014): 310–15. DOI: 10.1016/j.ijpddr.2014.10.003.

Meyer, William. "Faulkner's Patriotic Failure: Southern Lyricism versus American Hypervision." In *Faulkner and the Craft of Fiction*, edited by Doreen Fowler and Ann J. Abadie, 105–226. Jackson: University of Mississippi Press, 1987.

McCarthy, Cormac. *Suttree*. New York: Vintage, 1979.

Mitchell, George. *Mississippi Hill Country Blues 1967*. Jackson: University of Mississippi Press, 2013.

Muecke, Stephen. "The Fall." In *Joe in the Andamans*, 18–25. Sydney: LCP, 2008.

Nabokov, Vladimir. *Lolita*. New York: Vintage International, 1997.

———. *Pale Fire*. New York: Vintage International, 1989.

Nash, Richard. "'Honest English Breed': The Thoroughbred as Cultural Metaphor." In *The Culture of the Horse*, edited by Karen Raber and Treva J. Tucker, 245–72. New York: Palgrave MacMillan, 2005.

Nelson, Maggie. *The Argonauts*. Minneapolis: Gray Wolf Press, 2015.

Neimanis, Astrida. *Bodies of Water: Posthuman Feminist Phenomology*. London: Bloomsbury, 2017.

O'Gorman, Emily. "Belonging." *Environmental Humanities* 5, no. 1 (2014): 283–86. DOI: 10.1215/22011919-3615523.

O'Connor, Flannery. *Wise Blood*. 1952; rpt. New York: Farrar, Straus and Giroux, 2007.

Owen, Penny. "A Colorful Life, She's Riding Ol' Paint to Fame: Ryan Woman to Join Cowgirl Hall of Fame." *Daily Oklahoman*, October 29, 2000. https://oklahoman.com/article/2717491/a-colorful-life-shes-riding-ol-paint-to-fame-ryan-woman-to-join-cowgirl-hall-of-fame/.

Patton, Paul. "Language, Power, and the Training of Horses." In *Zoontologies*, edited by Cary Wolfe, 83–99. Minneapolis: University of Minnesota Press, 2003.

Peelle, Lydia. "Mule Killers." In *Reasons for and Advantages of Breathing*, 1–17. New York: Harper Perennial, 2009.

Ponge, Francis. *Soap*. Translated by Lane Dunlop. Stanford: Stanford University Press, 1998.

Pound, Ezra. *Make It New: Essays by Ezra Pound*. New Haven: Yale University Press, 1935.

Plumwood, Val. *Feminism and the Mastery of Nature*. New York: Routledge, 1994.

———. "Shadow Places and the Politics of Dwelling." *Australian Humanities Review* 44 (2008). http://australianhumanitiesreview.org/2008/03/01/shadow-places-and-the-politics-of-dwelling/.

Provensen, Alice and Martin. *Our Animal Friends at Maple Hill Farm*. New York: Random House, 1974.

———. *The Year at Maple Hill Farm*. London: Jonathan Cape, 1978.

Puig de la Bellacasa, Maria. *Matters of Care: Speculative Ethics in More Than Human Worlds*. Minneapolis: University of Minnesota Press, 2017.

Rasula, Jed. *This Compost: Ecological Imperatives in American Poetry*. Athens: University of Georgia Press, 2012.

Reckitt, Helena. "Forgotten Relations: Feminist Artists and Relational Aesthetics." In *Politics in a Glass: Case Feminism, Exhibition Cultures and Curatorial Transgressions*, edited by Angela Dimitrakaki and Lara Perry, 131–56. Liverpool: Liverpool University Press, 2013.

Redfern, Walter. *Puns*. London: Basil Blackwell, 1984.

Ritvo, Harriet. *Noble Cows and Hybrid Zebras*. Charlottesville: University of Virginia Press, 2010.

———. *The Platypus and the Mermaid, and Other Figments of the Classifying Imagination*. Boston: Harvard University Press, 1997.

Roberts, Monty. *The Man Who Listens to Horses*. New York: Random House, 1997.

Roe, Frank. *The Indian and the Horse*. Norman: University of Oklahoma Press, 1955.

Rose, Deborah Bird. "Judas Work: Four Modes of Sorrow." *Environmental Philosophy* 5, no. 2 (2008): 51–66. DOI: 10.5840/envirophil2008528.

Rose, Deborah Bird, and Thom van Dooren. "Guest Editors' Introduction." *Australian Humanities Review* 50 (2011). http://australianhumanitiesreview. org/2011/05/01/guest-editors-introduction/.

Rose, Deborah Bird, and Libby Robin. "Ecological Humanities in Action: An Invitation." *Australian Humanities Review* 31–32 (2004). http://australian-humanitiesreview.org/2004/04/01/the-ecological-humanities-in-action-an-invitation/.

Ruskin, John. *The Seven Lamps of Architecture.* 1880; rpt. New York: Dover Publications, 1989.

Schama, Simon. *Landscape and Memory.* New York: Vintage, 1995.

Schrader, Astrid. "Abyssal Intimacies and Temporalities of Care: How (Not) to Care about Deformed Leaf Bugs in the Aftermath of Chernobyl." *Social Studies of Science* 45, no. 5 (2015): 665–90. DOI: 10.1177/0306312715603249.

Sells, Michael. *Mystical Languages of Unsaying.* Chicago: University of Chicago Press, 1994.

Shakespeare. William. *A Midsummer Night's Dream.* New York: Penguin, 1967.

Shepard, Paul. *Coming Home to the Pleistocene.* Washington, DC: Island Press, 1998.

———. *The Others: How Animals Made Us Human.* Washington, DC: Island Press, 1997.

Shukin, Nicole. *Animal Capital: Rendering Life in Biopolitical Times.* Minneapolis: University of Minnesota Press, 2009.

Simms, Eva-Marie. "Eating One's Mother: Female Embodiment in a Toxic World." *Environmental Ethics* 31 (2009): 263–77. DOI: 10.5840/enviroethics200931330.

Simun, Miriam. "Human Cheese." In *The Multispecies Salon,* edited by Eben Kirksey, 135–44. Durham: Duke University Press, 2014.

Singh, Julietta. *No Archive Will Restore You.* Earth, Milky Way: punctum books, 2018.

Snyder, Gary. *The Practice of the Wild.* New York: North Point Press, 1990.

Spaid, Sue. *Ecovention: Current Art to Transform Ecologies.* Cincinnati: Contemporary Arts Center, 2002.

Spicer, Jack. *My Vocabulary Did This to Me: The Collected Poetry of Jack Spicer,* edited by Kevin Killian and Peter Gizzi. New York: Wesleyan University Press, 2010.

———. *The Collected Books of Jack Spicer.* San Francisco: Black Sparrow Press, 2002.

———. *The House That Jack Built: The Collected Lectures of Jack Spicer,* edited by Peter Gizzi. Middletown: Wesleyan University Press, 1998.

Stengers, Isabelle. "A Cosmopolitical Proposal." In *Making Things Public,* edited by Bruno Latour and Peter Weibel, 995–1003. Cambridge: MIT Press, 2005.

———. *Cosmopolitics I.* Minneapolis: University of Minnesota Press, 2010.

———. *In Catastrophic Times: Resisting the Coming Barbarism.* Translated by Andrew Goffey. London: Open Humanities Press, 2015.

Stephens, Beth M., and Annie M. Sprinkle. *Love Art Lab.* https://loveartlab.ucsc.edu/.

Stevens, Wallace. *The Collected Poems.* New York: Vintage Books, 1990.

———. "The Noble Rider and the Sound of Words." In *The Necessary Angel: Essays on Reality and the Imagination,* 3–36. New York: Vintage Books, 1951.

Stevenson, Robert Louis. *Travels with a Donkey.* New York: Heritage Press, 1957.

Stewart, Kathleen. *Ordinary Affects.* Durham: Duke University Press, 2007.

Szwed, John. *Space Is the Place: The Lives and Times of Sun Ra.* New York: Da Capo Press, 1998.

Taussig, Michael. *Mimesis and Alterity: A Particular History of the Senses.* New York: Routledge, 1993.

The Book of Live Stock Champions 1912. St. Louis: Hale Publishing, 1912.

Thompson, Charis. *Making Parents: The Ontological Cho-reography of Assisted Reproductive Technologies.* Cambridge: MIT Press, 2000.

Tsing, Anna Lowenhaupt. "Arts of Inclusion, or How to Love a Mushroom." *Australian Humanities Review* 50 (2011): 5–22. http://australianhumanitiesreview. org/2011/05/01/arts-of-inclusion-or-how-to-love-a-mushroom/.

———. *Friction: An Ethnography of Global Connection.* Princeton: Princeton University Press, 2005.

———. *The Mushroom at the End of the World.* Princeton: Princeton University Press, 2015.

Tsing, Anna, Heather Swanson, Elaine Gan, Nils Bubandt, eds. *Arts of Living on a Damaged Planet.* Minneapolis: University of Minnesota Press, 2017.

Van Dooren, Thom. *Flightways: Life and Loss at the Edge of Extinction.* New York: Columbia University Press, 2014.

Van Dooren, Thom, and Deborah Bird Rose. "Lively Ethography: Storying Animist Worlds." *Environmental Humanities* 8, no. 1 (2016): 77–94. DOI: 10.1215/22011919-3527731.

———. "Storied-places in a Multispecies City." *Humanimalia* 3, no. 2 (2012): 1–27. https://www.de-pauw.edu/humanimalia/issue%252006/pdfs/ van%2520dooren%2520rose.pdf/.

Van Dooren, Thom, Eben Kirksey, and Ursula Munster. "Multispecies Studies: Cultivating Art of Attentive-ness." *Environmental Humanities* 8, no. 1 (2016): 1–23. DOI: 10.1215/22011919-3527695.

Van West, Caroll. "Columbia Race Riot, 1946." *Tennessee Encyclopedia,* Tennessee Historical Society, October 8, 2017. https://tennesseeencyclopedia.net/entries/ columbia-race-riot-1946/.

Veselka, Vanessa. *Zazen.* New York: Red Lemonade, 2011.

Von Uexkull, Jacob. *A Foray into the Worlds of Animals and Humans.* Minneapolis: University of Minnesota Press, 2010.

Weil, Kari. "Autobiography." In *The Cambridge Companion to Literature and the Posthuman,* edited by Bruce Clark and Manuela Rossini, 84–95. Cambridge: Cambridge University Press, 2017.

———. *Thinking Animals: Why Animal Studies Now?* New York: Columbia University Press, 2012.

Weintraub, Linda. *To Life! Eco Art in Pursuit of a Sustainable Planet.* Berkeley: University of California Press, 2012.

West, Paige. "Spectacular." *The ABCs of Multispecies Studies.* http://www.multispecies-salon.org/spectacular/.

Wheeler, Wendy. *The Whole Creature: Complexity, Biosemiotics, and the Evolution of Culture.* London: Lawrence & Wishart, 2006.

White, Abbey. "The Out-of-This-World, One-Hundred-Year-Long History of the Moonpie." *Food and Wine,* September 20, 2017. https://www.foodandwine.com/articles/moonpies-history-one-hundredth-anniversary/.

Wolfe, Cary. *What Is Posthumanism?* Minneapolis: University of Minnesota Press, 2010.

———, ed. *Zoontologies.* Minneapolis: University of Minnesota Press, 2003.

Wolsak, Lissa. "An_heuristic_prolusion." *Raddle Moon* 18, no. 2 (2002): 81–91.

Woodward, Richard B. "Cormac McCarthy's Venomous Fiction." *New York Times Magazine,* April 19, 1992. https://www.nytimes.com/1992/04/19/magazine/cormac-mccarthy-s-venomous-fiction.html/.

Films

Ballard, Carroll, dir. *The Black Stallion.* Omni Zoetrope, 1979.

Coney, John, dir. *Space Is the Place.* North American Star System, 1974.

Eastwood, Clint, dir. *The Outlaw Josey Wales.* Warner Bros. and The Malpaso Company, 1976.

Jarmusch, Jim, dir. *Dead Man*. Miramax Films, 1996.

Myrick, Daniel, and Eduardo Sanchez, dirs. *The Blair Witch Project*. Haxan Films, 1999.

Stephens, Beth. *Goodbye Gauley Mountain: An Ecosexual Love Story*. Fecund Arts, 2015.

Zeitlin, Behn, dir. *Beasts of the Southern Wild*. Screenplay by Lucy Alibar. Fox Searchlight, 2012.

Records

"60 Words." *Radiolab*. WNYC Studios. April 17, 2014. https://www.wnycstudios.org/story/60-words/.

Charlie Poole with the Highlanders. "May I Sleep in Your Barn Tonight Mister." *The Complete Paramount & Brunswick Recordings, 1929*. Tompkins Square, 2013. Multiple formats.

John Denver. "Take Me Home, Country Roads." *Poems, Prayers & Promises*. RCA, 1971. LP.

Merle Haggard. "The Fightin' Side of Me." *Merle Haggard: 40 Greatest Hits*. Intersound, 2004. CD.

Royal Trux. *Pound for Pound*. Drag City, 2000. LP.

Sun Ra and His Outer Space Arkestra. "Nuclear War." *Nuclear War*. ATAVISTIC, 2009. Audiocassette.

Woody Guthrie. "Hard Travelin." *The Asch Recordings, Vol. 3*. Smithsonian Folkways, 1998. Audiocassette.

———. "Pastures of Plenty." *The Asch Recordings, Vol. 4*. Smithsonian Folkways, 1999. Audiocassette.

www.ingramcontent.com/pod-product-compliance
Lightning Source LLC
Chambersburg PA
CBHW070320240526
45468CB00025B/1193